D2.

HIGH DRAMA

Also by Hamish MacInnes:

International Mountain Rescue Handbook
Scottish Climbs 1
Scottish Climbs 2
Call-Out
Climb to the Lost World
West Highland Walks: One
West Highland Walks: Two
Look Behind the Ranges

Fiction

Death Reel

HAMISH MacINNES

HIGH DRAMA

Mountain rescue stories
from four continents

THE MOUNTAINEERS
Seattle

THE MOUNTAINEERS: Organized in 1906 "... to explore, study, preserve, and enjoy the natural beauty of the Northwest."

Published in Great Britain in 1980 by Hodder and Stoughton, London (ISBN 0-340-24559-X)

Published in the United States in 1981 by The Mountaineers, 719 Pike Street, Seattle, Washington 98101

Printed in the United States of America

Library of Congress Catalog Card No. 81-80500

ISBN 0-89886-031-8

CONTENTS

ILLUSTRATIONS

The Ogre[12]
Crawling down on two broken legs[13]
Doug Scott[14]

CREDITS

1 John Cleare	8 Riddell PhotoGraphics
2 Ludwig Gramminger	9 Tony Gazley
3 Photo Alex, Grindelwald	10 M. Glasgow
4 Swissair-Photo, Zurich	11 Paul Nunn
5 Horska Sluzba	12 Doug Scott
6 SRFW Foto-Archiv	13 Chris Bonington
7 Scottish Daily Express	14 Clive Rowland

Front of jacket photograph by Photo Alex, Grindelwald. Back of jacket main photograph by Scottish Daily Express. Top and bottom inserts by Ludwig Gramminger. Colour insert of a rescue team on An Teallach by Hamish MacInnes.

MAPS

ABOUT THIS BOOK

Come hither, you that walk along the way;
See how the pilgrims fare that go astray:
They catched are in an entangled net,
'Cause they good counsel lightly did forget:
'Tis true they rescued were; but yet, you see,
They're scourged to boot. Let this your caution be.

These words of John Bunyan are applicable today as they were to young Christian. This is a book about climbers that went astray, some "good council lightly did forget", others fell victim to the many hazards which beset those who frequent the high peaks.

There are many untold stories of men and women who fulfilled more than their duty as mountaineers and who, like the good Samaritan, "went to him and bound up his wounds". It is my hope that these accounts will convey some of the difficulties which beset a rescue team, or indeed the solo rescuer, often when all the odds are stacked against them: darkness, weather, fatigue, even fate. The stories I have chosen cover a period over the last thirty years; they don't always have a happy ending.

We have to look back a lot further than thirty years to find the origins of mountain rescue. Perhaps it is to Saint Bernard of Menthon that credit for the first rescue organisation should be given. Saint Bernard had high aspirations and based them 8,000 feet up in the Swiss Alps. Some time before 962 AD he founded the monastery which later bore his name. Its specific aim was to help travellers using the Grand Saint Bernard Pass. The constitutional edicts of the monastery stated that "the monks are to go out each day between the 15th November and the end of May, as they have always done." For over four hundred years those staunch men of God braved hail, rain and blizzard to guide people over the pass, many of the monks dying in this service.

Fortunately, the principle upon which this book is based, that of aiding the injured, hasn't changed over the centuries. It goes back to the origins of man, before the time of the meritorious Saint Bernard and the parable of the Good Samaritan. The following chapters have been written by rescuers, the rescued and by rescuers who themselves became the rescued.

To some these sagas may border on the macabre; but they are not intended to be so and anyone who regards this book in that light fails to comprehend the self-sacrifice and the stark facts of a rescue operation. One of the greatest forms of human endeavour is to pit your resources against the odds stacked up by a mountain. Certainly there's danger; experience, judgment and physical fitness must cope with that, but danger shouldn't be a deterrent. It makes one more aware. It's those who haven't experienced it who criticise. The late Geoffrey Winthrop Young in his poem 'Knight Errantry' compared the mountaineer with a knight errant. It's a good comparison. The chance of a climbing accident is an integral part of the sport; those who participate must also accept the possible consequences. Most mountaineers, however careful, realise that it could happen to them, for there are always objective dangers on a serious climb. It is a fact of life. You have to consider what you want to get out of the sport and just how far you are prepared to go. You may muster enough courage (some call it foolhardiness) to attempt a dangerous solo Himalayan climb, or you may prefer a gentle Lakeland fell walk, there is a degree of inherent danger in both.

One message stands out clearly from these contributors and that is their absolute sincerity. Each went to help others in dire trouble, often at grave personal risk and in the face of adversity.

ONE

An iron race the mountain cliffs maintain,
Foes to the gentler genius of the plain,
Who, while their rocky ramparts round they see
The rough abode of want and liberty,
The lawless force from confidence will grow,
Insult the plenty of the vale below.

'Hardihood of the Mountaineer', Thomas Gray

The Eiger North Wall will for ever stand as a milestone for those formative years of mountaineering, the 1930s, but it has also served as a gravestone for the unlucky who died on its flanks. The popular press had their first taste of mountaineering tragedy some fifty years before, when Edward Whymper's party crashed to their deaths on the Matterhorn. Though Whymper himself survived, he was obsessed with the stigma of this tragedy for the remainder of his days.

Most of the climbing fraternity as well as the public condemned those Eiger North Wall climbers who, they said, risked their lives and the lives of the rescuers who went to help them when they got into trouble. Yet those tigers of yesteryear were sensible young men who were only exercising an urge basic to all of us, to try something new, to conquer the frigid vertical heights by the most direct route to the summit. They were mostly of German or Austrian origin, possibly because the use of pitons and slings as climbing aids first evolved in the Eastern Alps and, without their assistance, such ambitious goals as the Eigerwand were then out of the question. Those who condemned this new breed of climber were themselves too timid to contemplate tackling such routes.

One can expostulate on the pros and cons of big wall climbing, but the courage of those who attempted those north faces as well as the courage of their rescuers is beyond question. For decades the Eiger drama has been re-enacted on page and screen, yet it will always demonstrate an extraordinary facet of human nature, this deep-rooted desire to attempt a problem, knowing full well the odds are against one.

Austria and Germany have always been in the forefront of mountain rescue development, especially in the pioneering days of big cliff rescue, where steel cables were first used in place of conventional ropes. The German Bergwacht, the Mountain Guard, were then the stars of rescues where the stage was some great alpine north face. Ludwig Gramminger was the leader of this determined band involved in what will remain probably the greatest sequence of mountain rescue operations of all time, in days when the helicopter wasn't the bird of mercy it is today. I have made many landings by winch wire on the Eiger North Face and I can vouch for the skill and the daring of the pilots on those operations. But their exposure to danger is brief, compared with the hours and even days spent by rescue teams in the past on the icy ramparts of this hostile mountain.

During the war most of Ludwig Gramminger's companions were away in the forces when in 1942 he got a call to go to the Eiskarlspitze in the Karwendal of the Austrian Tirol. A climber had fallen and was subsequently killed. It meant abseiling down a 350-metre face with the corpse. Perhaps the best introduction to Ludwig is to listen to his own description of how, when almost down the wall, his colleague, who had gone first to prepare the anchors for the ropes, had failed to complete the final belay on one of the steepest sections:

For the last abseil, I asked myself, had Stadler only put in one peg? I could only see one, but this was inconceivable. Was it an oversight as we were nearing the foot of the cliff? But there was no excuse for a single piton. It's dangerous enough roping off a solitary peg at the best of times, but frightening when carrying the additional weight of the body of a large man. Perhaps, I thought, the eight pitches which Max Stadler had already organised from the top had taken too much out of him? Anyhow, I secured myself to the peg using a sling, but didn't take off my abseil rope. When Michel, the other member of our rescue trio, arrived alongside using his own abseil rope, he could hardly get a footing as the wall was so steep. He too clipped onto the peg. As well as staying on my abseil rope I had taken the precaution of knotting it so that it couldn't creep through the karabiner brake I was using. Michel now came off his abseil rope, for he had to help me to change over to another rope for the final descent. To our horror we saw that his extra weight was making the peg bend and as if in slow motion it came out of the crack. I grabbed him and in so doing took some of his weight. In desperation he linked himself to me with a karabiner so that we were all hanging, two climbers and a corpse, on my abseil rope. After recovering from the initial shock we had to do some slick thinking. It was a good thing that I hadn't trusted that peg and also that I was attached to it by a sling, otherwise we would have lost the rope that Michel had transfered to it. We yelled down to Stadler to tie some pegs and a hammer to the end of this and in a short space of time we had sound anchors in place. We then lowered the dead man to the bottom of the face and quickly followed, glad ourselves to be down alive.

To climbers at least that's the sort of stuff that nightmares are made from, but it is only a small incident in the long rescue career of Ludwig Gramminger. The following adventures have been narrated before in various forms, but seldom by the rescuers themselves.

I

WE RECOVER THE BODIES OF OUR COMRADES

Eiger North Wall, 1935–6 by Ludwig Gramminger

In 1936 the Eiger North Wall was the last main unclimbed face in the Western Alps. German climbers had been much to the fore in the other great ascents; the Matterhorn North Face was climbed by the brothers Schmeid in 1931 and the Grandes Jorasses in 1935 by Rudi Peters and Martin Meir. That same year Wiggerl Steinauer and Hans Ellner scaled the North Face of the Aletschhorn. All these climbers came from Munich.

Climbing was just beginning to get public attention and the Eiger North Wall represented to many a vertical arena of drama and tragedy to which the accidents of 1933–6 were the curtain raisers. For this was the time of the first attempts on that notorious wall and the press were to have many a bonanza reporting and misreporting the assaults on the 1,800-metre high face.

It was again a Munich party that first set their hopes on this great North Face. Max Sedlmayr and Karl Mehringer were both members of the High Level Group of the German and Austrian Alpine Club. They left Bavaria in August, travelling by car to Grindelwald and took up residence in a hayshed at Alpiglen. Alpiglen snuggles in meadows at the bottom of the Eigerwand on the Kleine Scheidegg railway. Here they spent some time carefully studying the possible lines on the face. It was no easier then than now to keep your objective secret if the Eiger North Face featured in your itinerary and news leaked out that they were to attempt a direct route up the westerly section of the wall – straight to the summit.

They set off at three am on Wednesday, 21st August and after three days of hard rock climbing they reached the Second Icefield. Due to heavy stone fall here they had to bivouac early.

It was on that Friday night that the whole Eiger region was subjected to a savage storm. The face, which forms a northern bastion of the Alps, is a buffer to all the foul weather from that quarter; it attracts storms as a magnet attracts pins.

On the Saturday the telescopes of Kleine Scheidegg and Alpiglen were trained on the face looking for signs of the two men, but nothing further could be seen. They were known to be excellent climbers and were well equipped, so it was generally thought that they would have survived the blizzard. Unfortunately, dense cloud rolled in and blanketed the whole face and a heavy snowfall commenced. It got increasingly colder ($-8°C$ at Kleine Scheidegg) and the danger of avalanche on the face was considerable. On the Sunday around midday a portion of the wall was visible for a short while and then the two climbers were spotted higher up, presumably continuing the climb. But very soon the cloud closed in again and for the next few days not much more was seen.

Now with the continuing bad weather, the position of the two was critical and in Grindelwald preparations for a possible rescue were being made. In Munich our rescue group, the Bergwacht, received the following report at 9.30 am: "The weather conditions on the Eiger North Face are extremely bad. Today, Wednesday, 28th August it has snowed lightly on the upper slopes; in the valley it was raining. The snow is lying about fifty centimetres deep on the upper section of the face." A Swiss military plane had to give up a search on the following day because of poor visibility. There was nothing to be seen or heard, no signs at all. The face was under the constant observation of the Grindelwald rescue post, but the prevailing conditions precluded any mercy mission for the time being. Further reports arrived. In Munich our group was preparing to go to the aid of the missing climbers who would by now obviously be in a very serious condition. As soon as the conditions allowed, nothing would stop us doing everything we could to rescue our friends. We left Munich that same day at 9.30 pm in the Bergwacht Mercedes Kompressorwagen, driving through the night for Grindelwald. We had the best of equipment and rations and we departed in streaming rain convinced that we would bring help to our colleagues. There were four of us – Rudi Peters, Franz Hausstätter, Heine Sedlmayer and myself.

We arrived at Grindelwald around 9.30 am and our first call was at the rescue post which was also the guides' bureau, where we were given the run-down on developments to date. From this moment we were supported in every possible way. Herr Moser, President of the Grindelwald section of the Swiss Alpine Club and the manager of the Hotel Oberland, took care of our equipment and vehicle. Herr Direktor Grob from the travel office gave us lots of photographic material of the Eigerwand to study. Herr Direktor Luchtu gave us complimentary tickets for the Jungfrau railway. From photographs the guide, Fritz Steuri, and others showed us the line of the Sedlmayr–Mehringer climb and we weighed up the possibilities for rescue and recovery. In a short period of time we acquired a lot of facts. Later we took the train to Alpiglen where the missing men had made their headquarters. The bulk of their equipment – bivouac clothes, the second petrol cooker, spare sleeping bags, etc, were still in their hay-shed. On Tuesday the 20th, we were told, they had established a food dump on the summit, and, according to reports, set off on the climb on the Wednesday at three am. From observations made from the West Flank when taking up the food dump, they had formed the impression that they could climb the face in three days and had therefore taken less equipment and emergency food with them. From the hotel owner at Alpiglen we learned more about their proposed climb. One thing that was absolutely clear was that everyone who had seen them climbing was very impressed with their ability. The news of the first attempt on the Eigerwand had spread like wildfire. Two other Munich climbers, Haber and Prosel, who were holidaying in the vicinity, had already begun searching the day before, but due to the snow and stone falls they had had to give up.

We reviewed the overall situation and came to the conclusion that there was still some hope for Sedlmayr and Mehringer, if they had found a sheltered bivouac site. Swiss airmen had already flown across the face three times, for an hour on each occasion, but without success. Now it was very cloudy, though we hoped that the following day we should be able to search the wall ourselves with the telescope. We dumped our gear at the start of the climb for, in the event of a rescue bid, we should start from the same spot. Should the weather permit (which we doubted in view of the constant avalanches) we proposed setting out the next day. For the time being we stationed ourselves in a barn and, as agreed, sent reports on the rescue situation back to Grindelwald, from where Munich was informed. Friday, 30th August was a beautiful clear day. We travelled to the Eigergletscher station on the Jungfraubahn and there split into two groups. Haber and Prosel climbed the West Flank of the Eiger to get a view of the face from there. The rest of us went up the railway tunnel to just below the Eiger window. Here there are a few galleries giving access onto the wall. They were originally used for dumping rubble during the construction of the tunnel. We attempted to get on to the face by the gallery window closest to the route. It transpired that the conditions were as bad as they could be, but we still wanted to make an attempt. Peters went out on to the face belayed on a double rope. Because of the heavy snowfalls of the previous few days, it was quite wintry and during this time avalanches, some of them formidable, thundered down, often releasing great clouds of powder snow. Obviously, any search work would be very difficult in these conditions; the danger was so great that after a few hours we had to give up the idea of getting any further out onto the face. The rock was covered with an ice layer 10-cm thick; no sooner had we cut steps than they were immediately filled with cascading powder snow. So, back to the gallery window.

The Swiss flyers were not idle this day either; they took photographs, hoping that something would be revealed when they were blown up. From this visual material and various observations we concluded that a spine of rock on the Second Icefield would probably have seemed a logical line to the two mountaineers. So they had possibly left their bivouac equipment and rucksacks beneath it and attempted to climb it in reconnaissance. But they must soon have realised that it wasn't feasible and therefore descended to their rucksacks – this clambering up and down had been observed by a gamekeeper. They then bivouacked in a niche they had already found and probably due to the cold and the snow storm went to sleep never to awake. It seemed to all of us that something like this must have happened. To reach the Death Bivouac, as it was later called, in good weather would be possible only with great difficulty and risk. We would need to consider carefully whether it was feasible and indeed justifiable to undertake such a venture to recover two corpses. We decided to wait until the next morning. Two more Munich climbers arrived to strengthen our team, Hans Teufel and Albert Herbst.

The next day, Saturday, the six of us went up to the start of the face. From very early in the morning avalanches of stones and snow were hurtling down, as if trucks were continuously dumping their loads off the top. They were sweeping the wall like torrents. The marginal crevasses going round under the face were filled with avalanched snow. Despite the poor visibility, we decided to proceed to climb to the Eiger window in three parties. That was a wearisome business, traversing upwards, for one minute we were in an avalanche runnel that was so hard in places we needed crampons, then it was ploughing through fresh deep powder snow. At 14.00 hours the sun came out and all hell let loose. Avalanches like a great barrage opened up unpredictably all over the wall. It meant we had to take cover from these under overhangs and in holes as quickly as possible and wait until 19.00 hours when the sun had crept off the summit rocks. The face soon became quieter and in a short time everything was frozen, covered in ice. We were certain that the missing men could not be lying on the lower section of the Eigerwand, the middle of which is smooth and steep. In the event of a fall nothing would come to rest here. Tired and depressed we retreated to Alpiglen. There we discussed our efforts so far and resolved to go up the West Flank right to the summit the next day and from there descend the wall.

On Sunday, 1st September, we went to the Eigergletscher station again equipped with high-power binoculars and a tripod. The West Flank was certainly the easiest route to the Eiger summit at 3,975 metres, despite the fact that the conditions demanded good climbing know-how, and as we had to scramble up every ridge and eminence that gave us a clear view, great care was necessary. It was all in vain; we didn't see any sign of our friends. We reached the summit around midday and by descending the ridge a short way to the north-east, we had a good view of the North Face. To climb down this wall, however, was impossible at that time because several cornices overhung the ridge; there was besides two metres of snow lying on the summit and we could not find the food dump left by the two missing men. A descent would have required at least three bivouacs and indeed whether it would still be possible during the remainder of that year was the big question. Powder snow avalanches continually leapt down the face. So again we had to return to our base having achieved nothing.

On Monday another attempt was made to get on to the face from the Eiger window, but again it had to be called off as the weather conditions had hardly improved at all since Friday. With heavy hearts we now resolved to abandon the attempt because of the advanced time of year and the deep-winter-type conditions. It seemed impossible to us that the two could still be alive. We had tried everything humanly possible, but the unanimous view of the company was that not only would any further attempt put our own lives at risk, it would be irresponsible and foolhardy. The mountain was stronger than human skill or will. But we resolved that the following year we would come again and bring down our dead comrades and return home with them.

Back in Grindelwald everyone was most sympathetic over the fate of the two lost men. We took our leave and made arrangements with the Swiss guides that, should there be an unexpectedly fine autumn and the face become free of snow, we would return. We had experienced the fullest co-operation from all quarters, including the Swiss authorities.

The journey back to Munich was a bad one; it rained very heavily and we were still very preoccupied with the trauma of the search. At Berne the sun suddenly appeared and our spirits rose. We were starving but had little money and we wondered how we should overcome this problem. Then Rudi Peters had a bright idea. he knew a well-known writer who lived near Berne whom he wanted to visit. With luck, he said, we should get plenty of food there. He was right! A great spread was provided and we sat around the table and ate our fill. Nor did the hospitality end there; the writer's wife made us masses of sandwiches for our journey. But we had barely gone twenty kilometres when we came to a big orchard. We all agreed that this would make a delectable interlude as the apples were asking to be picked. Naturally, both sandwiches and apples disappeared in this impromptu picnic – climbers are renowned for their prodigious appetites. The journey back was a pleasant one after the rigours we had been through and our Kompressorwagen went like a dream; we were able once more to smile on life and enjoy the wonderful scenery and the fact that we were alive.

After a few weeks we heard from Grindelwald that pilot Oberst Udet with the mountain guide, Fritz Steuri, had made a flight across the Eiger face and had sighted one of the missing men at the Death Bivouac. He was sitting huddled up, face on hands, and the snow reached to above his knees. It was assumed that his companion was probably still in his bivvy sack buried under the snow. This flight proved that due to the heavy snow it would be totally impossible to recover them till the following year. For the victims' parents it was some small comfort to know at least where they were.

In the spring 1936 we were in touch with Grindelwald again. We received regular reports on weather and the snow conditions on the face. On 5th July I went with the then leader of the German Berg-wacht, R. Siebenwurst, to Grindelwald to arrange accommodation for our rescue team and to discuss the situation with the local guides. These men knew their mountain better than anyone and could give the best advice. We also intended to take a look at the face from the West Flank to see if a plan I had hatched would prove possible to put into practice.

On the West Flank at about 3,500 metres there is a gap in the ridge into which a chimney from the North Face leads. This chimney is some 150 metres long and links up with the band of rock that crosses the face (the upper limit of the Third Icefield). I now thought that we could abseil down this chimney by means of a 6-mm wire rope from a winch established on the ridge. Traversing the band would then not be so desperate as there were good belay possibilities at the junction of the ice and rock. But most of all the retreat and recovery of men and equipment could be guaranteed more quickly and safely. We wanted to get everything ready on the spot.

When we got to the Eigergletscher station we learned of an accident a couple of days earlier on the Schneehorn to two of our last year search helpers. Hans Teufel was dead, and Bertl Herbst injured in Lauterbrunnen hospital. After a successful ascent on the extremely difficult North Face of the Schneehorn, an ice peg had pulled out on the descent. Teufel fell and died instantly from a broken neck. Herbst only sustained a few grazes and bruises. He had to pass the night beside his friend on the ice and it was only the next day that his cries for help were heard by the Eigergletscher station. We enquired at the hospital after Herbst and were told by the doctor that we could take him back to Munich with us in a couple of days' time. All sorts of rumours were abroad; some said the pair had been in training for the Eiger Nordwand, others that the two had been sent out to see what the conditions were like with a view to recovering last year's victims.

After we completed the reconnaissance from the West Flank we descended and near Scheidegg met the first two recruits for an Eiger attempt that year, two Austrians, Edi Rainer and Willi Angerer. We visited them in their tent at the foot of the face. Both were splendid young men and made a good impression as climbers. The day we left Grindelwald they made their first recce of the wall. As for us, we drove round to Lauterbrunnen and collected Bertl Herbst. He was very depressed and could barely reconcile himself to the death of his friend. It was tough that the mountain had again demanded a victim, and very painful for him to return home without his climbing companion.

Once back in Munich we learned via the communications network we had organised that Rainer and Angerer had got company. Toni Kurz, a guide, and Anderl Hinterstoisser, a climber from Berchtesgaden, had set up their tent close by, having come from the Dolomites where they had climbed some of the hardest routes, including the North Face of the Cima Grande. They were apparently very fit and experienced. There was no rivalry between them; in true mountaineering spirit they made a joint reconnaissance climb and discussed their plans and proposals together. On the 17th the weather was somewhat better and on the 18th the two parties were able to make a start on the face. They had dumped food and equipment up to 3,000 metres.

The major difficulties began from the bivouac site below the Rote Fluh. Angerer and Rainer had already had an abortive attempt on this section. An overhang was passed on the right and the easier terrain reached by an extremely difficult overhanging crack, about the level

of the First Icefield. Now, however, steep smooth slabs blocked the
way to the Icefield. However Hinterstoisser overcame these difficulties with panache. He traversed using a rope in a pendulum
movement. They now reached the first bivouac site which had taken
last year's contenders two days. They had reached in one day the same
level as Sedlmayr and Mehringer's third bivouac. It was obvious to all
who watched that the two parties were moving well and working as a
unit. On the Sunday morning the four climbers were seen to leave
their bivouac. Shortly afterwards a veil of cloud encircled the mountain and nothing could be seen, but above the clouds the top third of
the mountain was showing throughout that Sunday. The reappear-
ance of the climbers was awaited with much anxiety. But nothing
happened. Neither party was visible beyond the spot where Mehringer
and Sedlmayr were seen for the last time the previous year, before the
storm enshrouded the mountain.

Shortly before eight am on the Monday the climbers were seen
again, continuing their attempt, albeit very slowly. But something
was amiss. Towards midday, shortly before the face was again
covered by mist, all four were back in their Sunday bivouac. There
was much speculation amongst the various observers manning the
telescopes. Had they given up? Were the difficulties insuperable? Or
had something happened to one of them that prevented their continuing? Several people noticed that one of the climbers didn't seem to
move so well as the others. It was thought that perhaps one of the
many stone falls that had been seen had injured him. Again cloud and
shreds of mist veiled the mountain and hid the 3,600-metre bivouac
site of the two parties from view. Anxious hours passed; everyone
hoped for the best. Another night came and went and by morning the
weather had again taken a turn for the worse; there was nothing to be
seen. Then suddenly for a brief moment the mists parted and the face
was clear. There was a mad scramble for the telescopes. The men
were seen on the Second Icefield above the Rote Fluh. They were
therefore retreating. It was easy now to see that one was injured, for
two of them were continually helping him. The descent with the
injured man was a very time-consuming business. At 8.30 pm they
reached the bivouac site that Sedlmayr and Mehringer had used for
their second night.

On the morning of the 21st July it was pouring with rain and above
there was fresh snow on the face. It would be hard to describe what it

is like to climb in such conditions after a frigid bivouac. Their rope must have been as stiff as a wire hawser (we were still using hemp rope at that time) and the rocks encased in a sheath of ice. Again clouds rolled in forming thick curtains; stone falls tumbled down and over the rock overhangs torrents of water and snow avalanches poured in continuous destruction. The traverse to them must have seemed impossible and so they resolved to abseil down the overhangs on the face below. They deliberated a long time over this abseil because the vertical and overhanging section below required several pegs and they only had a few. As the first one descended, a railway worker came out of the gallery window and called up the face to see if everything was all right. They called back, "All's well." It may have been the encouragement of finding themselves once more within shouting distance of other people. The linesman marked their position using a shovel as a pointer and went back to his work.

When he returned two hours later, he could hear cries of help from the face. He ran to the Eigerfenster station and telephoned the Jungfrau railway office for immediate assistance. There were three Wengen guides at the Eigergletscher station, sheltering from the storm. They were Christian Rubi, his brother Adolf, and Hans Schlunegger. A special train was ordered to take them to the gallery window, as the guides assembled their rescue gear – despite the ruling which had gone out that no life was to be put in jeopardy on the Eigerwand.

As the three climbed out of the gallery window, they were immediately assaulted by the violent storm raging on the face. It took all their strength to make a traverse of around 200 metres, running the gauntlet of continual stone bombardment and avalanches, until they were within shouting distance of the climber. His calls for help were getting increasingly more urgent. They heard, "Throw down a rope from above, no more pegs . . ." It was the cry of only one man. The guides shouted to him that it was impossible to get above him that day, he would have to wait until tomorrow. In agitation he shouted back "No, no, no!" It was terrible to hear; then he shouted something else about "Dead", but his words were carried away by the storm. The storm was so strong by then that the guides only just had time to withdraw to the gallery window before complete darkness set in. Between the crash of avalanches the man outside could be heard yelling for help like a wild animal. The icy face hurled back the inhuman, demented cries. It pierced everyone to the quick. Could he withstand the night?

Next day as soon as it began to get light the Swiss guides went once more through the gallery window and out on to the hostile face. The cries for help still came down from the wall. What must he have endured during this long night – yet he still lived! He grew quiet when he heard that they would now attempt to rescue him. They reached to within forty-five metres of the difficult section where Toni Kurz was hanging beneath an overhang in a single rope sling.

"Are the others still alive?" one of the guides shouted.

"No, they died yesterday. I am quite alone. One is frozen above me, one fell yesterday and the other hangs below me on the rope, he too is frozen – dead."

"Can you free yourself from the corpses? Try it and save as much rope as possible." Kurz climbed down twelve metres to his dead friend and with his ice axe cut the rope. Then again he climbed up to the other body and there, too, cut through the rope. The section of rope thus gained was frozen solid, but with incredible perseverance he began to separate it, untwisting the strands, with only one hand. (The guides had noticed that he only used one hand when he was abseiling, the other was frozen.) Only an experienced climber can appreciate what an achievement that was. When he had unravelled the frozen strands, he joined them so that he had a piece fifty metres long. He weighted it with a stone and lowered it to the guides. Hours had passed. One can but marvel at his will to live, his stamina! This man Kurz would have climbed the North Wall if the weather hadn't put a stop to it. Now the guides fastened a forty-metre rope, pitons, karabiners and hammer to the line and watched as it was raised by Kurz. (A second rope should have been sent up to the trapped climber.) Kurz hammered in the pegs and then the guides waited to see if he would pull the rope in any further. For a while he did; powder avalanches were meanwhile falling all around, but at last the rope stopped and Toni Kurz appeared over the overhang. He had therefore secured the rope above and was abseiling on it single. Slowly he came closer but the guides noticed the nearer he came, the more his strength ebbed. He was using a sit-sling for abseiling and the rope ran through a karabiner. There was no other method he could employ using only one hand. By holding the rope taut from below the guides gave him some assistance. But now he was coming to the knot where the ropes were joined. What would he do now? It would be impossible for him to get the bulky knot through the karabiner which was four metres above the guides. He realised this. Up till then his energy and his tenacious hold on life had been remarkable, now defeat threatened. Encouraging words were no longer of any help. The guides could see that suddenly it was all over. He tipped forward and didn't move any more. His face was red and frozen, his hands swollen and from his crampons hung long icicles. When it had appeared that rescue was almost achieved, his flame of life had been extinguished. Numbed and dazed, the guides took their difficult route back, immersed in the memory of the skill and courage of the young climber who still hung from the rope.

What happened on that Tuesday? What the misfortune was which cost the lives of those four young hopeful climbers we shall never know for certain. We have the sketchy details that Toni Kurz told the guides; climbers can only surmise the rest. The last one knows for certain of the party is that after the railway worker's call they decided to abseil down the eighty-metre overhang. This was because a retreat over the traverse was not possible. Hinterstoisser must have been injured by stone fall or avalanche and fallen either attempting this traverse or preparing a stance for the abseil. He took the rope and pegs for the abseil with him when he fell. Angerer, too, came off, either in the same stone fall or attempting to help his fallen comrade, but he remained hanging on the rope to which Kurz also was secured, held by a peg. Rainer was above them, at the beginning of the traverse, and must have frozen to death when, after Angerer's fall, he was yanked up like a puppet and left hanging jammed against the piton. Kurz was the only one not pulled off when all this happened, perhaps he was well belayed. The Swiss guides did all they could, we can corroborate that. There was nothing more that I could have done myself, taking into account the conditions at the time and the rescue methods in existence then. I was to learn a lot from these experiences and they helped us to develop new rescue techniques.

The police had raised the alarm and summoned our Bergwacht as soon as cries for help were heard on the Eigerwand and we had in fact arrived at the gallery window and were preparing to climb out, as the Swiss guides returned from their attempted rescue. Deeply shocked, they told us the story. We couldn't believe it. We could only inadequately thank them for their effort in trying to assist our friends, despite the terrible weather. It now remained for us to recover our dead.

The next morning we arrived at the gallery exit early. We took the same route as the guides had done the previous day. Again there was masses of new snow, and we had therefore to be very cautious. We fixed up a hand-rail, as we wished to take Kurz's body down to the gallery window. It was terrible seeing Toni hanging free on the rope some four metres out from the face and about three metres above our stance. We considered how we might get the body off the rope and down to us without it falling off into space. From its long exposure, Toni's rope was encased in ice making it as thick in diameter as a beer mug. We were amazed that the rope could withstand this weight of ice (it was forty-five metres long) as well as the weight of the body. There was therefore no way of getting up to the body by prussiking up the rope. We had with us a four-metre long pole and with a sling attached to the end of it we tried to get hold of a foot, arm or head and thereby belay him before he fell off into the depths when we cut the rope. We tried for three hours without success; when one of us got tired, another would take over, but it was all in vain. We were secured on a double rope; even so it was extremely difficult to move freely on our stance. We therefore decided to cut the rope without belaying the body and duly fixed a knife on to our pole for this purpose. He fell, as we had predicted, on to the smooth slabs a few metres below us. The ice broke off him and, separated from the rope, he shot down over the rock and snow runnels until he disappeared from our view. We would not be able to reach him until the following day in any case, but we wanted next to attempt to recover Rainer who was still hanging frozen above the great overhang. We crossed under the overhang a little further to the right and were then able to see him.

We knew the whole business was being watched through the telescopes at Kleine Scheidegg. On that lonely stance we discussed all possible aspects of recovering Rainer's body, but had to retrace our steps to the gallery entrance as we were under constant threat from falling stones. We knew it would not be feasible to effect the recovery in these conditions. Added to which, the dead man was completely frozen into the ice; once it thawed perhaps he would fall down unaided. So, wait a bit, we thought. There were now three bodies at the foot of the face; they would need to be recovered from Alpiglen.

In the evening we sat with the Swiss guides and Fritz von Almen, the owner of Scheidegg Hotel. It could be seen with all of them, in word or gesture, these tragic events had left their mark. Fritz von Almen told us a bit more about the route, with the aid of his big telescope, which was invaluable. Early on Friday we climbed up to the lower section of the North Face. This consisted of a whole series of steep snowfields with rocky buttresses in between and avalanche-scoured gullies. Everything had to be searched. But our diligence was rewarded – we found one of the fallen men, whom we later established to be Angerer, hanging in a steep gully. We wrapped him in a casualty bag and carried him down. The rest of the men not required for the transport continued searching. They found various bits of camera equipment and a watch. This was in the main gully into which everything from above is channelled. It was therefore where Toni Kurz must have shot down when we cut him free. Checking the fall-line, we saw a huge marginal crevasse at the bottom which in places was completely filled with newly avalanched snow. The parts of the crevasse that were still open were under constant bombardment from falling stones. So we had to abandon this to await better weather conditions before we could search it.

We did, however, find a second body that day. It turned out to be Sedlmayr from the previous year's attempt. So the mystery was solved; the two men must have been swept from their bivouac site by avalanches and carried down. But of his companion we found nothing.

Several days' searching went by and it was decided we could have another attempt at bringing down Rainer who was still frozen up in the crack. Our party was six strong; we climbed out of the gallery on to the face with enough rope to cross the Hinterstoisser Traverse at the end of which Rainer was suspended. We had to do the climb the same way as the climbers had done it. Steep sections of the face with broken rock led to the so-called Difficult Crack, which is very overhanging. The stone fall danger in this part of the face is considerable, for the stones come down in free flight from 400–500 metres above, over the Rote Fluh.

When we were standing on the band from which the Hinterstoisser Traverse drops down leftwards, we saw Rainer very clearly forty metres below. The ice had completely cleared. It took a while before we had four men up there and were all ready for the abseil – suddenly there was a strange noise and we couldn't believe our eyes – Rainer and the ice beneath him fell into the depths.

Shattered by this sight, we took a while to recover our senses. Actually we were relieved because who knows whether the recovery would have been completed safely? We now abseiled, and were very pleased to get back to the safety of the gallery window without incident, except for the loss of some ropes. We left them in place because they had been exposed to stone fall, so would be no more use for rescues, and they were used by later parties retreating from the Traverse.

During the following days we were again at the foot of the face and recovered Rainer from one of the marginal crevasses. We were unable to find Toni Kurz. There was still too much avalanche debris in the crevasses. We decided to postpone that search for a later date. In fact the conditions were such that his body wasn't recovered until the following year.

In a sense we left Grindelwald without success – we were not able to help our friends, but at least we were able to recover their bodies from the face and that was some comfort to their relatives. But what was as important was that none of our team suffered any mishap. We had been lucky, considering the conditions. In my mind it was as if our good intentions were rewarded with good luck.

When we got back home we kept ourselves prepared and equipped to rescue other climbers from the Eiger. For we knew that this face would feature more and more in the sights of good climbers; we were proved right.

2

The Eigerwand, 1957–62

The first British ascent of the North Face of the Eiger was a prize plum in our mountaineering orchard. I was well aware of this and during the spring of 1957 I contacted Chris Bonington who was then serving in a tank regiment in Germany to see if he was interested in attempting the climb. We were old friends and though I was aware that he hadn't climbed in the Alps before, I said in my letter to him, "Where better could you get such a fitting introduction to these Alps?" He wasn't totally convinced, but his spirit of adventure outweighed his common sense and we met in Grindelwald in July, 1957. Meantime, he had done a bit of Eiger research and was somewhat perturbed when he discovered that the wall then had only twelve ascents and had claimed fourteen lives. Anyhow, I managed to allay his fears, saying the climb was in the bag and, clutching a postcard with the route marked on it – our only guide – we set off. He didn't have much equipment and I gave him the plastic cover off my motorcycle to serve as a bivouac sack.

Our first acquaintance with the Eigerwand was of a passing nature, for after setting up a bivouac on the lower wall, threatening cloud caused us to scurry like squirrels for the valley and spend the remainder of our climbing holiday on the aiguilles of Chamonix.

A short time after that abortive pioneering attempt, where we barely tickled the soles of the Eiger, a rescue swung into operation on the north face which was a further instalment on this wide screen where Death invariably plays a principal part. It is a production where a 'hit' is a collision with a falling stone. The rescue of Claudio Corti from the Exit Cracks of the Spider confirmed Gramminger's faith in the use of steel cables for big wall rescues.

Ludwig's Bergwacht joined forces with Erich Friedli, a Swiss rescue team leader who shared a similar outlook to rescue work and techniques to Gramminger. Erich had assembled a formidable band of internationally known climbers on the summit when the Bergwacht arrived and the winch equipment was set in position for the very long operation down the face. Alfred Hellepart was lowered 320 metres on a thin steel wire to the trapped climbers. He reached Corti and discovered that Corti's companion, Stefano Longhi, was also alive 100 metres away. Hellepart succeeded in getting Corti up on his back, hauled from the top by the winch wire. But when Lionel Terray took over Hellepart's role and went down for Longhi, the radio failed and the attempt had to be abandoned. Longhi died, as did the other two men that had joined forces with them on the climb, two young Wurttemberg climbers, Gunther Nothdufft and Franz Mayer. After Longhi got injured, they had pressed on for help, leaving their vital bivouac sack with Corti who had exhausted himself trying to help his companion. After completing the climb, the two German climbers had died on the descent on the West Face of the mountain. Their bodies were not found until four years later.

I have avoided writing, or rather using a full account of this rescue as it has been well documented elsewhere, often with more than its fair share of hypothetical speculation on the actions and motives of the participants. The last words should perhaps be from Alfred Hellepart, for this quiet-spoken member of the Bergwacht was surely the hero of the operation. After a hellish night out on the descent with Corti, where a bivouac tent was torn to shreds by the wind, they continued down the following morning.

Alfred later wrote:

> Our small group of German friends stumbled down that last rock buttress to where the others were already waiting. Amongst those there were some who were more interested in making capital out of the whole business than in helping. We didn't want to have anything to do with these people. Up above we had become aware of something quite different, sacred to us, no one could rob us of these memories. We could understand each other without lengthy dialogue. This was apparent as we pressed hands and looked each other in the eye as we bade goodbye. May it always be so in the mountains.

Though I returned to the Eiger hopeful of the first British ascent, it was not to be. Like so many before me, heavy snow and bad weather made any attempt out of the question. However, Chris persevered and on one occasion with Don Whillans rescued Brian Nally from the Second Icefield. Nally's story as narrated in an interview for the BBC Documentary, 'The Climb Up To Hell', is one of the most moving in the annals of mountaineering. Brian had teamed up with a student, Barry Brewster, a highly proficient rock climber, though he didn't have a great deal of snow and ice experience. The previous year Brian had made the first British ascent of the Matterhorn North Face with a Scotsman, Tom Carruthers. Tom was later killed on the Eiger. I knew Tom well, he used to sleep under a bridge close to my house when climbing in Glencoe. There was so little room under this bridge that its occupants had to crawl about. He and his friends who frequented this doss were known as the 'Bendie-Bendie Boys'. Brian

Nally was a painter and like Barry Brewster came from southern England. Brian describes the climb:

> We approached the Hinterstoisser; it's not a very difficult move, but it's got quite a strange psychological effect. The Hinterstoisser is the Rubicon of this mountain. In theory, if you leave a rope on it to traverse, you can come back across, but in actual fact only a handful of men have crossed it and come back. No British party had been across. It was a setback and it happened to be my turn to lead. I was a little wary about it. I looked at the weather, almost hoping for it to be bad enough for an excuse to turn back. But it was clear. I looked down at Barry and he simply said "Best of luck, Brian," and that was it. That was the decision made and, once it was, everything settled into place. We went across, through this torrential waterfall, up a chimney and into the Swallow's Nest. We reached there just before nightfall and everything so far was going to plan. We were happy that night because the decision had been made, everything now was just to get to the summit. It didn't freeze that night, but we didn't worry too much about that.

After that bivouac they continued up on to the Second Icefield the next day.

> We got to the Second Icefield; we knew it was a long one, but the distance was enormous from where we were to the first rocks. It was late now and the Second Icefield was water, ice and slush. It was in very bad condition. We resolved to plough straight across rather than go for the rim. We decided to cut steps, firstly because the condition of the icefield wasn't good and, secondly, in case we had to retreat. So we ploughed across and the stones started coming down; we'd been through stone fall many times before, but we hadn't seen anything like this. The icefield was raked in every quarter and then suddenly all Hell would break loose. We turned in to face the ice and tried to dodge the big ones and hope the little ones wouldn't catch us, though we got hit several times. But we just pressed on and on. The icefield is incredible, it's endless . . . We were glad that the Second Icefield was over.
>
> Barry said, "There's a pitch of grade 5 up above." (This is one grade below the highest standard.) Now I belayed to a ring peg and

watched him as he set off up his pitch, the start of the Flat-iron. Higher up Barry put in two other pitons then he went out of sight . . .

Everything went quiet for a bit. The rope stopped, then paid out again. Suddenly, from high above I heard him yell "Stones!" In-stinctively, I dodged and kept close to the rock and at the same time I heard my name sharp and clear and I looked up and Barry was falling backwards through the air. He went hurtling past me, the two top pitons pulled out. He crashed on to the ice about a hundred feet below. For a moment I just stood there staring at the ring piton, not believing that it could have held and then I looked down at him. He was upside down on the ice. He wasn't moving. I stayed there for a minute and then I put a piton in and tied the rope to it and unroped, climbed up to the ring piton and hit it back in. Then I climbed down to Barry; he was very badly injured and uncon-scious. From the position of his body I came to the conclusion that his back was broken.

I formed a harness in the rope, took all the weight off his chest and hung him in the sling. Normally, it would have been quite a comfortable position. The stones were still coming so I started to hack out a platform and this took a long time. It had to be long and wide enough for his full length. I was grateful that he was uncon-scious, hadn't got any pain. When this platform was completed, I pulled him back into it, secured him and put him in the sleeping bag. Then I took my crash helmet off and put it on him and . . . and then tried to form a barrier between him and the upward slope. It was late in the afternoon by then and everything looked . . . every-thing was lost. It wasn't a question of just one of us being injured. This was the Eiger and it was both of us, you see. Once or twice I went up to the rock where I'd left some gear, brought it back and settled down for the night. I sort of placed myself between him and the upward slope and just waited for the morning. Stones were relentless. We were immediately in a path of one of the shutes that has a direct line to the summit where all the stones funnel down. We couldn't have moved to the right or to the left. We just had to stay where we were.

During the night I had to make the decision whether at first light I should leave Barry and try and go for my friends to help, or stay. It was obvious Barry was very badly injured; the point was, I couldn't bear for him to regain consciousness and me not to be there. It was a most terrible decision to have to make, and I spent the whole night trying to make it, but even at first light I hadn't made that decision. Because I wouldn't admit that he wasn't going to pull through and, though he'd been unconscious, he had moved once or twice, but he hadn't really woken. At first light I tried . . . tried to really make this decision and he appeared to stir a little, moved an arm and he seemed to regain consciousness a bit, so I went back again up the slope and got a stove, thinking that I'd make a drink or some soup or something if he could take it. I started to make this and he seemed to come to a bit. He opened his eyes and seemed to know where he was and who I was and said, "I'm sorry, Brian," and he died.

Everything went dark; it really was the end of – everything. First reaction was to go for the summit at any cost, because that's what we'd come to do; I couldn't bear the thought of going down. But time passed, I rationalised and came to the proper decision. So I secured him once more with ice pitons and cut the rope above him and took the rope, meaning to try for the descent. I went up again to the belay but came down once more to Barry and just stayed there for a little while. I couldn't bear to take any of the pieces of equipment that were so vital to me now. I couldn't bear to take the crash helmet or the ice screws and pitons. So I left everything just where it was . . .

I knew this was the last time I was leaving him and I started to go back up the slope; the stones had kept up all night, but they seemed to increase now. The whole field was raked from every quarter again. Suddenly, I felt this was bigger than usual; I started moving a bit faster and I was about twenty feet away from the rock when tons of rubble and ice came down; I was directly in the path of the rock avalanche. I raced for the rock and just got there, but turned round to see that this avalanche whisked Barry's body away and took it over the edge of the ice into the blackness. This was the cruellest thing that could have happened.

Chris Bonington and Don Whillans were not aware that Barry and Brian were ahead of them, having set out twenty-four hours previously. When Chris and Don reached the foot of the Second Icefield, they realised that the weather was worsening and decided to retreat.

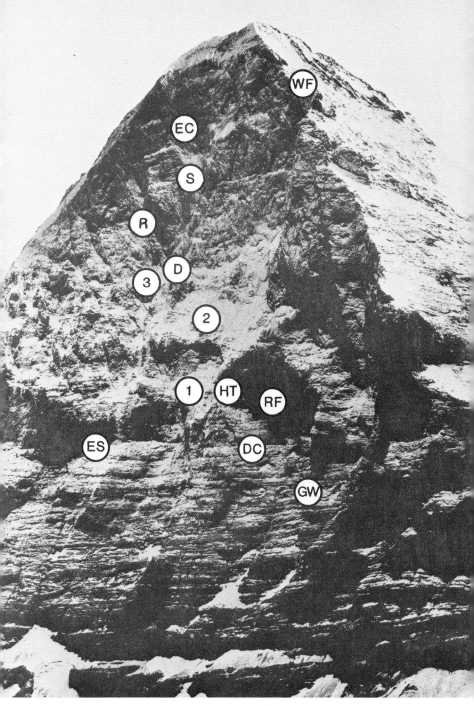

The Eigerwand: GW = Gallery Window, ES = Eigerwand Station,
DC = Difficult Crack, RF = Rote Fluh, HT = Hinterstoisser Traverse,
1 = First Ice Field, 2 = Second Ice Field, 3 = Third Ice Field,
D = Death Bivouac, R = Ramp, S = Spider, EC = Exit Cracks,
WF = West Flank.

The Mercedes Kompressorwagen in which the German Bergwacht drove through the night from Munich to Grindelwald in 1935.

Below left, a special plane to Berne was put at the disposal of the Bergwacht. Below right, Toni Kurz's body hanging free from the North Face of the Eiger on the ice-encased rope, 1936.

The rescue of Claudio Corti from the Exit Cracks of the Spider in 1957 confirmed Ludwig Gramminger's faith in the use of steel cables for big wall rescues; Alfred Hellepart about to be lowered 320 metres to the trapped climbers.

Moving down from the summit on the West Flank with Corti on the stretcher.

Corti safely in the bag.

The German Bergwacht return home after the Corti rescue, Hellepart second from left, Gramminger in the white cap.

South-West Face of the Matterhorn, showing the line of Lothar Brandler's fall, from F to the edge of the bergschrund, B.

Rescuers rescue themselves: the West Face of the Matterhorn at 900 metres with the couloir and the bergschrund (B) and the line of Brandler's fall. Brandler, who had been leading, came off and took Heckmair and Buschmann with him. Brandler (right) sits on his ice axe in a state of shock; Heckmair leans against Buschmann, left.

Gramminger about to take over carrying Anderl Heckmair who has broken ribs and a dislocated shoulder.

Heckmair, his legs secured to a bridge splint, is transported in the half-Akya stretcher.

The path of the avalanche in the Tatras.

Corridors were cut to probe for survivors.

They were just about to descend when two figures appeared from below. They were Swiss guides and they told them about the accident above and asked for their help. Chris and Don volunteered this without a moment's hesitation and set off across the vast expanse of the Second Icefield. They were continually subjected to stone fall and after a particularly bad one they looked across towards the Flatiron which was the direction it had come from and to their horror saw the tiny figure of a man being swept off into space. This was Barry Brewster. The guides promptly returned to the gallery window while Chris and Don pressed on towards Brian Nally who was visible as a mere speck of red at the top of the icefield.

Despite a storm, they got Brian down safely, a remarkable feat considering that Chris had lost his ice axe on the way up. The guides recovered Brewster's body from the bottom of the face. Later Brian Nally was presented with a bill of several hundred pounds for the rescue operation which he couldn't pay. This included a special train and the services of fourteen guides, which seems a bit ironical. It is also a sad reflection on journalism that for some unknown reason the train which was to take the soaked and exhausted climbers back to Kleine Scheidegg remained for almost an hour in the tunnel whilst reporters prised the whole story from Brian, who was still severely shocked.

Chris was to return to the Eiger later in that same year, 1962, and this time he was successful. Ian Clough was his companion, but even then death was at their heels, for behind them Tom Carruthers and an Austrian, Egon Moderegger, whom they had passed, had fallen to their deaths from the Second Icefield.

Now with helicopters capable of winching people off the most inaccessible parts of the face, the Eiger has lost much of its sting, but its place has been taken by other great walls in the Himalayas or the Karakoram; there will always be an 'Eiger'.

TWO

It was in the wake of the last war that I first made acquaintance with the Zmutt Ridge of the Matterhorn. As a kilted, inexperienced fledgeling, I was taken under the wings of two established canons of the mountains, George Ritchie and Derek Haworth, the first a solicitor, the second a doctor. With the objective of the Matterhorn's Zmutt Ridge determinedly implanted in our minds we made our way to the Schönbühl hut; our guidebook a postcard bought in Zermatt. My financial state was reflected in my lack of equipment; I didn't even have crampons.

The normal way to climb the Zmutt Ridge is from the Hörnli hut at the start of the ordinary route up the Matterhorn. We set out about two am when the saner Swiss dream of sheep in green pastures. In so doing, with only the light of a flickering candle lantern, we lost our way and inadvertently ventured into the jaws of the notorious Penhall Couloir which spewed rocks as soon as the sun touched the summit.

We endured the adventure, as did fortunately, Ludwig Gramminger and his companions several years later, for in 1956 in this same high angled corridor Ludwig was faced with the appalling prospect of getting his three injured companions back to safety, one of them gravely hurt. He describes the ordeal and, typical of the man, passes lightly over the momentous labour in rescuing his friends. It was an exacting test of his ability as a rescuer and of his proficiency as a mountaineer.

THE MATTERHORN AND THE BERGSCHRUND

by Ludwig Gramminger

In the summer of 1956 two climbers from Saxony, Vogel and Zireis, got into difficulties on the Zmutt Ridge of the Matterhorn. They had

come to Zermatt by motorbike with the intention of training on the
Matterhorn for an attempt later on the Eigerwand. They set up their
tent at the foot of the mountain on the banks of the Visp. The two,
both from Saxony, climbed to the Hörnli hut, spent the night there,
and then set off to climb the Zmutt Ridge and descend by the Hörnli
Ridge. They left their sleeping bags in the Hörnli hut. After eight days
the empty tent on the Visp bank drew attention. Police enquiries
indicated that the two had not returned from their Matterhorn climb.
The weather was very bad at the time this was discovered, but as soon
as it improved, a guided party and two guideless Viennese climbers
started up the Zmutt Ridge. After the Zmutt Pinnacles at the point
where one traverses into the Carrel Gallery (Carrel's Corridor), one of
the Viennese spotted a climber in front, above and to one side, wearing a red ski cap. At first he thought it must be the guide of the second
party but quickly realised that this was silly for they were behind. He
waited for the guide to catch up and pointed out his discovery. The
guide was puzzled and traversed across the face to discover a frozen
climber in a bivouac. The man had frozen to death in a sitting
position, secured to a peg. The guide took a few photographs, then
cut the body free and dropped it down the West Face. This upset Herr
Caplan, one of the climbers in his party, and he protested strongly
against the guide's action.

In Zermatt later the incident was discussed; it was a delicate matter
for the father of one of the missing men, Herr Vogel, had already
offered a reward for the finding of his son's body. It was perhaps
fortunate that from the photographs one couldn't tell if it was Vogel's
body which had been found or his companion, Zireis. After these
events the weather became very bad, the guide announced that he had
made a search for the body, but had found nothing.

Some time later Herr Vogel came to the offices of the Bergwacht in
Munich and asked for their help to locate his son's body. He said that
he had no further confidence in the Zermatt guides. I had to tell him
that after the recent bad weather and heavy snowfalls high up, there
was very little prospect of finding the missing men that year. "Even
the best Swiss guides would have small chance of doing so," I added.

Understandably, Herr Vogel continued to press for a search, so I
relented and promised to organise one right away. For my companion
I chose my old friend, the guide Anderl Heckmair who was then
nearly fifty, and as the weather had just turned for the better, we

decided to leave immediately for the Valais. It was 1st October, 1956. At the last moment Herr Vogel brought along two men to accompany us, two friends of the missing Saxons, Lothar Brandler and Klaus Buschmann. We weren't enamoured of the idea but, as there was room in the car, we agreed.

In Zermatt we first spoke to the police, then with the guides, to discover if anything else had been found in the meantime. Nothing had, so all four of us went up to the Schönbühlhütte on the west side of the mountain, accompanied by a Swiss lady. At the hut we met Ludwig Steinauer and he promised to keep the Schönbühlhütte open, as it had already closed for the season. We had brought up with us a half-Akya stretcher with transport wheel. The weather was fine but very cold, which was good for our task.

Early next morning we set off from the hut and crossed the Zmutt Glacier to the foot of the Matterhorn's West Face. The Swiss lady remained in the hut. In about two and a half hours we reached the bergschrund. This was some two to four metres wide, with a fifteen-metre high vertical ice flank to climb on either side. There were also two snow bridges which proved very difficult. The lower slopes and the avalanche cone under the face yielded no trace of the victims and we came to the conclusion that in all probability the dead were buried under the masses of new snow. We roped up to search the area above the bergschrund to the start of the rock face, and to take a look into the couloir coming down from the Zmutt Ridge.

Anderl told Klaus and Lothar that they, too, should rope up and try to cross the bergschrund and the ice slope. Klaus, who tried first, didn't manage it, but Lothar then had a go and succeeded in reaching the upper edge of the dangerously steep, smooth ice cliff above and got a good stance. The vertical distance was about fifteen metres. Now Anderl and I made a serious error. We didn't go as a two-man rope, but attached ourselves with karabiners from our chest harnesses to the rope from Lothar, belayed above. We all reached the upper stance and let Lothar go on right away. Above, the conditions were good and without thinking too much about it, we were able to climb together on the rope using our twelve-point crampons and axe points. The going was excellent on the hard firn. It was at an angle of about 50°. It was a mistake, but we didn't give a moment's thought to the fact that one of us could make a false move; we only had eyes for the icefield around and above us which we were scouring.

We had already put a few rope's lengths behind us; but moving together without resting was too strenuous for me and I was puffing and panting.

I called to Andel who was second on the rope above, "I'm going to untie from the rope and traverse over to the left to the Zmutt Ridge and get on to the rocks. Perhaps I can find a good stance there. From there," I added, "I can search the upper section of the face with the glasses."

"Right," he shouted back. I unclipped from the main rope and moved up to the left, where I had to cross a small hard gully down which stones hurtled in the afternoon when the sun was on the West Face.

I was scarcely a metre above this gully when I heard a noise above. I looked up and couldn't believe my eyes. A man was shooting head-first towards me. It was Lothar Brandler, who had been leading. It all happened so quickly and the reason I didn't get torn off with him was because I had already crossed the gully and was out of his direct descent line. Anderl's attempt to arrest the fall with his ice axe failed as Lothar was already falling too fast and the firn snow was very hard with ice beneath. I saw the whole thing clearly as if in slow motion. Anderl now swept past me, plucked from the face. I shouted to him, I forget what now, and then saw Klaus, the last man on the rope, receive a terrible jerk; he was projected off backwards, as if by cata-pult, down the mountain without being able to do a thing about it. Helpless, I could only watch, numbed, unable to intervene. It was dreadful to see one, then the other, whipped off into space, to see arms, legs, axes, rope, tangled, flailing, whirling down the gully, and then to watch them disappear over the edge of the vertical cliff. It was a fifteen-metre drop – had they fallen into the open bergschrund? Far below, I was able to make out the avalanche cone again and I waited anxiously to see if they would reappear there where it ran out, but no. I now feared that they had fallen into the schrund. I shouted and listened alternately. Nothing.

Thoughts jumbled in my head; I had to force myself to consider carefully what to do – I can hear myself now, how I counselled myself out loud: "Wiggerl, you must think very carefully what is to be done!" It was as if I was rooted to the snow, standing there on the steep slope to one side of the hard gully, with four of the twelve crampon points in the firn and clutching my axe. I felt very alone; I

dared not make a wrong move – those below needed me. It would
have been dreadful had I fallen too . . .

Two of the others had lost their axes in the fall. They were still
sticking in the ice of the gully. Ice axes can be very useful items on a
rescue operation, for splinting and transporting the injured. I must
retrieve them, I thought. Carefully, step by step, I climbed downwards, then across and I had them. I could move well enough with
two, but with three – what'll I do with the third one, I asked myself? I
was tempted to stuff it across in my chest harness, but that could be
dangerous if I should fall too, so I hung it by its wrist loop to one arm.
With extreme care and yet not slowly I reached the top edge of the
bergschrund and the fifteen-metre ice wall. At last I could see what
had happened and was somewhat encouraged. Two of them lay close
together on the steep slope below the schrund, the rope ran up from
them and into the crevasse. So one of them had fallen into this and the
other two swept right over it and were now held by the rope. It
should therefore be possible to get the one in the crevasse out. I
shouted and then shouted again, and at last received a response, from
the man in the crevasse. I asked him whether he was injured, but he
only said he would see if he could climb up the rope. I called down
that I would soon be there to give him a hand. The two others were
lying motionless and I feared the worst.

But first I had to direct all my concentration on the difficult descent
of the ice wall with the three ice axes as a handicap. Immediately
below the open bergschrund yawned blackly, too deep to see the
bottom. I moved with circumspection, careful in case something
should break off, or in case I should fall, yet at the same time angling
diagonally down so that I shouldn't fall into the crevasse if I did slip. I
have forgotten how I managed to get down this tricky little wall
without assistance. I certainly had luck on my side – with a last strong
leap I reached the other side of the crevasse and stood beside the
rucksacks that we had left there. In the meantime, the man in the
crevasse had climbed up the rope and was now out, and I greeted him.
It was Lothar Brandler.

When I saw his face I was shocked but without letting it show – it
was badly lacerated and covered with blood, and then I saw that his
hands and arms were in the same state. He talked in strange, disjointed
fragments and I realised he was suffering from shock. His behaviour
confirmed it – he didn't look at me and even wanted to throw the two

rucksacks down the steep slope of some 250 metres. I had difficulty getting him down to the others. I carried the rucksacks myself and as I descended I could see that Anderl Heckmair was lying crumpled, unconscious and bleeding very badly from a gaping wound in the back of the head. Klaus Buschmann lay on his back, groaning loudly. He was having difficulty in breathing. I examined him and saw that he was not in fact badly injured. This eased my mind somewhat, but Anderl was quite still.

I told the two Saxons to clench their teeth firmly and only do what I told them, at the same time belaying them both to their ice axes. Then I encouraged them to help me get Anderl settled more comfortably. As a first measure I bandaged his nasty head wound, and as I was doing it, he awoke for a brief moment and though semi-conscious, complained of pain in his right shoulder and arm. I had a closer inspection and saw he had dislocated his shoulder. He passed out again. His unconsciousness was now to my advantage and his; with some exertion I managed to get his shoulder back into place. He awoke immediately after this operation and right away recognised the Dent d'Hérens North Face which was the first thing he saw. He named it but didn't connect it with his situation. He didn't remember the accident or why he was there. I was touched that he recognised me right away and immediately said, "If Wiggerl's here, then everything will be all right."

Like Klaus he was having great difficulty with his breathing. I realised this could only mean broken ribs. After this preliminary first aid, it was now important to get them out of the danger zone, off the steep slope. Above, the sun was creeping across the West Face and we could expect stone falls soon. The gully above was like a cannon barrel aimed directly at us, only awaiting the final triggering of the sun. Therefore we had to get out of the firing line as fast as possible, but how?

I gave the two young men precise instructions once again, securing them, one close in front of me, the other behind. They were like zombies, almost immobile, not with it, and I had to shout at them sharply to urge them on. There was no alternative; the urgent thing was to get Anderl down.

Only when we had safely reached the bottom of the slope and traversed round a bit to get out of the danger zone, did I take notice of the other injuries of all three. Luckily, I had plenty of dressing

material. As far as Lothar was concerned, after taking care of abrasions
to both arms, the worst was over; Klaus also had severe abrasions as
well as bad bruising to his back and his difficulty breathing. Later it
was confirmed he had a broken rib. Anderl was in the worst state.
Fortunately, the dislocation was now reduced and I strapped his arm
to his chest. But I was particularly worried that he couldn't hold up his
head; it kept dropping on to his chest or falling to one side. I considered what this might mean. Then from a pair of nylon over-
trousers I made a kind of cravat, a collar, wide, thick, strong and yet
soft. There was an immediate improvement. Further investigation
suggested that the difficulty in his breathing must be connected with
other serious injuries. I was aware that he must have several broken
ribs. I had a big over-anorak with me and used this as a strong support
bandage-wise over his chest. This was extremely painful for him but I
felt it would be the best thing in the long run. But what could I do
about the many contusions Anderl had suffered? He was unable to
move on his own and was in great pain if he tried to do so. It was
impossible for him to stand on his own; I had to support him continually. First I tried to lay him on his back, but that presented further
problems; I realised then that the lumbar vertebrae must be damaged.
I tried all possible ways of getting him into a carrying position so that
we could move him without causing him undue pain. The best seemed
to be if he leant sideways on to me, clinging to the straps of my
rucksack with his one good hand, his left one. I secured the rucksack
firmly to my back, then put my right arm round his waist and grasped
his belt. By this means I succeeded in easing things for him so that he
could take tiny steps, albeit with great pain. There was no other
choice, this was the only way we could, with luck, hope to get back to
the hut in daylight. Perhaps, given time, he might have got along
better by himself. But he could only put one foot ten centimetres in
front of the other, not a centimetre more.

    We were all still wearing crampons. So we painfully progressed.
Later when the snow surface became soft, I took off Anderl's
crampons. Every twenty or fifty metres I had to call a halt. The one
way Anderl could rest was for me to go behind him, a little higher so
that he could lean against my chest and sit on my knee. I very quickly
lost all feeling in my feet in this torturous 'resting' position. For me
these stops were the worst of all. But how could we have made this
difficult journey otherwise? I had thought of all sorts of possibilities:

such as attach him to the rucksack and carry him, but he would have suffered unbearable agony like that. No, this was the best, I concluded.

There was the additional problem of the two young men. I had to safeguard them across crevasses and supervise their every movement. Whenever it was time for a rest, the one in front would simply drop to the ground and the other would similarly crumple behind me and I could do nothing but look on. Anderl and I had difficulty instructing them in the simplest basic mountaineering rules; things like climbing down a glacier with crampons. I had to shout loudly, it was the only way I could get through to them. I knew that we still had in front of us a steep pitch of blank ice and that there the greatest difficulties awaited. Once at this impasse, I had to safeguard them step by step downwards, and then follow with the immobile Anderl. At every crevasse I had to traverse until it was a mere crack; only there was it possible to cross. Anderl still took the tiniest of steps. We had already been going five hours and finally had the glacier behind us. But now came rock and moraine that was almost more difficult than the ice. The good thing about this section was that finally I didn't have to worry about the two young men. There was no longer any danger, no crevasses, no fear of slipping; it was just wearisome. We could see the Schönbühlhütte and from time to time tried calling. But there was no-one to be seen.

After another hour, we heard shouts and saw climbers descending the moraine, which we had to reach to gain the hut. We were overjoyed and I was enormously relieved to see them. It would have been quite impossible for me to have overcome the sixty-metre high moraine wall without the help of a rope and a belay from above. Now a climber with a rope came down towards us, which enabled this last obstacle to be overcome.

Above, on the edge of the moraine, was the track to the hut and once there I would be faced with a difficult decision. With the help of the climbers I could be in the hut with Anderl in half an hour, but ought we not get all the injured down to Zermatt right away? Even with assistance from the climbers from the hut we couldn't get the three injured men down to the valley in less than four hours. It had already taken seven from the scene of the accident to the hut path. Moreover, we were all shattered. I tried to talk to Anderl, asked him how he felt. He was of the opinion that if he could rest and be taken care of in half an hour at the hut that would be best. I agreed that to get him into a good comfortable position was top priority. Also he, like the rest of us, needed rest.

We carried Anderl up to the hut in a rope seat, as quickly as possible, but I could see that his condition had deteriorated. That night I stayed up very late working out the method for transporting Anderl down to Zermatt. The Swiss lady, too, had her hands full after our arrival, taking care of Anderl who was completely helpless. The pain of his bruises got steadily worse and began to swell badly. There was also the problem of Lothar and Klaus. Klaus's contusions were giving him a lot of trouble now. He was covered in blue patches with terrible black swellings. I thought by morning he would surely be unable to use his limbs.

I got up very early and got our half-Akya assembled ready to carry Anderl. It was padded with our sleeping bags so that he would be more comfortable, with his legs secured to a bridge splint. Lothar and Klaus seemed to be completely incapable of movement. I explained to them that only exercise would ease their condition and allow them to move again. Once more I had to use strong words to get that message across. Two of the Swiss climbers helped me with the difficult business of evacuating Anderl to Zermatt and things went better for the two young Saxons once they got going. Anderl was reasonably comfortable on the journey and I was now thankful that I had let him rest in the hut overnight. It had been the right decision.

Arriving in Zermatt, we went straight to the doctor in the hospital. This was purely to have a look and see what was broken. Our resolve to get Anderl back home right away, come what may, was unchanged. He was given a firm, wide strapping over the whole chest. Luckily, the hole in his head turned out to be only a cut, probably caused by his ice axe. His shoulder was back in place and was in order, but it was established that he had a fracture in his cervical vertebrae.

Our car was in St Niklaus and when we fetched Anderl from hospital the next morning, the doctor expressed doubts about the wisdom of the long journey. But we made up a bed padded with sleeping bags by pushing the front passenger seat right back without its back rest. Lying with his legs bent, he travelled without pain over the Furka and Oberalp Passes, then through the upper Rhine Valley. After crossing the border at Oberstdorf, we took Anderl to hospital. A thorough examination revealed that he had also a fracture to a lumbar vertebra together with a fracture of the right clavicle. Six ribs were broken. Since the ribs forced Anderl to lie perfectly still, no plaster cast was necessary for the vertebrae.

Anderl, the first conqueror of the Eiger Nordwand, passed his fiftieth birthday in the hospital. We were both thankful it was all over; after all, we realised, it could have been a lot worse. I have often speculated on what would have happened if I hadn't untied from the rope above the bergschrund. All four of us would then have lain injured on the glacier and help, if it had come at all, would certainly have been too late. Above all, the fact that Lothar Brandler, who was still very young at the time, took the lessons of the accident very much to heart was gratifying. Later he gained extensive experience in ice techniques and, already being a fine rock climber, developed into an outstanding mountaineer.

THREE

Beware the pine tree's withered branch;
Beware the awful avalanche!

'Excelsior', H. W. Longfellow

An avalanche to the layman is often simply regarded as a mass of snow shooting down a mountain, just like a load of sand or gravel being tipped off a truck. The word avalanche is an all embracing one conveying everything from rock falls to soggy messes of slithering mud and earth which can be a serious problem in some countries in the spring thaw. Then there are the thoroughbreds of ice, powder snow, wet-snow and an assortment of slab avalanches, or indeed combinations of all these.

Avalanches are just one of many dangers sprung on the unwary by mountains. They can descend with devastating force, but they are not all in a hurry. A small wet avalanche can tumble down a slope as if it had all the time in the world, but its more flighty brother, the airborne powder avalanche can scour a face in a blast of destruction, reaching speeds of over 200 mph. It can rip reinforced concrete to pieces, leaving only a skeleton of steel and reduce villages and even towns to their foundations.

Up till the early 1960s very little notice was taken of avalanches in Britain. It is true that climbers were injured and killed by them on occasions, but they were considered to be an act of God. Later, however, once the ice climbing revolution got under way in the mid 1960s, the number of mountaineers on the hills rose dramatically in winter; and so inevitably more were caught in avalanches.

One of the earliest recorded avalanches in Scotland is shrouded in folklore and legend, but the bare facts are interesting enough. A certain Captain MacPherson was known as the 'Black Officer'; he was a despised recruiting officer, with whom many felt they had a score to settle. At one time he was reputed to have given a ball at Ballachroan and sent invitations to all the young bloods of the district. Though it wasn't a fancy dress ball, the wily captain had laid out a selection of smart red coats for the young men to try on, which they did with alacrity and laughter. Once resplendent in the uniforms they had signed their destiny. The captain's soldiers descended and pressed them into the service of the King. But in the end it was the Almighty who took vengeance and so the people of the district considered his death a fitting judgment.

On the 11th January, 1800 by the new calendar, but Old Yule according to the reckoning of the time, MacPherson and four other Highlanders went to Gaik, a remote bothy in the Cairngorms, to stalk. There were no witnesses to the catastrophe, other than perhaps a golden eagle or a red deer, when the avalanche thundered over that lonely lodge. The five men were buried and killed.

It was probably a wet-snow avalanche and it took the lodge apart as if it were made from old orange boxes. When a search party went up to look for the overdue hunters they were flabbergasted at the devastation, but they didn't have any tools with them to dig down to where the lodge had been, so they returned to Speyside and came back the next day with reinforcements, picks and shovels. They recovered four bodies including that of the Black Officer. The last man had been carried some way by the avalanche and was found much later in the year when the snow melted. The tremendous grinding force of the avalanche had twisted the hunters' guns which were found in the debris of the building. The accident created a lot of speculation at the time, for the Black Officer was said to to have been a buddy of Auld Nick as well as having other nefarious associations. A predecessor of McGonagall wrote:

> . . . Gashed, torn by the demon, the merciless foe,
> In Gaick lie their corpses deeply swathed in the snow.

It is said that to be involved in an avalanche is to have one foot in the grave. When I began to take an academic interest in snow structure and avalanches in the early 1960s, I had already fallen foul of three, so I had more than a passing interest in them and, presumably, I already had a foot in three graves. Abiding by the axiom "better late than never", I read all I could on the subject. Some may wryly point out that as I've been engulfed in three more avalanches subsequently, these

studies haven't done me much good! But most of these personal
encounters and rapid descents were either in the Himalayas when
caught out in bad weather, or on actual rescues on ground where, like
a sensible angel, I would normally have feared to tread.

I resolved, however, to do something constructive about avalanche
search in Scotland after looking for a buried climber, Professor Lata,
who had been swept down in a small avalanche from the Aonach
Eagach Ridge in Glencoe. It was really an apology for an avalanche –
a narrow ribbon of snow which had slid down like a stair-runner for a
thousand feet. But it was wet snow with virtually no air content.
Burial in such liquid porridge, should there be no air trapped between
the snow boulders, is fatal. The Professor's companion got free and
fortunately survived. I had my dog with me when we started searching for the buried climber, but in those days we had no dogs trained
for avalanche search and when she started to dig enthusiastically at the
edge of the debris, which I thought was an unlikely place, I called her
away. Next day we found the Professor's body where the dog had
been digging.

In 1965 the Scottish branch of the British Red Cross sponsored my
visit to the Swiss Avalanche Dog Course based near Davos. When I
returned I started the Search and Rescue Dog Association and we held
the first training course in Glencoe that winter. Though the dogs were
to be primarily used for avalanche search, we incorporated in their
training summer search technique, for locating people lost on hill and
moorland. We had made a start.

I wasn't the only person with an interest in snow structure. Eric
Langmuir, then the Principal of Glenmore Lodge, a government
training centre in the Cairngorms, was engrossed in the subject and
later became a leading authority on avalanches in Britain.

Eric made countless climbers and skiers aware of avalanche danger
and also of the fascination of snow in all its varied forms. He invited
Miloš Vrba, a Czech, to visit Scotland and lecture on the subject. At
that time Miloš was an avalanche expert with the Czech Government
and a member of the Horska Sluzba, their national mountain rescue
service.

I first met Miloš when he came to Glencoe to talk to our rescue team
and next day he gave us a demonstration on the hills. He surprised us,
after he had taken a snow profile, by saying that he considered the
snow unstable and dangerous. We were even more surprised next day

when we found that he had been right. The snow had avalanched overnight.

Miloš is a stocky man with precise speech and a perpetual twinkle in his eye. We became good friends and later Eric and I visited him in Czechoslovakia. Our whistle-stop tour with the Horska Sluzba included a short stay in the Low Tatra; country not unlike the Cairngorms with rolling hills which seem to invite you to walk them. In winter they are snow-covered and give a feeling of infinite space; in the forests on the lower slopes silence prevails, only broken by the soughing of the pines. The sort of area where one could imagine Good King Wenceslas with foot-weary page hirpling through oxter-deep powder.

But the sequence of events which Miloš now relates are not tranquil. It all started on a day in 1956 when hell broke loose in a thunder-like peal.

AN AIRBORNE AVALANCHE

Detective work in the Tatras by Miloš Vrba

The forester walked up and down in the roomy chamber of his old wooden lodge, hands in pockets, gloomy, nervous. Nobody remembered such a relentless snowstorm as this at the beginning of March. Yet there was no sign of any change. On the contrary, it had been getting from bad to worse. It was nearly dark in the room. The snowdrifts more than half covered the small windows and the cloudy daylight hardly got in. The cribs were empty and the deer were hungry. But it was quite impossible to think of going out with food for the poor animals. The best friend of the middle-aged bearded man did not share his master's troubles. The dog slept quietly in a corner.

If he could at least have a game of cards with the loggers above. In normal conditions twenty minutes' walk would take him to their hut and he could have a good time in a warm smoky room with those hard woodsmen, some shuffling, cutting, dealing; others telling stories into the night. Now, only a fool would try to go there.

Living in such a lonely place was not a simple matter. One must be constantly busy. Inactivity in solitude makes people nervous and quarrelsome. No doubt the loggers above did quarrel, especially at cards, but at least they had a choice. Among twenty people you can always find a new partner either for companionship or for a quarrel. However, to live only with a quarrelsome female under one roof, that's martyrdom, the forester reflected. No pipe allowed, each microscopic bit of rubbish discussed. Now such a clattering of pots and pans in the kitchen; it gets on one's nerves.

The loggers could at least swear at each other, man to man, and give vent to their furies. Twenty lumberjacks have a rich verbal reserve! But there were not twenty today – only nineteen. Jim left yesterday. Did he make it, the forester wondered? Probably, he reached town all right. It must have been difficult, though. If one could but telephone. However, as usual, the wires were broken under heavy icing and snow. The underground telephone cable will probably never be laid. No-one worries about such a forgotten forest lodge in the mountains and who would spend money for twelve kilometres of telephone cable? Certainly not the telephone company.

Time was dragging terribly. It was only half past nine in the morning.

There was a deep-throated rumble and the dog suddenly jumped up. It was always afraid of thunderstorms. It was true, though, that long low roar was really strange and there was no lightning. A thunderstorm on the 8th March? It was not usual, he thought, but here, in the Low Tatra of Czechoslovakia, it was not exceptional. We sometimes even have them at Christmas and New Year, so it's not so surprising, he assured himself.

The dog showed no inclination to go on sleeping. On the contrary, he grew restless and was obviously frightened. He followed his master step by step as the forester paced the low room, for he too felt uneasy. Finally, he sat down. So did the dog; close to the chair, staring at his master's face.

"Did you hear the thunder?" the grey head of the forester's wife appeared in the half opened door.

"Yes." The terse answer indicated that her husband did not feel like talking.

Nevertheless, the woman continued, "It's said to be a bad harvest when thunderstorms come so early."

Another deep thundering roar; this time stronger. The old wooden house trembled on its foundations. Still, no lightning, though that thunder must have been very close.

The dog howled and hid under the bed.

Darkness fell and a great wind broke tree-tops, some of which fell on to the roof. There was a crash of glass in the loft. Even the forester was taken aback. In order to camouflage his concern he reached for the pipe which was normally strictly forbidden in the room because it produced an awful smell, but now his wife did not take any notice. She only crossed herself and prayed.

"May be it's the Last Day," she said quietly, resigned to what may come.

"Perhaps Old Nick will take you off to hell," the forester replied jokingly in an attempt to boost their morale. He wanted to keep his wife in the room. Fear brings people together and they were both frightened. The dog slunk out from beneath the bed to under his master's legs.

The forester finally filled his pipe and lit a match. His hand shook. Neither of them could think of anything to say – it seemed as if time had stopped. They were not able to share their anxiety and to express their emotions. They both, however, instinctively felt that something must have happened, something quite terrible.

Their uncertainty was shattered by a heavy blow on the lodge door. The dog ran to it barking like mad, followed by the forester and his wife. When he opened it, a cloud of whirling snow burst into the passage and a man fell over the doorstep. They drew him in and quickly closed the door.

It was John, one of the loggers from the hut above. He was covered in blood and dressed only in a torn night-shirt. His bare legs were partially wrapped up in material obviously torn off the shirt. He was now unconscious, having passed out as soon as he fell through the doorway, and had multiple bleeding surface wounds but, at first sight, nothing more serious. They laid him gently on the bed.

He soon came round and opened his eyes.

"Tell me, Johnny, what has happened?" the forester asked quietly, but urgently.

"Explosion . . . There was this great blast . . ." John said with difficulty and closed his eyes again.

"Take care of him," the forester ordered his wife, "I'm going up there with the dog!"

The walk in deep powder snow and through muscle-aching drifts reaching a height of two metres was exhausting for both man and dog. The forester had the advantage as he wore snow-shoes, while the dog's paws sank deeply into the powder and his master was obliged to help and even carry the poor animal over deep sections.

The snowstorm permitted only limited visibility – a mere couple of steps and the forester quickly lost any idea of distance and time. It seemed to be an endless white hell. He felt tired and was obliged to have a rest and leant against a tree. Immediately he was alarmed for he realised that it was one of the last trees and beyond nothing but a white emptiness. Where is the forest, he asked himself? Where are the old high spruces? He must have lost the way, he thought. But that was out of the question. He knew the way as well in darkness as in daylight, summer or winter. The forest had simply disappeared!

He stepped forward like a sleepwalker, having forgotten about his dog. The beast followed, wallowing through the snow masses. Fighting on through the whirling whiteness the forester reached a drift that looked like a swelling wave. Up until now he had sunk deeply into the white cover despite his snow-shoes, now the walking was surprisingly easy. He felt a hard base lightly covered with powder snow. He scraped away that thin surface layer and saw an ice-hard brownish snow beneath, full of stones, earth, twigs and needles. Incredible! What had happened, he wondered? Everything around had changed and now this strange snow! An explosion? What sort of explosion?

The dog sniffed, barked briefly and ran uphill, quickly disappearing in the whirling snow. The forester followed the dog's prints and soon he heard the sharp bark that he knew was a sign of some important discovery. Indeed, when he saw the dog it was digging and sniffing the snow.

When the forester came nearer he shuddered. The dog had uncovered two human bodies buried in the surface snowlayer. He quickly removed the snow from their heads and recognised two of the loggers. They were alive. He shook them and thumped their backs hard. This crude treatment seemed to have the desired effect for they opened their eyes, and stared dully but did not respond to the forester's questions. The dog did not mind their miserable condition. He jumped, barked, wagged his short tail with joy and licked the cheeks of his good friends.

The forester praised the dog and was about to tell it to sit when the animal disappeared. It had got a fresh scent. The warning barks changed to friendly ones and in a couple of minutes it returned out of the white snow-screen, jumping cheerfully in front of two men – evidently people it knew. The forester saw it was two young lumber-jacks from another forest camp close by.

It was chance that they had left their mountain hut in a neighbour-ing forest, for they had run out of food. Taking shelter from the storm on the way back they, too, had been frightened by the "thunder". They had been heading back to their hut when the forester's dog scented them. Just as well it did, for its master would not have been able to evacuate the two men who were buried and they would surely have died if left.

"Hello, Charlie!" the older of the two men addressed the forester, "what the blazes has happened here? It doesn't make sense. We called at your lodge. Your wife's crossing herself and talking about Dooms-day, John's lying on the bed bleeding and blabbering something about an explosion and these two blokes here looking as if they have just fallen from the moon. What the hell is going on?"

"As I see it, lads, a big avalanche must have come down. I've never known anything like it. I can't even imagine how it could be possible in this deep forest and so far from the mountains. But, no doubt, it was an avalanche. And I'm afraid that all the others from the hut must have been buried. You had better get these two to the lodge quickly, in case they are seriously injured."

"Right," said one of the woodsmen. "We'll take care of these two."

"Good. Then I'll have a quick look round with the dog," returned Charlie, "to see if there is anyone else to be found. Afterwards I'll go down to the village to ring for help. Our phone's out of order, as usual."

Though the dog worked well, it didn't find anything else. Finally it went out of the avalanche cone and sniffed at the base of one of the remaining trees. The forester assumed that the dog had lost interest, so decided to discontinue the search and go down to phone. However, just then the dog barked, calling him.

"What's the matter, you old fool?" he spoke to the dog good-naturedly. "You're outside the avalanche path here." But nevertheless he unwillingly went over to it, and quickly changed his opinion of his canine friend. The dog was no fool, for under a thin powder layer there were dark red spots of blood in the snow. Not only blood but also traces, shapes, strange impressions: not from bare feet, nor boots, nor snow-shoes. Simply shapeless hollows leading away from the tree, but surely made by a human being not by an animal.

The dog went on sniffing at the tree. However, he did not lift up his hind leg, as he would have done had another animal left its visiting card, but stood up on his back legs, his fore paws against the tree trunk and continued sniffing. The forester was puzzled because he saw above only broken branches, as on the other remaining trees. However, with careful examination he found hanging from the tree trunk a long drop of freezing congealing blood, almost black in appearance. Looking up again he saw a weird sight: a piece of John's night-shirt on a broken branch, high above the snow level.

What on earth had made John climb the tree? he asked himself. He had presumably fallen down from that branch, hurt himself and afterwards crawled downhill, leaving those strange hollow indentations with his knees which he had protected with torn pieces of his night-shirt.

There were too many unknown factors about this whole tragedy; he must get help urgently. Before noon the forester rushed into the village headman's house and described the situation, whilst still getting his breath.

"Charlie, I cannot believe that it was an avalanche," the headman said. "Couldn't it, after all, have been an explosion as John said? Tell me, have you ever seen or heard from your father or grandfather of an avalanche in the neighbourhood of your lodge? Don't forget that great barrier of forest separating you from the avalanche slopes higher up! I'm almost sure . . ."

"You're quite right, Tom," Charlie interrupted, "but time is running out. Whether it was an avalanche or an explosion is all the same now. Sixteen people are very likely still buried and another three lie in my lodge, perhaps critically injured. Do something! Telephone for help!"

"But, I've no idea what to do. Who've I got to call?"

"Everyone! Mountain rescue service, police, army, hospital, fire brigades. Simply everyone. The more the better! We need a lot of people, shovels, picks, saws, axes, food, bulldozers and I don't know what else. They will know. But, for heaven's sake, make those phone calls, Tom! Every minute is vital."

"Yes, I understand, Charlie. But I think you had better do it your-self!"

That day, in the early afternoon, I received a cable: AVALANCHE ACCI-DENT LOW TATRA SOUTH. NINETEEN PEOPLE BURIED. AVALANCHE EXPERT NEEDED. COME PROMPTLY BY AIR-TAXI. CAR WAITING AIRPORT BANSKA BYSTRICA. The cable was signed by Joe, Rescue Chief of the Low Tatra South district. Joe was my good friend.

Great! In a trice everything turned upside down. The accident happened 400 kilometres as the crow flies from Prague where I was up to my ears with work. Instead of concentrating all my thoughts on the main problem of what to take with me, I began to speculate where the avalanche accident might have happened. I was a little confused be-cause I knew very little of those southerly slopes of the seventy kilometre-long mountain chain. The majority of that hillside was inaccessible then, far from roads and railway, without hotels, lodges, marked routes, downhill runs, chairlifts or ski-tows. Really, virgin mountain country with the only exception being the southern part of Chopok.

Deliberating on these things I lost a lot of precious time. But in spite of this I landed at Banska Bystrica airport by five pm and immediately went on by mountain rescue service car. The young man who met me couldn't tell me much because he himself knew little. He was, however, a skilled driver who, in spite of the twisting narrow roads, snowdrifts and ice, covered the fifty kilometres to the village of Dolna Lehota within the hour.

It was from this village that the SOS call had been sent several hours previously, a small Slovakian mountain village in the old style, with low wooden cottages, a quiet idyllic place. But when I arrived this was no longer the case. Military vehicles, soldiers, lighting and tele-phone cables were everywhere with the unhappy villagers looking on in amazement.

I didn't have much time to take all this in but was impressed how much had already been done. I sensed that there was a good feeling of fellowship amongst the rescuers, a voluntary unit, a blend of intellect, will and technical expertise whose common aim was to save human lives. Aware of these high ideals, I entered the village headman's house.

It now served as the headquarters of the commanding officer. This high-ranking army officer did not let anyone forget that he was appointed as lord of the avalanche and that everybody must comply with his orders without hesitation.

"You're late!" he greeted me with those tense words and a firm hand-shake. "Will you have a drink?"

"Thanks."

"Let's start immediately," he continued, "you are said to be an avalanche expert. Let's hope so." He looked at me steadily. "As you have probably seen, the army has undertaken the rescue operation, as we have the necessary equipment and men. But you must help us because we have no experience with avalanches. My second in command is avalanche commander above in the search area and he's been told to carry out your orders. The position is this," he cleared his throat, "there are about two hundred people above. Tomorrow, if necessary, there will be three or four hundred. You are fully responsible for their safety. Do you understand? You must safeguard them against further avalanche danger!"

"No, sir, I do not agree to your conditions!"

My reply took the officer unawares – he wasn't used to being talked to like this. His mouth closed with a click of teeth – I continued before he recovered.

"After eight days of snowfall there is a general avalanche hazard. That's all I can tell you. If you have taken on the overall responsibility for this rescue you must also reckon with the risk. I can only assure you that I'll assess the snow situation on the avalanche slopes above as soon as it is possible. Now it is getting dark and I can't do it until first light. I must tell you, too, that I've never been in this region before. I don't know it and won't tell you any fairy tales!"

"All right," he said slowly, "your points sound sensible. I'll ring up the avalanche commander. You go up there in about half an hour. I'll give you a tracked vehicle and a driver at your permanent disposal. Here is a large scale map of the area and I won't try to influence your decision tonight. It's your decision whether you will let the rescue go on, or stop it till tomorrow. I have ordered a helicopter for the early morning to observe the situation from the air. You will want to use this, I presume."

"For heaven's sake, no helicopter, no airplane, no noisy machinery at all!"

"Why the hell not?"

"The noise and the air turbulence of low flying aircraft could release additional snow masses and cause avalanches that might threaten your soldiers and the others as well."

"Yes, I see," he mused, rubbing his chin. I think he was beginning to appreciate that there was more to an avalanche than a pile of snow.

We went up as far as the forest lodge. The narrow road had been cleared and made wide enough for vehicles moving in one direction only. The traffic was controlled by the police.

Beyond this, I had to walk. It was not far, some 400 or 500 metres as far as I could judge in the dark. The trail was hard packed and wide, having been trampled by hundreds of feet. Somewhere in the dark to the right a diesel engine throbbed and the battery of lights ahead indicated my final destination.

In the harsh glare of searchlights I felt myself lost amongst a mass of busy people, mostly soldiers. However, Joe walked out from the dark, having seen me. Instead of friendly words of greeting he shone a powerful light on six mangled corpses lying on the dirty snow.

I was shocked. It was such a horrid spectacle that I was obliged to transform it in my imagination and thought of it as a Shakespearean tragedy in a theatre. A velvet-black background contrasting with the sharply illuminated foreground, the lights being focussed upon the terrible scene. A brilliant arrangement of light and shadow, indeed; Shakespeare himself wouldn't have prescribed such a cruelty. The only woman among those six corpses was scalped. Her long black hair laid out beside her bloody bald head.

". . . hardly 900 metres above sea level . . . no avalanche as yet . . ." I caught only fragments of Joe's speech; he must have been speaking for some time. I was full of horror and couldn't concentrate. I was simply not there.

". . . we wanted to probe but it was quite impossible . . . ice-hard snow . . . probes bent and broke . . . what do you say to this system of lengthwise and transverse corridors?"

"What? Sorry, Joe, I didn't get that."

"Parallel corridors or channels! Two metres apart. It was my idea to dig them and to probe horizontally from within. The snow is hard on the surface only, whereas one or two metres down it's possible to probe. When I saw so much manpower and tools it occurred to me to make use of them. It seems the only possible way to search the avalanche tip. There are also lots of tree trunks in the debris that must be cut. Do you think this is a sensible method of searching?" he asked me anxiously.

"Sure. Good work, Joe. I doubt whether such an idea would have occurred to me. Really first class. But tell me, why did you start just in this area? Was it intuition or lucky chance?"

"Neither. We started to dig in the same place where the forester's dog discovered two living men and where the forester himself found traces of one man who wasn't buried, but fell down . . ."

"Yes, I know. I've heard the story already," I told him. "Nine victims found in such a small area! Incredible."

"Yes, that's right. These six were discovered at a depth of about two metres. The dog couldn't scent them. It isn't a trained avalanche dog, of course."

"Your corridors are pretty deep. About five metres, aren't they?"

"Some even seven metres!" he returned.

"Joe, I think there are too many people concentrated in one area. Isn't it possible to enlarge the search area?"

"You had better tell it to the commander. He's just coming. I'll introduce you."

The avalanche commander was a young officer of lower rank. At first sight he appeared self-confident and energetic. I realised he expected something different where I was concerned. He surely thought I'd be some sort of superman, with an inscrutable expression, who would confidently point in an instant to where the missing ten persons were to be found. Instead, I presented the figure of quite an ordinary human being called an avalanche expert. Fortunately, he was immediately called to the phone in the signals tent, so that our first impressions were brief and we didn't exchange a word.

Later, when he returned, he came with an inconspicuous man.

"This is the forester," Joe made the introductions.

I immediately found the forester sympathetic; he was a man of the outdoors.

"Would you mind, Mr . . . , I am sorry, I didn't catch your name?"

"Call me Charlie like the others used to." He nodded towards the avalanche debris.

"Well, Charlie," I began, "could you tell me the story of the avalanche from the very beginning? You seem to be the only reliable witness and I must know all that's happened."

He described the events as he knew them, slowly but briefly. Suddenly I had a feeling of being observed by somebody. I was, but it was the dog who'd fixed his bright amber gaze upon me. When our eyes met I smiled and the dog wagged his short tail – our friendship was sealed.

Charlie noticed this and said, "This is my dog, Brok. I'm sure he's the only hero of this terrible day, though he's not aware of it."

"Tell me, Charlie, can you locate the lumberjacks' hut?"

"No, I can't. Everything has changed, and I'm puzzled. Maybe tomorrow in daylight. However, I still haven't finished the avalanche story," he continued. "I don't understand why John climbed that tree over there, you can see it silhouetted in the dark. What do you make of it?"

"Have you tried talking with him since he came round?"

"No, they took them all off to the hospital."

"I'm puzzled as well, Charlie. I don't understand it either."

Joe, Charlie and I sat down on a broken tree trunk near a fire made by the soldiers. The fire slowly sank down into a snow hollow. Brok, making the most of the pleasant heat, was cuddled upon a sack and soon fast asleep.

The young officer came back. He had probably received further orders from the C.O., for he immediately asked me for instructions.

"I understand," I answered, "you are in command of about 200 soldiers and policemen."

"Correct," the officer agreed, "most of them are working on the avalanche, the rest on the road, the generator and communications. There are also the cooks, lorry and bulldozer drivers. Then there is the medical staff. There are another sixteen mountain rescue personnel. However, they are under the command of the rescue chief here." He nodded towards Joe.

"Have you really sixteen people available, Joe? I've seen about half that number. Where are they all?"

"I'll tell you later," Joe said mysteriously.

I thought Joe's reply odd, but didn't pursue it just then.

"Tell me," I addressed the officer again, "when did you discover those six victims?"

"About three hours ago. They were found practically all at once, certainly within fifteen or twenty minutes."

"And since then, what else did you find?"

"Nothing. Oh, yes, there was a pocket watch belonging to one of the dead men."

"I see." I deliberated, then continued, "I think little more will be discovered in that area. A lot of people are wasting their energy and they cannot work properly as they are too concentrated. Let's arrange the search more effectively. Unless you have any objections, sir, I would recommend you to allow only fifty people to work here to enlarge the corridors, and another hundred should start the same operation at the end of the avalanche cone and work uphill."

"Are you sure that the missing ten men may be there?"

"No, I am not. But this is normal procedure for avalanche search if no other facts are known, and at the present I don't know any other facts. Unless someone can give you further information that could change my instructions? No? Well, I haven't, for example, any idea of where the hut was. I cannot, therefore, but recommend that you start digging at the end of the avalanche tip."

"All right, sir, I'll do it according to your instructions," the officer agreed, "but I have another twelve soldiers at my disposal. Am I to let them work here or send them down to the end of the avalanche tip?"

"No, I've an idea how best to employ those twelve men. I have seen that the rescuers piss any old place on the avalanche. Tomorrow morning an avalanche dog from High Tatra will arrive and such distractions will interfere with its work. Have these twelve men build latrines somewhere in the wood. Nobody should be allowed to pollute the avalanche further. You must give these orders immediately."

The officer's face was a picture of disenchantment. Such a mundane matter, piss houses indeed!

Up till then Charlie had been silent and meditatively smoking his pipe, but when the officer and Joe left he turned to me.

"I think you are right that nobody else will be found in this hollow. I was well acquainted with all the people from the hut. Those discovered in this small area, including John and the two men found by Brok before noon, came from one village and lived together in one room."

"And what about the dead woman?" I asked.

"She was their cook. Loggers from another village lived together in the second room. There was always rivalry between those two groups. The women caused most of the quarrels. You can well imagine the situation: eighteen virile men and two wives. The corridor between the two rooms often formed a boundary that couldn't be crossed."

"Wait a minute, Charlie! Eighteen men and two women. Unless I'm mistaken, that's twenty people and not nineteen! I was told that there were nineteen people in the hut, not twenty!"

"That's right," Charlie answered slowly, "one of them, called Jim, left for town yesterday as he has to stand trial today. He sells pigs on the black market and is charged with tax evasion. That swindle has saved his life."

"Did he live in the same room as the others discovered here?" I pointed to the holes in the avalanche.

"Yes, he did and, as I said, all in that room have been found. Now we must concentrate the search for the ten missing people from the other room."

It was midnight. The snow had stopped falling some time before; the wind had dropped, but now fog slowly crept in. Anonymous figures moved in it like blurred shadows on a screen.

Charlie with Brok had left half an hour ago and I sat on the broken tree trunk alone, thinking. They were not pleasant thoughts. I was helpless and could do nothing but wait. There was too little known about the circumstances of the tragedy and the known fragments of the jig-saw didn't help me to find a reasonable solution.

A phantom-like figure coming out of the damp fog turned out to be the long absent Joe. He was accompanied by a pleasant smell of warm food for there was a soldier with him with a dixy of hot goulash soup. I suddenly felt awfully hungry because I had not eaten since morning.

As I tucked in, I asked Joe, "How many men did you say you have?"

"Sixteen, and tomorrow morning there will be another fifty coming from other districts."

"I've been wondering about your sixteen merry men. Where are they all?"

"Well, ten of them are working with the soldiers. They are probing the snow between the corridors and six are high up the valley above us monitoring any snow movements."

"Have they a radio transmitter?"

"No, we haven't any, but I gave them two flare pistols and instructed them to go up along the verge of the remaining forest as far as the mouth of side valley which is about 800 metres above."

"Yes, I know where it is. I've studied the map I got from the C.O. What's the precise function of those men?"

"They are to listen carefully. Should they hear a roar of a further avalanche they are to fire a warning flare. That's the agreed signal for the soldiers. They would then immediately run away from the avalanche tip into the forest."

"A sound idea, Joe! I only hope you don't believe that this precaution will be of any use?"

"I don't, really. It's only a safety gesture. A matter of psychology. I have been simply obliged to do it. I'm sure you understand."

"Sure, Joe. But now let's talk in earnest. Do you know this region? If so, tell me whether we are threatened by any further avalanche release. It's your subjective opinion I want to hear, not any theoretical precepts."

"That's a difficult question, Miloš. To tell you the truth, I don't know the area well enough. I've never been here during the winter season before. This region's not of interest to skiers or climbers. But I was here once in late summer, about three years ago. To the best of my recollection, the upper forest margin is two or three kilometres uphill. Above that there are grassy and steep slopes of about 30° inclination, reaching as high as 1,900 metres. Perfect avalanche runways. A lot of avalanches must hurtle down those slopes every winter but nobody worries about such a huge deserted area, inhabited only by real bears or by bears like Charlie here." He smiled good naturedly towards the other end of the tree trunk where the forester and Brok had returned and were about to sit down. Charlie had brought a bundle of branches and a bag of pine cones. I looked back at Joe.

"Go on! As yet you haven't answered the most important question: whether there is additional avalanche hazard or not."

"I don't know. Maybe yes, maybe no. What do I know of the snow masses up there? In two seconds a new avalanche could bury all of us and I don't want to talk about it any more. But tell me why are you so firmly convinced that the avalanche must have come from above? It might be a local snow release. Don't forget the great distance from the avalanche slopes! Between our present position and those slopes there are curved, narrow and afforested valleys. Also, the valleys themselves are not that steep. I worked out their inclination is only between

5° and 15°. No more. In my opinion too little for an avalanche to travel such a great distance, to overcome such obstacles and to reach down to here."

"I don't agree with you, Joe. An avalanche of enormous mass, energy and speed can do it. I've no doubt that the avalanche came from above. Look at the map, Joe! The margin of the forest runs pretty zig-zag. What does that mean? That's a result of previous avalanches, though none of them travelled as far as this one. Such avalanches may occur four or five times within a millenium; probably beyond human memory, especially in such a remote region. Though I haven't yet seen the situation above, I'm pretty sure about it. But I'm anxious on another point. The valley above is interconnected with another. The avalanche came down through one of those valleys and the valley through which it came is no longer dangerous because it has avalanched – all that snow is down now and cannot produce any additional avalanche. I'm worried about the other valley where perhaps no avalanche has been released as yet. Or, it might have been a double avalanche that came down through both valleys at the same time and merged into one stream of enormous energy just above the loggers' hut. That would be the most favourable condition for us."

"I cannot tell you anything further about that problem until daylight, Miloš. Then I'll send patrols to investigate."

Until daylight! I was told the same by Charlie when I asked him to locate the hut. Daylight was a question of another six hours. These thoughts ran through my mind. The trapped people might be alive and in need of help. Every lost minute may mean life or death, not only to those buried somewhere in the snow mass, but to all of us. Even now I didn't have any idea what was above. Could I take this appalling risk? Hadn't I better tell the commander the truth and ask him to stop the operation until daylight? I didn't.

I was frustrated and angry about my inability to do anything further. The commander returned just then. My face must have reflected my thoughts. I forgot even to thank him for the soup. He gave me a slip of paper.

"Something from headquarters. Not important for me but you will perhaps find it interesting," and he went off again.

It was a record of a telephone call with the hospital where the three who had been rescued were being cared for. All were suffering from severe shock. The two found by the dog still could not speak. They had internal injuries. John had only superficial wounds. The most interesting part of the message was his version of what had happened for he had recovered sufficiently to give a statement.

Before the catastrophe he was asleep and was awakened by a deep thundering. He was going to look through the window to see what was the matter but just as he reached the window a tremendous explosion tore the hut asunder and he was catapulted into the air. After what he thought was about twenty metres' flight he landed on the top of a spruce and fell down through the branches. His only thought was to protect his legs with pieces torn off his night shirt. somehow, he reached the forest lodge. He couldn't remember anything more.

I got up and went to Charlie at the other end of the log. He had been busy working on something in the snow using twigs and pine cones. He also used a shovel from time to time.

"Look, Charlie, your problem is solved. John didn't climb the tree. He landed on top of it after a twenty metres long airflight."

"What?" He stared to me incredulously, his pipe in his hand.

"Here, you'd better read it yourself." I handed him the slip of paper. He read it slowly, probably several times. Meanwhile I observed his work. When I finally understood what he had done I was delighted. It was a relief model of the valley before the catastrophe. The valley was slightly curved. The steep hillsides were completely afforested, trees simulated by cones pressed into the dirty snow. The stream flowing through the valley was marked by means of twigs and thicker sticks were used for three-dimensional models of the two buildings, the forest lodge and the loggers' hut. This last model attracted my particular attention. It was situated on the same side of the valley as the forest lodge, on a plateau above the stream. The natural shape of the plateau had possibly influenced the location of the building for it was at an angle to it, so that one end of the hut bridged the stream on the side closest to the mountain. It seemed that Charlie had not yet finished this part of his task, because behind the hut he had heaped a high steep pile of snow without any cones on it.

"Haven't you finished yet, Charlie?" I pointed at this heap of snow.

"Yes, that's done," he answered absent-mindedly. "The rest of the hut was hidden behind a rock. That's the best I can do for a rock." He started to fill his pipe, his thoughts now obviously elsewhere. For me he had just uttered the most important fact, though he hadn't realised it. Until now all the known facts had fitted together but, unfortunately, did not give me a clear picture of events as a whole.

"That won't do. It's out of the question!" Charlie said finally in disappointed tones, brooding still on the message from the hospital.

"Why, what's wrong, Charlie?" I asked briskly. "With the help of your model you'll be able to locate the hut in a few minutes, using John's landing tree as a starting point."

It was a stupid oversimplification of mine, and I made an awful fool of myself by such a rash conclusion. Charlie stared evenly at me.

"It doesn't make sense," he said flatly. "The hut was situated two or three hundred metres uphill from here and from John's landing tree, as you call it. Besides, it was on the opposite side of the valley. Look here," he pointed to the inner curve of the valley model, "that's approximately our present position. A pretty long distance to the hut, isn't it? John must have landed on another tree, if at all. Not here. But then why is a piece of his bloody shirt still hanging on that tree, over there?" He pointed with his pipe.

"Why didn't you tell me sooner that the hut was situated so far off? It was my first question!"

"You asked me the exact position. An approximate one you can find on your map."

"No, I can't. The map is older than the hut, so it's not marked."

The forester turned his back upon me, kicked furiously at the snow model and sat down on the broken trunk. I felt deflated, but didn't say anything further and walked away into the dark and the fog.

Later, much later, when I went over that critical bit of information again, I realised my unforgivable mistake in accepting John's initial information. A man who is projected from a disintegrating hut by an unknown force cannot reliably determine how far he has been hurled. Information from eye-witnesses of any catastrophe is often wrong, being as it is influenced by fear, shock and a common human failing to exaggerate – though in John's case exaggeration was to prove to be the last thing we should all be accusing him of.

But for the present, was I perhaps being too meticulous – wanting too many details? Success, I thought, is for those who don't ask but give orders. Yes, I really had been about to call my driver, go down to the village and tell the commanding officer that the avalanche was beyond my experience and knowledge and that I was going home.

It was, however, lucky that I was also annoyed, having felt an injustice. A voice within me whispered, calling me a coward who wanted to leave the battlefield before the fight was decided. I was annoyed by my own shortcomings, but also those of others. No, I'd stay, not just because of the buried people, though they were probably dead, I'd stay because I'd demonstrate that I could get to the bottom of all this chaos and find the avalanche victims. But it would be a different Miloš Vrba who'd take over. Now there wouldn't be any more "Can you . . . would you be so kind . . ." Now it would be straight from the shoulder, "You must!"

Meanwhile, I went over to the end of the avalanche tip where the corridor digging and probing was in full swing. The officer and Joe immediately joined me.

"No traces yet," the commander reported reproachfully. "I'm sure this search area is quite useless."

"Carry on!" I retorted, ignoring his poignant remarks.

"At first light over 400 people will arrive," the commander continued stiffly. "Are they to dig here or somewhere else?"

"Ensure that they have the necessary tools, and are instructed about the emergency. At daylight you and the forester will go with me, Joe, uphill to study the situation. Later I'll give my instructions on procedure."

"Yes, sir!"

Joe was evidently surprised by my changed attitude and using our friendship as a lever he tried to humour me by making a joke, but I didn't react and told him, "At the first sign of dawn, Joe, you will send two patrols up to investigate the avalanche situation in both valleys. They will take two-way radios to inform me of the immediate situation."

"We haven't any radios, you know that," Joe objected.

"The soldiers have and they will lend them to you."

"That's quite impossible," the commander protested. "No civil person may use the army's frequencies. You must ask the commanding officer for special dispensation."

"You will do that," I replied. "One of your operators will explain to the mountain rescue team how to operate the equipment. We shall start at six o'clock sharp. One of your radio operators will also come with us."

I left then. Both I knew were angry, but so was I. It was cold during those long hours before dawn. I preferred, therefore, to walk about within the circle of light cast by the searchlights and fire. The rough snow surface littered with broken trees and branches made the walking difficult. For something to do I decided to investigate the opposite side of the valley.

The valley was about thirty to forty metres wide, really slightly bow-shaped, the area where the search was being conducted forming the outer curve. On that outer margin, about 200–300 metres uphill was where the hut had been. But how, I asked myself, is it possible that until now all the victims located were at the inner curve of the valley, and how is it possible that the trees on that outer curve are hardly damaged, whereas here the majority of them are smashed? That was at variance with principal physical laws and with my experience as well. After all, everything flowing, streaming, running and rolling is pushed outside on a curve, not inside.

I couldn't understand these anomalies, though I spent a long time investigating each particular spruce with the beam of my torch. My self-confidence sank again; the whole affair seemed a mystery.

A gloomy, foggy and watery dawn arrived. We started uphill, climbing the avalanche path. Charlie with Brok took the lead, followed by Joe and me and finally the commander with a radio operator carrying a transceiver. We went up slowly for it was rough going, though the slope wasn't steep. The shapes of the trees disappeared in the fog, and the valley grew wider. We didn't talk, not only because of the difficult terrain, but also due to the strained terms we were all now on. It seemed an endless and exhausting trip. Finally, Charlie stopped, looked round in the fog and turned to the left. We followed him. In front of us a rock rose out of the fog.

"Here it is," Charlie said.

"Are you able to mark out an approximate ground plan of the hut?" My voice sounded hoarse and breathless.

"I'll try, though the snow must be about seven or eight metres deep here."

He began to measure the distances step by step. Joe helped him, having brought up an armful of branches to mark out the walls.

Meanwhile, it got brighter and the fog lifted. I saw with interest the smashed trees on the steep hollow hillside above the rock and to the left of it. The piled-up timber made a crazy sight, as if a giant had smashed trees with his hands and tossed some with their tops upper-most above the rock, while at the head of the slope tree-tops were pointing down.

Suddenly, the radio operator raised his hand, drawing our attention to a signal coming in. The rescue patrols had reached the point where the valleys joined and reported that the avalanche ran down through the left valley only. The right-hand valley had been blocked by a ten metre high ice wall. They asked for further instructions.

"Bad news," I said, "tell them to go on separately to investigate the snow situation above."

"And you, sir," I said to the commander, "give orders that the support party which is due must not go into the avalanche tip. They will wait in the hillside wood for orders!"

"I cannot keep all those people waiting," the officer protested, "I was ordered by headquarters . . . Watch out, avalanche!"

We all quickly looked up, automatically pressing ourselves to the rock. Only the dog kept quiet because his animal instinct did not register danger. There wasn't any. The supposed avalanche was only a high wall of white snow which appeared out of the dissipating fog about thirty metres from us. In fact, it was the second step of the existing avalanche which had stopped not far from the hut. Probably it originated from the snow transported in the avalanche cloud which settled in that area after losing the majority of its energy, and thus formed an immense mass of white snow, contrasting sharply with the dirty avalanche tip coming out from the bottom of the terrible white-ness. The frontal wall was about ten metres high. Maybe even more.

"Joe, have you ropes and ice axes?"

"Yes, of course."

"Well, send four or five of your men to investigate the stability and hardness of that mass of snow. Very carefully!"

Charlie had almost completed his work. Both rooms and the corridor were already marked and he was just indicating doors and windows with sticks. I was busy observing the hillside opposite. The fog had gone so that I could clearly see every detail on that slope, though it was 200–300 metres from our position. An extensive bow-shaped area of smashed trees piled up in the same curious shape as on the slopes above us. All the broken trees on that distant slope had their tops lying towards us, however, and here I realised they tended towards the inner avalanche curve where John and the others were discovered. The full significance of this came to me. Take it easy, no hastiness, the inner voice whispered, and I smiled to myself. I was sure of everything now. It had all dropped into place.

"Charlie, tell me – No, I'll tell you. John and the other victims who have been found lived in this room," I pointed at his hut plan, "in the room which was over the brook facing the mountain."

"Do you read my mind or did someone tell you?" Charlie returned, looking surprised.

"No, I worked it out myself. I even know where . . ."

In that moment we were interrupted by another report from one of the rescue patrols. The men climbing up the right-hand valley had discovered a tip of a big avalanche that had stopped about 300 metres before the bottom. They thought that avalanche may have been released at approximately the same time as the other one, as there was only a thin layer of powder snow covering the debris.

"That was your first 'thunder', Charlie! Now, everything is clear, gentlemen. Let's get started."

"I don't understand," Charlie murmured, perplexed.

"Neither do I," Joe added. "What were you about to tell us, Miloš?"

"Simply," I said, "that I think I know exactly where the ten missing persons are to be found. Just here," I pointed. "Or, say, within a distance of fifty metres downhill. Not more."

"Sir, will you be so kind as to express your theories more clearly?" The commander's tone was petulant. "I must do something with the men waiting in the wood. There are almost 500 of them now."

"Clearly? Yes, and briefly! It was an airborne avalanche that came down in two waves from different directions and of different energy. The first one was a pressure wave of immense power. That wave ricochetted within the valley like a billiard ball. I understood what happened for the first time after having seen the patterns made by the smashed trees. The pressure wave destroyed the front part of the hut. John and the others living there were blasted and hurtled a distance of 250 metres in the curve of the valley. Not twenty metres, Charlie! John really landed on that tree, he didn't climb it. He fell down, out of reach of the additionally flowing snow. The others were not so lucky and landed in the avalanche stream where they were buried. The avalanching snow, mixed with wood and stones, rolled down in the second wave. Those slower flowing masses of lower energy destroyed

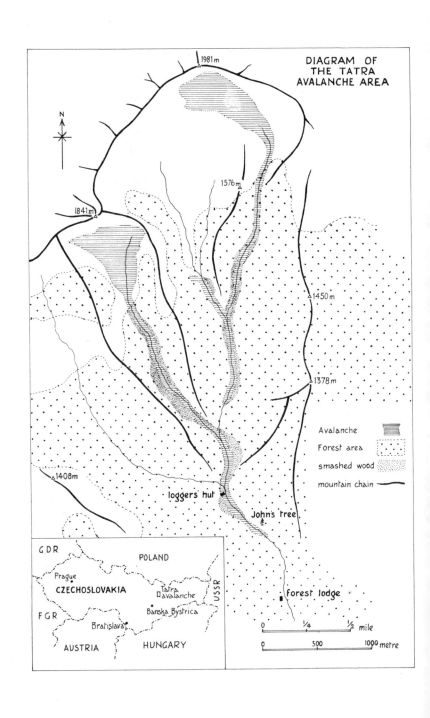

DIAGRAM OF
THE TATRA
AVALANCHE AREA

N

△1981m

1576 m

△1841m

△1450 m

△1378 m

△1408m

loggers hut

John's tree

Avalanche
Forest area
smashed wood
mountain chain

GDR
POLAND
Prague
CZECHOSLOVAKIA
Tatra
avalanche
USSR
FGR
Banska Bystrica
Bratislava
AUSTRIA   HUNGARY

forest lodge

0   ¼   ½ mile

0   500   1000 metre

the back part of the hut hidden behind the rock here. The missing people living there must have been buried either in the base of the hut or dragged down along the outer curve of the valley, not too far off."

"Your orders, sir!" The officer asked impatiently, unimpressed with my dialogue.

"All your people with tools will come here, immediately," I said. This space where the hut was situated and an additional strip, say twenty by a hundred metres downhill, must be turned upside down as soon as possible. The organisation is your business."

"Yes, sir." He dashed off.

"Joe, I want to know urgently the result of investigation of that wall of white snow."

"Right, I'll see to it."

Charlie came over and said, "Last night. I was mad. I'm sorry."

"Charlie, I share the same sentiments – about myself. I talked like an idiot. Let's both forget it."

The commander proved to be an excellent organiser who knew how to direct a large number of people in those difficult conditions and how to allocate particular tasks to the right personnel.

Joe brought a report on the white snow wall and I was a little alarmed. The mass was rough and hard enough, though not so ice-hard as the dirty avalanche tip. This was good. But they had also found long narrow deep cracks in the snow.

"Longitudinal or transverse?" I asked.

"Longitudinal ones, and in the lower part only," Joe explained.

"If the cracks were transverse, I should be afraid of a glacier-like creep downwards. However, I don't understand the longitudinal cracks, I cannot explain those."

"Neither can I," Joe added.

"Tell them to keep a close eye on them."

Meanwhile, the soldiers dug a deep pit and had now uncovered the damaged floor of the hut. We decided to try the avalanche dog. But the animal refused to go down into the deep pit and the handler had trouble getting the dog to work. Finally, the dog got a scent at the back right-hand corner. Within a few minutes two victims were found. Two dead men were pressed against the timbers of the back wall, both still holding a hand of cards. There were no visible injuries. The doctor judged that they very likely died immediately after burial because no traces of ice were found in their mouths and nostrils.

Further victims were discovered soon afterwards, outside the former hut. The ninth corpse lay thirty metres downhill. Altogether eight men and one woman were found by eleven o'clock. The tenth man was missing.

"Charlie, what's the matter? Nine people again. Where can the tenth be? Haven't you any idea? Did he go into town with Jim?"

"That's out of the question."

"What about the out-house?"

"Dug out already. Destroyed, but the door was found in the frame and was closed from outside."

After a short noon break, Joe proposed to enlarge the area searched by making another corridor. I agreed, then remembered the snow mass above us and asked about the cracks. No change, was the report and I forgot about that problem for the time being, unfortunately.

I was occupied with another idea. I decided to make contact with the hospital, and question the lumberjacks to see if they had any idea of the whereabouts of the missing man. Charlie had told me his name. The reply was prompt: a few minutes before the catastrophe he took a bucket and went down to the brook for water.

"Charlie, do you know their path to the stream and the place where they got water?"

"Exactly."

The last phase began. The path to the stream ended only a few metres in front of the white snow wall. A wide corridor was quickly dug. A lot of people were at my disposal and they worked in relays. The pit at the foot of the white wall was soon twelve metres deep. But when both the corridor and the pit were complete, nothing was found. Not even the bucket. The soldiers standing on the bottom of the hollow reported that the brook was completely dry.

"Did you say dry?" Charlie wondered. "The brook was swift and never iced up even in severe winters."

A shiver went down my spine. There was something odd here! I was not surprised that the last victim wasn't found but I was by the absence of the stream.

"Look . . . look, there!" Joe cried, "the wall's giving way!" He immediately fired a warning flare.

The emergency worked perfectly. Everyone took his shovel, saw, axe or pick and ran up the hillside into the wood. In two or three minutes an immense snow block slowly broke out, rolled over and a fountain of water shot up from the white wall as if under the power of Moses' rod. Then the dirty stream cascaded downhill. Within minutes the search corridors and the avalanche tip were flooded.

A water avalanche! Something nobody had expected. Not snow but water threatened several hundred people. Thousands of tons of snow had formed a natural dam that collapsed due to the digging of the pit and corridor at the foot of the white snow wall which was actually a dam.

I stared helplessly at the streaming water and felt suddenly exhausted. Yet one of the last memories of that terrible avalanche rescue I'll never forget. An officer came from somewhere and though soaked and muddy he reported, "Sir, nobody is missing, nobody has been hurt. Some tools, several covers, one tent and one telephone have been swept away."

"Thank you very much," I managed to mumble.

It all happened many years ago, on March 8th, 1956. And the reference book facts when finally pieced together read like this: At 9.40 am two bulky powder avalanches released in a remote region of the Low Tatra mountains. One of those avalanches contained 1,590,000m^3 of snow, weighing 380,000 tons and travelled a distance of 3,500 metres from the rupture zone. This great mass ran down into a narrow, curved and afforested valley. The immense avalanche, reaching a speed of about 250 kph was pressed into the valley neck. In that critical section the mass exploded in the air and turned into an avalanche cloud. The pressure wave and the avalanching snow buried nineteen people. Sixteen of them did not survive. Twenty-five hectares of an old forest were smashed. It took eighteen months to clear the smashed timber and the same time for the avalanche snow to melt. The last victim was found by the forester's dog six weeks after the accident, having been buried under an overhanging bank of the stream.

FOUR

I

The Helicopter Revolution

I first met helicopter pilots Markus Burkard and Günther Amann in September 1973 when Dougal Haston and I were landed by winch wire at the Eiger's Death Bivouac. That lower, Dougal's first, must have been quite an initiation. Being in the rescue business, I had done many previous lowers, often in bad conditions, so it wasn't quite so alarming for me, but to be whisked up from that awesome face on a slender steel wire, out over the verdant pastures of Alpiglen, gives one pause for reflection with 7,000 feet of space beneath your crampons! It was Günther who was piloting on that occasion and it wasn't until the following year that I flew with Markus. Whereas Günther is inclined to be introspective and quiet, Markus is more carefree, though no less careful than his colleague. These two pilots have saved many climbers and skiers in difficulties in the Swiss Alps.

The insurance service provided by the Swiss Mountain Rescue Flight, though inexpensive, is second to none. Its pilots, like their compatriots doing the same job in Chamonix, have proved beyond doubt that mountain rescue with helicopters is by far the most efficient means of taking the injured off mountains.

Helicopter winch rescue originated in Britain where it was developed for Air-Sea Rescue. It was first used in the Alps in 1961 on the East Face of the Watzmann, a peak near Berchtesgaden. The aircraft used was an old Sikorsky. Though many different types of helicopters are in use for rescue work today, the French Alouette has been the most popular workhorse and its souped up small brother, the Lama, is one of the few helicopters which can lift its own weight; it also holds the world altitude record of almost 41,000 feet.

The Eiger North Wall didn't succumb easily to this helicopter revolution. Here, too, as with other 'firsts', psychological barriers had to be broken and it wasn't until 1970 that Günther, as a rescue exercise, lowered Rudolf Kaufmann, a Grindelwald guide, on to various parts of the face, the Spider, the Flatiron and the Ramp. This was an amazing breakthrough, but prior to this the helicopters had played a combined operations role. For instance, a rescue team was flown to the summit ridge in the winter of 1970 with winching equipment and an injured Japanese climber was taken up from the Exit Cracks. Fixed belays were established at the top of the mountain, at the finish of the Ramp and the North Pillar, which meant that in the event of a rescue taking place in weather too severe for a helicopter to operate, normal winching procedure, as pioneered by Ludwig Gramminger and Erich Friedli, could be swung into action with the minimum of delay.

During the summer of 1970 that astute master of the telescope, the late Fritz von Almen saw from his base at Kleine Scheidegg that one of two Italian climbers had fallen, close to where the unfortunate Corti had bivouacked many years before. He informed the authorities and at dawn next day a rescue party was flown to the summit ridge and a guide lowered by winch wire to the scene of the accident. Angelo Ursella, a climber from Udine, had fallen thirty metres and unluckily some coils of his rope had caught round his neck. He was immediately strangled. His friend, de Infanti, was whipped off his belay, but being uninjured, managed to climb back up to his stance. The guide got de Infanti to the summit shortly after midday. Ursella's body was recovered later.

In September of that same year, the first exclusive helicopter rescue was done on the face. Günther Amann was the pilot. The circumstances leading up to this rescue, which fortunately ended happily, were rather bizarre. Two German climbers, Martin Biock and Peter Siegert, started up the original route. They were both strong climbers. Siegert, for example, was one of the first to try the Eiger Direct in winter and was also a member of the party that made the first winter ascent of the Matterhorn North Face. However, the Eiger didn't seem congenial, for at the Difficult Crack Biock dropped the rucksack he was hauling up a pitch and, though they recovered it some two hundred metres below, Siegert's crampons had been lost. One advantage of their close proximity to the 3.8 window was that it made commuting possible and Peter dashed down to the Stollenloch window, took a train to Grindelwald, where he bought a new pair of crampons and was back on the climb with Martin by midday.

By now the sun was causing havoc and the usual stone trundles had started down the Hinterstoisser, so they decided to get to the Second Icefield via the Japanese Route, up the Rote Fluh. This is the intimidating overhanging red wall to the right of the Hinterstoisser. It was whilst bivouacking in hammocks from this huge overhang that night that they discovered their stove had been damaged in the fall and couldn't be used. For some reason best known to themselves, they decided to carry on next morning, but by the evening had only reached Death Bivouac. When they were at this fateful ledge the weather broke with a vengeance, typical of the Eiger, and the next two nights were spent at this isolated eyrie.

On the second night they signalled for help by torch and Kurt Schwendener, the rescue boss in Grindelwald, set the rescue machine in motion. The weather was still bad next day and in case Amann couldn't get in with the Lama, Schwendener also arranged for a group of guides to be ready at the Stollenloch. Despite intermittent cloud Amann got close enough to the bivouac to speak to the two Germans using the helicopter loud hailer, for he was not absolutely sure that they now wanted to be rescued. In the past many climbers had retreated from Death Bivouac and above, and it was assumed that these two were uninjured. Later, when the cloud cleared, Amann saw that they had abseiled two rope lengths to the side of the Flatiron and here they made definite signals that they wished to be picked up.

Rudolf Kaufmann, the guide, was lowered to the tiny stance (the size of a biscuit tin lid) and Biock was hoisted up and taken to Scheidegg. Fifteen minutes later both Siegert and Kaufmann were winched aboard in safety. In all, the rescue had taken less than an hour.

Between 1973 and 1977, I did many flights with Günther Amann and Markus Burkard connected with filming and T.V. Most of the winch lowers were either on the North Face or on the West Flank. My last trip with Markus in 1971 was a hurried one. I had a meeting in Zürich about a possible live T.V. climb of the face and I had to check on one or two points, which meant a flight to a ledge high on the West Flank on a cold September morning. I had only four hours to complete this work. The well known Swiss climber and guide, Hans Muller, was with me and when Markus dropped us off on a snow-covered ledge, it felt both lonely and cold. The mountain was in the first grip of an early winter. The helicopter landed close to Kleine Scheidegg, keeping in radio contact with us for the return trip.

When our survey was completed we called Markus on the walkie-talkie and he picked us up. On the descent I asked him if he could fly close in to the Japanese Direct route to enable Hans to check on some ledges which we were wanting to see. Hans had done the route in both summer and winter. Markus nosed the Alouette into the wall like a dog scenting a lamppost, until we were below the great overhang above and to the right of the Rote Fluh. He then eased the helicopter beneath this so that the deafening roar of the rotors and the gas turbine bounced down on us from the rock roof. It was both exhilarating and frightening, yet he was in perfect control. His only apparent concern was before he took the machine beneath the rock when he asked Hans if the overhang was solid. Hans had assured him that it was. This is typical of the confidence which these pilots have in their crew, for both the winchman and the guide have to be experts also and equally cool in a crisis. Markus wasn't worried when he took us under that overhang and Günther wasn't scared when he dropped Dougal and me off at Death Bivvy and other places on the wall. When Markus in the following narrative talks of almost crashing the helicopter on a rescue, he must really have been out on a limb.

2

A CAULDRON OF WIND

a pickup at the Dossenhütte by Markus Burkard

On Friday, 11th November, a group mostly of younger climbers from Belfort in France started from Rosenlaui in the Bernese Oberland for the Dossenhütte. The weather was fine, the sky cloudless, but the forecast was very bad. A depression had been threatening for days.

The group camped below the moraine, in the Gletscherhubel area and started the ascent on Saturday. As the day wore on, the expected bad weather front reached the Rosenlaui area. By evening it started to rain heavily, turning later to sleet and snow. Two days later, on the Monday evening, the Swiss Alpine Club rescue leader in Meiringen received a report from Belfort that several people were missing. Later when I was on duty I heard about these seven overdue climbers. The operations leader told me what he knew and I assumed that they were waiting in the Dossenhütte for better weather and a helicopter to pick them up. There are ten days' emergency provisions in the Dossen-hütte and plenty of wood but, unfortunately, no telephone.

On Monday it snowed without stopping from ten am onwards. For a while even the Brünig Pass was only passable with chains. Winter had started with a vengeance. Later on that Monday night an un-usually severe storm raged over the Alps and on the Tuesday morning I heard on the news that the met. station on the Säntis had recorded a wind speed of 140 km per hour. During the night we were awoken several times by the noise of the storm. I had forgotten about the seven climbers, because the weather was so bad that a flight to the Dossenhütte was out of the question. A telephone call from operations headquarters shortly before nine am changed the situation completely!

A twenty-two-year-old climber from Belfort had reached Rosen-laui absolutely exhausted and raised the alarm. He, with the six others, had left the Dossenhütte on Sunday morning, two days earlier, and had tried to descend to the valley. When they left, it had already been snowing all night, so they attempted the descent under the worst imaginable conditions. The normal route through the Dossenwand, threatened by avalanches, seemed too risky and there was no choice but to climb to the Dossensattel and reach the valley via the Rosenlaui glacier.

Three of the climbers got as far as the first icefall at 2,500 metres. There they were left behind as they were unable to go further. A seventeen-year-old boy reached the shelter of the Dossen bivouac with a fourteen-year-old companion. The youth who later was to raise the alarm continued the descent accompanied by his girl friend. They failed to locate their tent at the Gletscherhubel campsite, an hour above Rosenlaui and were therefore forced to bivouac in the open. During the night the girl died from exhaustion and hypothermia. This was the sad news I was given.

Just then thick clouds made a flight impossible and so the rescue leader in Meiringen had to go about organising a rescue party from the

Hasli. We promised help as soon as the weather improved. Rosenlaui was to be the meeting point. At Interlaken Urs Menet, the mechanic on duty with me, made the Alouette 319 ready for take-off. I obtained the latest weather reports. They promised some temporary improvements due to the strong winds. At 3,000 metres wind speeds of fifty knots and gust up to sixty-five knots were reported. Above Interlaken there was a patch of blue sky. Shortly after 10.30 am Peter Winterberger reported that the Dossenhütte was clearly visible. We took off.

I had a sinking feeling – a glance at the peaks was sufficient. Everywhere the same picture presented itself; snow showers, wisps of cloud which rose, dissolved and reappeared, gusts of wind shaking the helicopter. Above Meiringen the valley was completely clear of clouds. We flew up to 2,000 metres and cast our first glance in the direction of Rosenlaui. Seen from the air, this glacier is one of the most beautiful of its kind, but today there was a storm above the ice. Everything seemed to be moving. The snow swept along the rocks, was hurled high in the air and formed eddies which jumped like dancers over the crevasses. A dim light lay over the scene. We flew into this cauldron and into the lee of the big Wellhorn. Terrible gusts of wind caught the Alouette. We were hurled upwards and the next moment we were hit from above, then once more pressed down into our seats. I required the full range of the controls in order to keep the machine in the air. I felt sick. During my thirteen years' helicopter experience I had seldom encountered such winds. This was hell. I flew a full circle 200 metres above ground. It was impossible to keep a look-out for people. I could reach the radio-controls only with difficulty, as this meant lifting my arm off my knee and this impaired my steering. There was nothing I could do – the force of the gale was overwhelming. I could not tell from which direction the wind was blowing – it seemed to be everywhere. On my right the snow swept over the rocks in the direction of our flight. On Urs' side was a counter-wind blowing across the glacier. I did not know what to do.

After circling for the second or third time, far away – 300–400 metres higher – we saw two figures, one of whom was waving. They were standing near an icefall where the huge crevasses begin. This meant flying higher, further into the cauldron. I simply had to overcome my feelings and control myself. For a moment the thought crossed my mind that the tremendous winds might snap a rotor-blade or ruin the tail rotor. I was terrified to crash out of control on to this cruel glacier. The upper end of the glacier was hidden by clouds consisting of snow and ice crystals. The cold hard snow swept in from a westerly direction and continued horizontally over the icefall.

Now we were above the two men. Only with difficulty could I keep the stick steady in my hand. It was being shaken by the strong bumps and the upwards and downwards currents. There was no question of flying on course. We thought that we would never get anywhere near our men. Still, I could not simply leave them, I imagined the long steep climb which the rescue party would have to face. I saw the threatening clouds on the Dossensattel on my right. The victims had been fighting for their lives for the last two days in this hell composed of wind and cold. Ice axes, half-buried rucksacks, ropes and scattered bits of clothing protruded from the snow. It was a horrifying picture. A landing was impossible as the angle of the glacier was too steep. At the utmost I could touch down with the nose-wheel and hover at the same time in order to try and get the victims on board. But first I had to get near enough. It just had to work! I was thinking of Sigi long ago on the Monte Rosa glacier in the south-west wind and of that avalanche disaster behind the Testa. Here, however, was the Rosenlaui glacier. I fought, I was frightened, I cursed, I was furious with myself and the profession I had chosen. Twenty times I asked Urs where the wind was blowing from; he probably thought I had gone crazy.

The first attempt ended twenty metres above the party; on the second we flew as fast as an express train over them, although I had chosen the same direction. During the following attempt, shortly before landing, we were caught in the down-current so badly that I had to open full throttle. The huge crevasses came towards us so fast that I believed we were going to crash. At the last moment I managed to pull away. The new turbine had to give its maximum power. I could not consult the confounded T4 instrument any more. This was the moment when I wanted to give up. What was the use of smashing the Alouette and risking our lives? Urs did not say a word, but as a glider pilot he knew what we were up against. We headed towards safety, but after thirty seconds I had to turn back and try once more. Finally, we succeeded in touching the ground with the nose-wheel. Urs opened the sliding door and I shouted at him to keep an eye on the rotor. We were in a cloud of whirling snow. I had to correct the

Alouette's position continually – it was like holding a bucking bronco. The silhouettes of the two men were my only landmark. Snow whirled through the cabin like dust. I was ready to take off at any moment before the rotor hit the snow.

Now the incredible happened. The two men did not stir. One of them was lying in the snow, secured to a red rope. Both held their heads hidden behind their elbows. The extra blast of the rotor-blades seemed to take their breath away. Urs made signs, I shouted which only served to soothe my nerves; the others could not possibly hear anything, but it helped me. Now one of them looked back – he understood that we could not land. My starboard main wheel was half a metre above ground and the Alouette was bumping. Several times the stick was at the end of its travel. I wanted to take these men on board, fly away, never to return.

Now one of them dragged the other over the snow to the helicopter. He was crawling like a worm over the ice. He must have been at the end of his tether. I wondered whether the two were tied together with the rope. If one of them was inside the helicopter and I had to take off suddenly, the other one would be left dangling on the rope, a potentially dangerous situation. However, it never came to that. When both men were at the level of the sliding door, outside my field of vision, I felt blinded. Everything around me was white, snow and ice.

I was left without any landmark at all. I had to take off, called to Urs to check that nobody hung on to the helicopter – and we were away. Like this we would never get anywhere and the only alternative was to fetch a guide to help us. If only all went well! I gave a radio message asking for someone to be ready and flew back to Rosenlaui. There we met Fritz Immer and Peter Winterberger, both guides used to flying. For reasons of balance I only wanted one of them. We shed all unnecessary material in order to be as light as possible. I did not even switch the engine off as I had to turn back at once to rescue the men before the weather made this impossible.

After starting I managed to warn Fritz Immer over the intercom to hold fast. The wind was as strong as before and snow eddies were whirling everywhere. The gusts from the Wellhorn shook us and I tried to meet them as well as I could. I was caught in an impossible situation where there was no way out; I simply had to carry on.

After several further attempts I managed to touch down on the ice

with the nose-wheel, choosing a blue, half-buried rucksack as a
beacon. Fritz Immer jumped on the glacier and now everything
happened very swiftly. The younger man almost flew into the cabin,
the older one, completely exhausted, was hauled in. Over the radio I
could hear Urs' heavy breathing. Much strength was needed to carry
the completely apathetic, almost paralysed man on board. I kept my
eyes on the blue rucksack. Whether it was the wind or the moving
men which caused my correcting manoeuvres, I did not know. I took
off even before the door was shut properly, relieved to have rescued
two. But during our descent I started to count: one raised the alarm,
his companion is dead, two are on board – where are the remaining
three?

On arrival I needed to stretch my legs and left the Alouette for the
first time. My stop-watch recorded sixty-five flight minutes. During
this time one flies from Interlaken to Zermatt, round the Matterhorn
and back again. Normally our flight would have lasted twenty
minutes, but now time was immaterial. I talked to the seventeen-year-
old boy, who seemed to me in a reasonably good state. He kept on
saying: "Nous sommes sauvés," (we have been rescued). He had
spent two nights in the bivouac on the Dossen. This morning he had
returned to the icefall and wanted to accompany the remaining three.
However, only one was still alive – the forty-year-old man lying in
the back of the helicopter. The woman had died during the first night.
Marc, the seventeen-year-old companion, died the following day.
Both lay buried under the snow.

A fourteen-year-old boy was still at the Dossen bivouac. Twenty
times at least we flew over this small hut, but there was no sign of
anyone. Once more we flew back, Fritz Immer jumped out of the
hovering helicopter, ran the fifty metres to the hut and fetched the
shivering boy. He dragged him by his belt over the snow. The boy's
legs kept buckling under him. Into the cabin they went and we were
off.

The three unfortunates on the glacier would have needed a further
thirty minutes in order to reach the safety of the Dossen bivouac.
They were not fully equipped and totally unprepared for a change in
the weather. The boy was merely dressed in blue jeans and walking
shoes.

We took the survivors to hospital. The forty-year-old man's
temperature had fallen to 32°C. He was completely exhausted and his

will to live at a low ebb, I do not think that he would have lived to see the arrival of the rescue party. Nobody can imagine what he must have gone through; to be helpless at the mercy of a storm for two days and nights; to have to watch one's wife dying and a cheerful seventeen-year-old collapsing, losing consciousness, never to wake again. It must have been terrible for him to wait and suffer up there, all alone. I am in no position to judge what they did wrong – nobody can do anything about that now.

Three people died. The guides found the two women later and when the wind had abated, we flew them back. The Rosenlaui glacier is Marc's grave. Officially, he is considered missing, but he is lying somewhere under the snow and has found his eternal rest in the mountains he loved. It is a sad story: in spite of having rescued several people and done our utmost, we cannot feel very happy.

On landing after a difficult flight, before we switch the radio off, it's customary to say thank you to each other over the intercom.

FIVE

Scottish hills to the visiting tourist, perhaps blessed with fine weather, may seem serene and gently inviting. Indeed they often are in summer and even in winter when the weather gods smile on these northern latitudes, but in storms they can reveal their Jekyll and Hyde character and be as savage as a rabid dog.

There are three tales in this chapter, each illustrating endurance and dedication to one's fellows. They are from three distinct areas of the country, the Cairngorms, the Central Highlands and the West. One is of the longest burial under an avalanche which anyone has survived in Britain, another of the tragedy which overwhelmed a band of experienced climbers on what is normally a gentle mountain path and the last a tale of bravery seldom equalled in war or peace.

I

Avalanche on Beinn A'Bhuird

Visitors to Royal Dee-side generally get the impression that the valley of the Dee is a tranquil place – as indeed it is – while the gently rolling Cairngorms look no more forbidding than a school of slumbering whales. However, three distinct features, weather, altitude and sheer size, can transform those leviathan-like peaks into deadly killers of the unprepared.

Much of the high ground is over 4,000 feet, but the height is deceptive because the mountains extend over a vast area; here one has much further to walk in order to reach a climbing area than in most other regions of Scotland. The weather is probably the most dangerous single factor. The Cairngorm tops form elevated plateaux whose height and open nature offer little obstruction to the high winds which, in winter especially, sweep in with alarming rapidity. These winds can soon sap a climber's strength and have a dangerous chilling effect.

The ferocity of Cairngorm storms has to be experienced to be believed. At the Ptarmigan Restaurant, on the forehead of Cairngorm, wind speeds of 150 mph have been recorded. It is not an exaggeration to say that severe weather in the Cairngorms rivals that found in any part of the world. In a blizzard it is an arctic no-man's-land.

Ben Macdhui (4,300 feet/1,300 metres) is the highest mountain in this range and, incidentally, the second highest in Britain. It is connected to Cairngorm by a broad plateau which nowhere falls below the 3,600-foot contour. The westerly slopes of Ben Macdhui fall steeply to the Lairig Ghru: this is a pass which connects Spey-side with Dee-side, and it lies between the portals of Braeriach and Cairn Toul on one side and Ben Macdhui on the other. It is twenty-seven miles from Aviemore to Braemar. No accommodation exists for twenty-two miles of this journey other than the odd bothy or barn. One such haven to the traveller, on the Braemar side, is Derry Lodge. For many years this isolated game-keeper's cottage was the home of Bob Scott who was head-keeper for Mar Estates. (Mar Lodge Hotel is a famous stalking and fishing centre near Braemar.)

Bob is a generous character, as free with his fund of tales as with his hospitality. He has been 'father' to succeeding generations of young climbers from Aberdeen: such well-known mountaineers as Bill Brooker, Tom Patey and Jim McArtney started their climbing apprenticeship from his hay barn in the shadow of these hills. Bob took his role as guardian of the glen seriously. He felt that, living as he did in that remote yet popular area, he had a certain responsibility towards travellers. On a bad night he used to place a lighted candle in his window as a beacon for belated and lost walkers trudging through the Lairig Ghru down from those featureless tops.

His candle was lit as usual one wet, autumn night some years ago when, between 1.30 and two am, there came a knocking at his door. As he jumped out of bed, dressed only in his shirt, he realised that it was terrible night of rain. It was bouncing like bullets from the roof of his cottage.

"Who's there?" he shouted above the cacophony of wind and water.

"We're lost," came a feeble reply.

"Are ye ladies or men?" asked Bob.

"Ladies."

"Weel, wait there a minute and I'll put on ma plus-fours," answered Bob, going back into his bedroom.

When he opened the door he saw that they were two girls; both appeared in a bad way, shivering, saturated and obviously wishing that they had never heard of the Cairngorms.

"I canna tak ye into the hoose," he said in his broad Dee-side accent. "It's full up. But we'll go oot tae the bothy and I'll soon get a fire going for ye."

In no time he had a big fire roaring in the bothy and went back to the house for food. After a few minutes he returned.

"A've brought ye half a loaf and a've brought ye a bit o' butter. A've got eggs and a've got cheese and a've got jam," he added, "Noo, ah don't think ye'll starve!"

One of the girls, who was as pale as plain flour, said, "We'll have to take our clothes off and there's no blind on the window." She pointed up to the solitary pane of glass which rattled in the driving rain.

"Och, ye don't need to bother with a thing like that here," he replied, laughing. "There's naebody aboot and a'm a married man, ye ken." Then he gave them two large great-coats which he said they could use to sleep in amongst the hay in the corner. From the doorway, he asked,

"What time do you want wakened at?"

"About seven would be fine," said one of them, shaking water from her flimsy cotton anorak.

"Goodnight then," said Bob as he left them.

In the morning when he went out to wake them up, they were sleeping, as he later recalled, "just like two corpses". He invited them in to breakfast and over the meal they told him what had happened. They had stayed the previous night at the Youth Hostel at Aviemore. When they asked the warden there whether it was possible for them to cycle through the Lairig Ghru he had told them – probably jokingly – "Sure, people do it every day." Since the girls came from Birmingham, they assumed that the route over the pass followed a rough road at least. However, as the going became progressively worse they were forced, much to their disgust, to carry the bicycles. Finally they decided to abandon them and continue on foot, intending to return to collect them the following day. But they were caught by darkness and became hopelessly lost. The rain had been growing steadily worse and eventually formed a seemingly unending downpour. At last, when they thought that they could go no further they saw the light in Bob Scott's window.

The next day, in better weather, they retraced their steps of the previous night and returned safely to Derry Lodge with their bicycles.

Not all the tales associated with Derry have such happy endings. Climbing conditions were poor on the 28th December, 1964. Earlier that month snow had covered the tops, crisp and deep but not necessarily even. This had consolidated and formed a good, hard base in the gullies and on the faces. However, about the 27th a fresh fall of snow occurred and the hills were then plastered. But, despite this, the temperature was unusually high for December. It didn't bode good for climbers. It didn't bode good for four men, carrying heavy rucksacks. They asked Bob if they could use his bothy for a few days. As usual, he told them that they could stay as long as they liked – provided they kept it clean and tidy.

"Whit dee ye hope to do, lads?" he asked.

Robert Burnett, the eldest of the party at twenty-eight, replied, "We hope to do some hill-walking, we've got a few days' holiday."

"Weel, watch the gullies just now," warned Bob, kicking at the snow under his tackety boots. "This stuff is very wet still."

Early next morning Bob was over collecting wood from the stick shed close to the bothy when the four lads emerged. The weather, though better, still had a damp, muggy feel about it; there had been no overnight frost.

"Morning, boys," he greeted them as they shouldered their rucksacks. He could see that they were well equipped. "Heading off?"

"We'll just take a walk up Beinn a'Bhuird," answered Burnett.

"Ah well, take care then, as I telt ye," warned Bob. "I dinna like these conditions."

"Oh, we'll be all right," rejoined one of the others. "It's an easy climb."

They set off for the hill but one of them – he looked the youngest – came running back for something he had forgotten. Bob watched him as he hurriedly departed again to catch up with the others. He never imagined that, within four hours, the lad would be dead.

That day Bob and one of his gillies were traversing the lower slopes of Beinn a'Bhuird hind shooting. They saw no sign of the four lads, although they must have been descending from the summit while the keepers were on the southern slopes of the mountain. The climbers came off the South Top and were at this time in a gully which had a very big build-up of snow on the true right bank. One of the party, Alister Murray, was slightly to one side of the rest.

Few mountaineers, even today, take sufficient heed of possible avalanche danger. In 1964, though many climbers had been involved in avalanches, these didn't receive much publicity. People accepted them fatalistically – largely as an act of God – if they ever thought about them at all, just as they accepted unpredictable stone fall. I don't suppose it entered the boys' heads whilst they were walking over the snow cover, that the mass of snow in the gully was poised, only requiring the smallest vibration to trigger an avalanche. Avalanche it did. Starting with a fracture twenty feet wide, then extending across the slope as if severed by an invisible guillotine. It was a classical, wet-snow avalanche, starting initially from a fracture of wind slab.

Murray managed to keep clear of the main force of the avalanche but his companions were swept away. With considerable presence of mind he noted where he had last seen them and stumbled down the avalanche tip which extended several hundred yards down the gully. There was no sign of his companions but he shouted for them as he descended. The avalanche he judged to be about ten or eleven feet deep. He eventually gave up the search and did the only thing possible; he went down to find help at Mar Lodge. From there, at 5.50 pm, he telephoned Braemar Police Station.

In Braemar P.C. John Bruce answered the call. There was no organised rescue team in the area; in those days there were just a few locals who would go out in an emergency and evacuate a casualty, even though they themselves were inadequately equipped. Jim Fraser, a quiet-spoken Aberdonian, was then living in Braemar; a few years previously he had started a horn-carving business in the village. As he was a keen hill man, always willing to help, John Bruce went round to see him as soon as he had contacted headquarters. He also told John Duff, the other policeman in Braemar, who had recently arrived there. There was no police Land-Rover in the district then, but a local farmer, Mr Pottinger, had one, so John Bruce contacted him to see if he could assist. This small party, with Gordon Fraser, a Mar Lodge

game-keeper, P.C. Alexander Souter from Ballater and Jock Farquharson, who worked at Mar Lodge, climbed into the vehicle which
spun up a rough track to just beyond a wood, close to the bottom of
the gully. They considered themselves fortunate that the accident was
so accessible; a most unusual occurrence on Cairngorm rescues.
Gordon Fraser, the game-keeper, was the most familiar with the area
so he acted as guide.

It wasn't a bad night, though there was no moon, but the stars gave
enough light to allow them to see the outline of the peaks. There
were, however, a few black areas in the night sky which indicated
clouds and this didn't suggest any improvement in the weather. They
found the bottom of the avalanche tip without much trouble. In those
days even the official rescue teams which had already been established
in the Highlands had only a vague notion of how to conduct a proper
avalanche search. Nevertheless, the Braemar party worked their way
up the avalanche tip, probing at random with some long, bamboo
poles they had brought along, and about a hundred yards from the
bottom of the avalanche they located the first man. They found him
by pure chance in their random probing, buried three feet deep in
avalanche debris. It was Alex McLeod who at twenty was the
youngest member of the group. He was dead.

By the time they had dug him out of his icy tomb the light from
their torches was reduced to a dull glow. They realised that they
would have difficulty even getting back to the Land-Rover, for the
weather was deteriorating and it was really dark now. There was no
hope of finding anyone else that night. There was no sign of the other
two buried men in the area where Murray had thought they might be,
nor was there any answer to the rescue party's frequent calls. The only
thing they could do was to return at first light and conduct a more
thorough search.

It was three am before they got back to the Land-Rover. On the
way they met Dr Irvin, the local doctor, and told him they had
only found the one man. The doctor confirmed that McLeod was
dead.

Next morning the Land-Rover crawled once more to a point just
beyond the wood. Ahead they could see the elephantine bulk of Beinn
a'Bhuird encased in a dazzling mantle of snow. The scar of the avalanche was visible but looked small and insignificant on the massive
south flank of the South Top. From this summit a broad, easy ridge

eases down in a southerly direction, forming a blunt nose known as Bruach Mor; the avalanche gully is to the south-west of this and in summer holds a stream, the Alltan na Beinne, a tributary of the Quoich Water which in turn flows into the Dee between Mar Lodge and Braemar.

That morning they had gathered a few extra helpers, including at least one member of the Steele Combo Ecosse Band who were playing at Mar Lodge at the time. The noise of the Land-Rover's engine broke the still of the lonely glen; when it was cut there was a momentary hush. Suddenly, a man shouted:

"I can hear someone calling!"

There was no doubt about it. From somewhere up in the direction of the avalanche tip there was a cry: "Help . . . Help . . ." It seemed so incredible that they could hardly believe their ears – they were absolutely positive that there had been no shouts the previous night for the wind had been too light then to drown such vigorous cries.

Grabbing their rescue equipment they proceeded up the slope as fast as possible. They passed the shallow and empty grave from which McLeod's body had been exhumed. The shouts were coming from the brink of a small, iced-up waterfall, somewhat higher up than Murray had indicated. Hastily, they went round the side of this and saw above them, in the debris, a hand sticking out of the snow and moving – it was whiter than the snow.

"All right, lad, we've found you. We'll soon have you out," shouted Jock Farquharson.

Though still breathless from the dash up the slope, they quickly dug round the buried man, careful not to injure him with the shovels. It proved to be a difficult task, since both his feet and the lower part of his body were encased in ice. When a wet-snow avalanche is subjected to pressure, as it often is in its rush through narrow parts of a gully, it rapidly freezes once it stops and pressure is released. This is what had occurred in Robert Burnett's case. It had also become colder overnight and so any melt water which was about – probably the snow round his body melted by body heat – refroze and encased his exposed skin, for his shirt, pullover and anorak had been pulled up by the force of the avalanche. The ice adhered to his body as if it had been bonded with a powerful adhesive and when it was removed his flesh resembled a pin-cushion as a myriad of needlepoints oozed blood. Even using a pen-knife they had difficulty in removing the ice and large areas of skin simply peeled off. His hands were in a similar state for he had been frantically digging for hours; he was badly frostbitten.

It was then 12.30 pm. He had been buried for twenty-two hours – the longest avalanche burial survival recorded in Britain. The previous night, when the rescue team was searching, he must have been unconscious and this fact probably played a considerable part in saving his life, for someone unconscious uses less oxygen and isn't subjected to the same degree of shock as a fully conscious person. Burnett was put on a stretcher and taken down to the Land-Rover; an ambulance picked him up at Mar Lodge and took him to Aberdeen hospital.

Meanwhile, the search continued for the one remaining man, Alex McKenzie. The rescue party again employed the bamboo poles to probe the avalanche tip. At 2.30 pm, as they were growing despondent at the prospect of failure, Jim Fraser finally located him; he was about three or four feet below the surface. He lay face down with the snow packed tightly about him. They knew before they dug him out that he was dead.

Later, when Burnett was interviewed in hospital in Aberdeen by Sergeant Massie of Bucksburn, he criticised the rescue team for abandoning the initial search despite the fact that their torches were dead. Even with later knowledge of avalanche search and rescue, I feel that the small volunteer party from Braemar made the only possible decision. Jim Fraser, now a member of the Search and Rescue Dog Association, thinks that if he had had an avalanche dog that night, Burnett would have been located with the minimum of delay, and he's probably right.

Burnett, I gather, took up pot-holing after his accident – the confines of a narrow pot-hole shouldn't hold any terror for him after his burial under the snows of Beinn a'Bhuird.

2

THE WELLINGTON AND THE STORM

New Year on the Corrour Track

To the north of the Rannoch Moor and south of Loch Laggan, in the wilds of the windswept no-man's-land of Ben Alder lies Loch Ossian;

a loch which takes its name from the most famous of Celtic bards. It is desolate country by any standards, especially in winter, where for months it can retreat under a blanket of snow. In olden times it was the hunting ground of Scottish kings, who had their base on an island on Loch Laggan, now, alas, submerged beneath industrial waters, for the loch is a hydro-electric reservoir today. Much of the lower ground round Loch Ossian is also submerged under a green sea of unimaginative coniferous uniformity: Forestry Commission planting.

Desolation, like beauty, is in the eye of the beholder. To a few discerning people the land round Ben Alder is a sanctuary in the bosom of Scotland. Only the thread of the West Highland line to the west intrudes on this haunt of the red deer, the golden eagle and the fox.

It was in December 1942 that a Wellington bomber number L7867 of B Flight, RAF Lossiemouth, took off on a cross-country day training flight. The weather was cold and blustery at Loch Laggan and on the peaks sleat hissed down. Visibility was bad. The pilot took the plane down through cloud to below 5,000 feet, thereby disobeying specific instructions. About 1500 hours it crashed into the summit of Geal Charn, 3,714 feet, just north of Ben Alder.

Duncan Robertson was then head-keeper of Corrour Lodge which snuggles amid trees at the north-eastern end of Loch Ossian. That evening the kitchen door burst open and a man dressed in a flying suit staggered in. Quite coherently, he asked the startled housekeeper if he could take his harness off. He was Sgt. P. E. Underwood, RAF, the tail gunner of the Wellington. After establishing that his five fellow crew members were all killed, he had struggled down from the summit to the Lodge unaided.

Nine years later, again in the month of December, a survivor loomed out of one of the worst storms for many years, into the shelter of that snug kitchen, to announce that four men lay dead up towards the pass to Ben Alder.

The friends one makes in youth often have a lasting influence, especially climbing companions. There's an impetuous tendency to stick out your neck, mostly through lack of knowledge; nevertheless, upon this foundation experience is built, as well as mountaineering common sense. The obvious isn't always so apparent when you don't have anyone to show you the ropes! When I started climbing there were no climbing schools, either outward- or upward-bounding. The modern inmate of such establishments is crammed with instant knowledge and in such academic circles the snow hole is regarded with the sanctity of a church, and map and compass the bible and staff of the wayfarer.

When John Black, John Bradburn, Sid Tunion and I lifted our eyes to the hills it was with an abundance of enthusiasm and a distinct lack of equipment: an old hemp rope, clinker-nailed boots and, if we were lucky, a karabiner and sling between us. We had to make do with the minimum of gear, yet I feel that our shoestring education had a lot of compensations. It taught us to be self-sufficient and self-reliant, principles much lacking today. Now we have occasionally to go to the assistance of a party on a mountain that may only be 'fatigued' and require an escort (often an ill-tempered one) back to the road.

Tragedy overtook those early climbing friends of mine one cold December in 1951. The events which befell this party and also included Sid's wife, Ann Tunion, had nothing to do with lack of equipment or lack of knowledge, for by then they were all experienced mountaineers with several years on the Scottish and Alpine peaks behind them. It was a type of accident which still happens today. The adversary is not mountain or avalanche, but the weather and that most insidious killer of the unwary, exposure.

I first met John Black, John Bradburn and Sid on the Cobbler, a small, savage, terrier-like peak which stands boldly above Arrochar at the head of Loch Long, some thirty miles from Glasgow. For generations it has been a kindergarten for budding rock tigers from the city. Its mica schist grudgingly offers the smallest wrinkles as a substitute for holds and when wet, which it often is, it makes the crags as slippery as oiled leather.

John Black was a lean-faced, serious man with deft movement who had the analytical mind of an engineer. John Bradburn was also in the engineering business, being a draughtsman: quiet spoken, always well dressed and giving the air of one contented with life. Sid was from tough stock. As a lad with his brother Sandy, he thought nothing of walking into the depths of the Cairngorms from Aberdeen where he was brought up. Aberdonians are hard men on the hills and Sid was no exception. All, including Sid's wife Ann, were honorary office bearers of the Glencoe Mountaineering Club, based in Glasgow. Though I was never a member, I used their bus at weekends and climbed with them. We taught ourselves the vagaries of the sport and rejoiced in the freedom of the hills. Another young climber who sometimes joined us was Jimmy Grieve. Those were carefree days and on a Saturday we used to rendezvous at Glasgow's St. Enoch's Square and take the bus to Glencoe or some other far-flung highland destination. We even went to the Alps in the bus on one occasion.

But to return to the Glencoe Club party of New Year 1951. Hogmanay is a time for revelry in Scotland where the national drink is patronised with a fervour which must gratify the Exchequer. Climbers usually head for the hills at this festival; some to ensure their discomfort insist on camping on mountain tops, a peculiar diversion, you may say, when the summits are in the path of the North Atlantic hurricanes.

The Glencoe Club party decided to take in New Year 1951 at Ben Alder cottage in the Central Highlands. It is a snug abandoned bothy on the shore of Loch Ericht that seems to beckon the weary traveller, and it is reputedly haunted by the ghost of a hanged man. The area is wild, with no roads and even the trails owe an apology to the walker. It was close by that that sprightly Jacobite and alcoholic, Prince Charlie, took refuge in Cluny's cave, a rustic hideout by all accounts which, if it didn't operate on smokeless fuel, at least had a backdrop of grey Ben Alder cliff which would obscure any smoke signal to keen-eyed redcoats.

There are seldom good climbing conditions at the New Year, but being a perennial optimist I myself repaired to Glencoe that year with Charlie Vigano, a member of the renowned Creagh Dhu Mountaineering Club, in the hope of stealing a route before the Old Year escaped. Anyhow we agreed there was little climbing on Ben Alder and in those days I didn't go a bundle on either history or ghosts.

John Black, John Bradburn, Jimmy Grieve, Sid and Ann Tunion left Queen Street Station, Glasgow, on a Fort William train. Their intention was to get off at the remote halt of Corrour which comprised a brace of incongruous buildings and two lonely signals, set amidst god-forsaken country on the easterly frontier of Lochaber. On the train were other mountaineers with similar intentions, members of the Scottish Mountaineering Club who knew the Glencoe climbers. Dick Brown was one of the S.M.C. party. With him were Dr Malcolm Slesser, Stanley Stewart, Gordon Waldie and several others. Dick Brown takes up the story:

I think the first sign that things were going wrong that holiday was at Bridge of Orchy station when the train stopped. I went up the platform to see the driver, for I knew that the guard had been celebrating and you have to make arrangements for the train to stop at Corrour, it's not a regular halt. On the way along the platform I met another climber who told me that there was no point in going to see the driver, for both he and the fireman were in much the same state as the guard.

The train jerked out of the desolate station of Orchy and skirted the Rannoch Moor. We did stop at Corrour, however, though as the train was long and the station short, the manoeuvre of stopping the guard's van at the platform was not successful. The Glencoe party, who had their rucksacks with them in the carriage, got out smartly. But not so us, for our gear was in the guard's van beneath a mountain of other luggage. The guard came along and shouted, "You've got two minutes to get your stuff off." He then disappeared, but he was true to his word: the train pulled away before all our rucksacks and skis were unloaded. Stan Stewart and I were still on board and Stan, who incidentally is a solicitor, rushed into one of the compartments and pulled the communication cord. But the New Year breakdown in communications obviously extended to the communication cord. The train kept going. It was pulled again and the one-time merry guard came storming down the train, as black as an Atlantic depression, asking who was responsible.

I said to him as he barged in, "If you don't stop this train, I'll go right up to Fort William and make a complaint. I'm warning you!" The guard, realising that I meant what I said, released the vacuum brakes and stopped the train about a mile and a half beyond Corrour station.

By the time we got all our gear assembled on the snow beside the line, the day was well advanced and the weather nasty. Several old women peered through the steamed-up windows of the train with worried expressions, wondering where on earth we were going on such a night in such a place.

Malcolm Slesser, meanwhile, left behind with some of our equipment close to the station, had climbed the signal post to see if he could spy the wayward train. He couldn't, so he trudged up the line to try and make contact with Stan and myself.

Sid Tunion's Glencoe party had already got a lift in a lorry going to Corrour Lodge. It had waited some time for our group, but eventually had to leave without us. So we set off laden with skis and rucksacks to the Youth Hostel (which has no warden) at the south-westerly end of Loch Ossian, just off the dirt road to Corrour Lodge. There we spent the night.

Sid's party had a drum-up of beans and soup in the woods close to the Lodge and then, shouldering their packs, headed up the snow-covered track towards the pass leading to Ben Alder cottage. It was about 8.30 pm and though it was snowing a bit, there wasn't a great deal of wind. Anyhow, they knew that it was a fairly straightforward trek up over the pass then down to the cottage. They had heavy packs, with enough food for several days. They even had a pressure cooker.

They had been going about two hours, having covered some two and a half miles up the glen, when they found that the snow was too deep to continue. John Black, Sid and Ann Tunion decided to bivouac for the night, as they had plenty of equipment. They were at the junction of the Uisge Labhair and the Glas Choire streams at a place called the Tramp's Grave. John Bradburn and Jimmy Grieve carried on, but a short way beyond they, too, decided to bed down for the night.

At about six o'clock the next morning John Bradburn and Jimmy Grieve decided to push on towards the pass. The weather had worsened overnight and a strong south-westerly wind was blowing. Sid's party awoke about two hours later after an unpleasant night and decided, like their two friends, to continue. It was easier, they thought, to go with the wind in the direction of the pass than to fight it. They also knew that John and Jimmy would be worried if they didn't show up at Ben Alder cottage. But the weather was so desperate now that John Black, Sid and Ann couldn't roll up their sleeping bags. In any case the rucksack straps were frozen solid, like steel bands on a packing case. It was quite impossible to open their packs to stuff the frozen bags inside. They didn't have much to eat, despite the fact that they had ample supplies of instant food in the form of chocolate and shortbread. In such an environment, in cold, damp and the cutting blast of the wind, one doesn't have the inclination to linger over food in any form. The overriding desire is to get to hell out of the strength-sapping blast.

Meantime, back at the bottom end of Loch Ossian, the S.M.C.

party made their way after breakfast along the rough road to Corrour Lodge. Stan Stewart remembers that day well:

> There was now a very strong south-westerly wind blowing where we were. The temperature was just around freezing or a little above. There were blatters of sleet and big wet flakes melted on landing and the gusts whipped up spray dervishes from Loch Ossian, so that the air was filled with cold moisture. Even with the wind at our backs we were soaked. I was wearing an old Home Guard great-coat, cut to jacket length, which I had proudly thought to be my personal armour plate, proof against anything. But its hidden qualities included a large capacity for absorbing moisture and by the time we reached the far end of Loch Ossian we were only too ready to sink our pride and beg the shelter of the estate bothy.

The keeper, Andrew Tait, after looking over the wretched soaking party, asked them where they were headed, and when they said Ben Alder cottage, he asked, "Are you from Gartnavel?" (a well-known mental institution near Glasgow). But like most Highlanders, the keeper's bark was worse than his bite and he took them to a snug bothy and ordered his men to cut a pile of firewood for them. The keeper's boss, Sir John Stirling Maxwell, the owner of the estate, was also a member of the Scottish Mountaineering Club.

A short way up the pass a life and death struggle was being enacted. It was about 9.15 am when Sid's party, fighting their way up the glen, met John Bradburn and Jimmy Grieve coming back. This was at Lochan Allt Glas Choire. John Bradburn told them about the bivouac they had and how at six o'clock they had pressed on with the gale whipping the fresh snow into a frenzy. But they had found that they just couldn't make it and had decided to come back. They all now turned into the wind and headed back towards Corrour Lodge.

At about ten o'clock Jimmy decided to abandon his rucksack. Today, such irrational behaviour is recognised as a sign of impending exposure. So far he hadn't appeared too bad, just a bit slower than the others. Presently it was John Bradburn's turn to act strangely; he threw his torch away, complaining that it was too heavy! When they reached the bivouac site which Sid's party had used the previous night the rest decided to abandon their rucksacks. Though the storm had been too bad for them to eat a meal, they did have some chocolate –

probably about three ounces each – as well as some butterscotch. Ann, who had been sick earlier, had fortunately recovered.

John Bradburn and John Black broke trail, always a soul destroying and energy absorbing task. Then Sid and Ann gave them a break. The wind was so strong now that they had to lean steeply into it and keep moving, otherwise they would have been blown backwards. Hailstones straffed them, projected by the worst storm for years in an area renowned for severe winter weather. Not long after this, only about half a mile beyond the bivouac site, Jimmy died. Half a mile further John Black and Sid collapsed. Vainly Ann tried to shelter them from the blast, but to no avail; they both died. John Bradburn was somewhere ahead. Ann left the boys about 1.30 pm and managed to reach the Lodge in under two hours.

At the bothy the S.M.C. party had made the most of the relative comfort; the previous night both Malcom Slesser and Dick Brown had produced chanters and there was a light-hearted competition in the intricacies of piping, with the pibroch (classical pipe music) being discussed and played by the log fire. Outside the storm raged. It created havoc throughout Scotland, bringing down trees and causing widespread structural damage. A short time after 1.30 pm the S.M.C. group heard the heavy tread of keeper Andrew Tait's boots outside the bothy. He opened the door and announced: "Look here, there's a woman in my house. She tells me there's four dead men in the glen. Can you come and give me a hand?'

With the keeper and two of his men, the climbers found the bodies of John Bradburn, John Black and Sid in the fading light. Jimmy's body was located the next day. During the night Andrew Tait had made up stretchers with saplings and jute sacks and with the help of the deer ponies the bodies were taken down to the Lodge.

It is easy to appear complacent over the passage of years and say such things don't happen to experienced mountaineers any more. Now we are aware of the dangers and the sudden onset of exposure. In 1951 exposure, if indeed anyone thought about it, was assumed to be a gradual process. Its symptoms are now well known to include faulty vision and irrational behaviour; manifest in this party as they abandoned their rucksacks and John Bradburn threw away his torch. Or was it? Certainly they must have been suffering from exposure, but leaving their packs might have just saved them by diverting their last straws of energy to locomotion rather than carrying a burden. One can hypothesise endlessly on the tragedy, but the fact is that they were reasonably well clad with windproof though not necessarily waterproof clothing, and of course damp soaks away vital body heat like a deadly wick, with a wind in excess of fifty mph and an actual air temperature of 32°F. The effective chilling temperature that day must have been in the region of −10°F.

John Black suffered from asthma, and I remember Sid on some occasions lagging behind when we were climbing. It was only later, after I knew him better, that I discovered he suffered from a pelvic war wound. He had served in the Royal Artillery. These may have been contributory factors.

The accident rocked the Scottish climbing fraternity to its roots. Here were four climbers, and I can personally vouch for their fitness, who were adequately equipped with plenty of food, who died on what is usually an easy mountain path. It just didn't seem possible, yet it happened.

Ann survived unscathed except for the terrible trauma of losing her husband and three friends. A short time later the Glencoe Club was disbanded.

3

DUEL WITH AN TEALLACH

Just occasionally one hears of an act of bravery which seems to go far beyond the bounds of rational action. It may be someone saved from drowning by a complete stranger or a child snatched from the teeth of a blazing inferno by a passing samaritan, but usually such acts of mercy are of short duration, at least those which involve a single rescuer, though both lifeboat crews and various teams of rescuers can be exposed to danger for long periods.

The striking thing about Iain Ogilvie's attempt to save his friends on an ice-bound mountain in western Scotland is that it was a protracted effort by one man. There was no other alternative, for to have left his friends and gone for help would have certainly sealed their fate. As it was they had a chance, however slim, if he stayed with them and moved them to a safer place on that hostile peak.

But first let me describe the mountain in question, An Teallach, which means the Forge in Gaelic. Heading north towards Ullapool in north-west Scotland, one first catches a glimpse of the castellated peaks of An Teallach from the Dundonnell Forest beyond Garve. It's not a forest of trees, but a deer forest, squelchy bogs, bouncy heather and of course deer. The road to the doorstep of An Teallach forks left from the A835 to Ullapool. Skirting the Corrieshalloch Gorge, it weaves downhill on the Road of Destitution, a name inspired by starving natives of the area who built it during the potato famine of 1851 – payment was made in potatoes!

This road gives the best tourist's view of the mountain; few peaks in the British Isles can vie with its rugged profile, it looks as if it was carelessly built by a crazy architect. What one can't see from the Road of Destitution is Toll an Lochain, an inkwell-like lochan huddled beneath the great cliffs. Around it for threequarters of its circumference An Teallach bends like a cross-cut saw. The highest peak is Bidean a'Ghlas Thuill (3,483 feet/1,062 metres). Eight further summits curl round the lochan to the west and south, the southerly aspect terminating in An-Sail Liath, the Grey Heel.

On the 17th April, 1966, three friends travelled north from London and parked their car in a lay-by off the Destitution Road. They were Iain Ogilvie, fifty-three, a member of the Alpine and Scottish Mountaineering Clubs; Charles Handley, fifty-nine, known as 'Tommy', who was of the Alpine Club and Climbers' Club, Peter Francis at thirty was the youngest member, a good rock climber – but he didn't have the snow or ice experience of the other two.

Shouldering their packs they climbed to the col east of An Teallach and made a high camp. There was an unusually heavy covering of snow for the time of year – moreover, it was extremely hard; as hard as Iain Ogilvie, with his wide knowledge of Scottish conditions, had ever experienced in early spring.

It is not uncommon for parties traversing An Teallach to pitch camp to the east of the mountain as these three friends did, otherwise the traverse would be a long day. Furthermore, they welcomed the solitude of the Highland snows. The scenery alone pays dividends to those prepared to carry a tent into this hinterland. Few places can rival the sheer grandeur of the cirque of An Teallach, while to the north, the horizon is dotted by peak upon peak endowed with such magical names as Cuinneag, Bein Dearg and Cul Beag. Beyond Ullapool on the fringe of the North Atlantic are the Summer Isles, small idyllic jewel-like islands on a romantic sea-board.

The object of this particular expedition was to go over all the ten tops of the An Teallach range. The first peak of the day was Sail Liath. Ahead, the peaks clustered in a series of icy pinnacles with a great precipice of 1,500 feet falling to Toll an Lochain. On their right they passed the gaping mouth of Constabulary Couloir, first climbed by Dr Tom Patey and members of a police rescue team. Presently the three climbers arrived at the main obstacle on the traverse, the face of Corrag Bhuidhe Buttress, in summer a steep rock face, in winter often plastered in snow and ice.

It was lunchtime when Iain Ogilvie and his two companions reached the summit of Sgurr Fiona. During the morning they had enjoyed traversing the top of Sail Liath, the four pinnacles of Corrag Bhuidhe and Lord Berkeley's Seat, a draughty and exposed 'armchair' which is a promontory on the ridge. From below this last point an easy snow slope led them to the top of Sgurr Fiona and they realised that the main difficulties were now behind them.

At this stage, Tommy and Peter decided to miss out a subsidiary summit to the west, Sgurr Creag an Eich. Iain, however, had finished his sandwiches before them and, as he was feeling fit, he decided to take in this top. He asked his friends if they would wait for him and this they agreed to do, Tommy adding, "But if we get cold, we'll move on slowly and if there's any difficulty – anywhere that needs a rope – we'll wait for you."

So Iain set off to bag his peak.

He had covered almost half the distance along the snowplastered ridge to Sgurr Creag an Eich before he looked back and saw that Tommy and Peter already had the rope on and were climbing down the ridge of Sgurr Fiona towards Bidean a'Ghlas Thuill. Since the understanding was that they would wait for him, should the rope be required, he concluded that they must have thought that the rope wasn't really necessary for someone of his own ability, but that Tommy had thought it prudent to have Peter safeguarded as he wasn't so experienced.

As Iain considered this possibility, he turned and looked back again. He could see them quite clearly, silhouetted against the bright northern sky, now drawing slightly nearer as they by-passed a rocky step on the ridge. He stopped to watch them. Neither was moving now and he wondered if they were debating the best line of descent, or were they going to wait there for him? He went on but soon turned round again; for no obvious reason he was feeling distinctly uneasy. To his horror he saw they were both falling, sliding down the steep, hard snow at a high speed, hopelessly out of control. They shot over one low cliff, then over another where the rope caught and they were left hanging on the snow face. There was no movement, no sound, just silence.

Iain Ogilvie describes what happened:

I ran back to the col and put crampons on over my tricouni-nailed boots. I recalled as I ran that Peter Francis also had crampons and Tommy had nailed boots the same as mine. Once at the col I found that I was at their level, but to reach them involved a long but fairly straightforward traverse of a quarter of a mile over hard snow interspersed with scree patches. On a later visit in summer I found that there was a deer track along this line but, of course, with the snow cover there was no sign of it then. The snow was banked up against the upper cliff on which they hung and it was much steeper than it is in summer. Several jagged rocks protruded from the slope down which they had fallen and I saw, as I approached, that the rope was snagged on one of these, so that they were both hanging from it. The particular projection on which the rope caught was very small and obviously had only a hair-trigger grip. If, I told myself, I could get them onto safer ground, then the most sensible thing to do next would be to go for help.

There was another vertical drop below them, but about thirty feet away to one side there was a steep tongue of snow and ice leading through the difficult sections below. I couldn't see to the bottom of it, but I realised that this was the best chance – my only hope of getting them down. This was essential, as I couldn't leave them where they were to go for help; it would take hours and, though they both appeared to be unconscious, it was just possible that one of them would come round and any movement might have sent them crashing once more down the face.

All this took only seconds to run through my mind. I quickly cramponed over to where they were hanging and discovered that they both had severe head injuries. With some difficulty I secured their rope where it was already caught. They were tied together with a fifty-foot length of full-weight nylon climbing rope and I had a further 120 feet in my rucksack. I went down to Tommy and tied him on to an end of my rope; as there was no suitable anchor to which I could tie him, I drove my ice axe into the steep slope for a belay. I then cut the rope on which he was hanging so that his weight came on to the ice axe on my rope. I had secured the other rope at the rock spike so that it wouldn't run free with Peter on the end of it once it was cut.

I then swung Tommy across the hard snow in a pendulum motion to the top of the tongue of snow – my only hope. Once he was on the correct line of descent, I proceeded to lower him until he was out of sight over a bulge. When all the rope ran out there was still considerable tension on it, so I knew that he hadn't yet reached the bottom. I had no alternative but to descend the steep slope. Using my crampons, this stretched me to the limit of my capabilities, for I had no ice axe, as it was holding Tommy, and I dared not put any more weight on the rope because the belay wasn't all that secure. My two friends had lost their ice axes in the fall and the only thing I had in lieu of an axe was a piton hammer. I tried to drive it in above me as I kicked the points of my crampons into the snow. Suddenly, as I was inching down, I slipped and fell over a short rock step of about six feet, landing on my chest on the slope beneath. The snow was still iron hard here and, even as I tried to regain my breath, I knew that it was imperative to stop: otherwise I would be killed. Putting my full body weight on to the head of the piton hammer, so that the short spike bit into the snow, I slowed up and scraped to a halt. I was shaken, bruised, but otherwise uninjured. I had been carrying two rock pitons which I had intended to use to bring Peter down, but these were lost during my fall.

I worked my way over to where Tommy was hanging at the end of the rope and realised that I would have to secure him before I could go back up to release the rope and get my ice axe. I had with me an ice screw but the surrounding ice wasn't suitable for it, so I had to jam it into a crack in the rock nearby. I realised that it had only a fifty-fifty chance of holding, but things were getting desperate; risks had to be run.

I was now able to use the hanging rope as a handrail since Tommy's weight had been transferred from it to the piton, and I quickly reached my ice axe and descended again without further incident. This time I lowered him a complete rope's length, using the ice screw as a belay. When the rope was paid out its full length he had reached the foot of the Torridonian Sandstone rock bands and was at the top of another steep snow slope. I climbed down to him and started to cut out a ledge in the hard snow. All this, I later discovered, took a great deal of time, but eventually it was completed and I laid him out on this cold ledge and covered him with most of my clothing.

I then started back up the slope for Peter. As I removed the rope from the screw at Tommy's last belay on my way past, the screw actually fell out of the crack and bounced down the slope. I had been right – it wasn't secure! However, I told myself that this was no time to think of narrow escapes.

When I reached Peter I suspected that he was already dead but, having come all this way, I decided to try and lower him down. As I now had both ropes available I could secure him from much further up the slope. Also, I had my axe which made my own position safer, though unfortunately, I had to use the axe again as a belay for the second lower to Tommy's ledge, because the ice screw had vanished.

After a lot of hard but uneventful work, I brought him down to Tommy's level. I knew then that I would have to run the gauntlet once more and descend the treacherous slope without an ice axe. There was no alternative for once more the axe wasn't safe enough to risk our combined weight.

"The last ten feet down to where Peter hung were at a steep angle. I slipped again. I might have saved myself with my hammer, I suppose, but I tripped on Peter's body and pitched headlong over it. In seconds I was travelling at an alarmingly high speed. As soon as I tried to dig the hammer pick in, it was snatched from my hands by the force of my fall. I shot down about 500 feet, hitting two rocks sticking out of the snow en route. Fortunately, I stopped before running on to the scree and boulders at the bottom. I was badly bruised and skinned and, as I found out later, I had slipped a disc in my neck.

By this time it was after one pm. There was no possibility of getting up again. Even if I had managed to reach them there was nothing more that I could do. The only course left open was to go down for assistance and return with help. I knew also that I must get down for my own survival, as there was no shelter and it promised to be a very cold night. All my warm clothes were covering Tommy. Even the prospect of going for help was a bleak one. I had five miles to travel and 2,000 feet to descend down the rough valley from Coire Mor an Teallach. It was 5.30 pm before I reached a crofthouse at Ardessie, from where I telephoned to Dr Tom Patey in Ullapool.

As soon as Tom had the message from Iain Ogilvie, he alerted the local police sergeant, Roddie Lovat, who in turn contacted his headquarters in Dingwall. Both Ross and Sutherland Police Rescue Team and the RAF Kinloss team were told of the accident.

Tom arrived in his Renault at the croft house at 6.30 pm. Meanwhile, Iain Ogilvie had not been idle: he had marked on his map the exact location of the accident.

Iain had not met Tom before. "My first impressions of Dr Tom were very true of the man. He took my map, listened patiently to me for about half a minute, and then said, 'If you got yourself all the way down from there on your own, the district nurse can deal with you. I must get up before it's too dark. Tell the rescue party to follow.' "

Tom Patey was born in the small township of Ellen in 1932. With the wild Cairngorms as his playground in his early years, he grew up with a high degree of physical fitness which, combined with his natural musical talents, made him the ideal companion for hard, long climbs, followed by nights of song. Tom was a song-writer and a singer who had a magical touch on his accordion. He was involved in quite a number of rescues in north-west Scotland and, devoted a considerable amount of his precious spare time in helping to train the local police, for he shared my view that you can't teach people to rescue on mountains until they have learnt to climb.

Tom set off dressed as usual in a pullover, an old pair of dark trousers, with an anorak tied about his middle, and a great coil of rope slung over his shoulder, grasping his old ice axe. He followed the trail of blood left by Iain Ogilvie. In an hour he had covered the distance – which gives some indication of his fitness – but he had trouble in locating the two men. They were both dead when he found them. It was 8.30 pm as he started to cut steps down the slope for another 500 feet in order to help the other rescuers.

He saw them coming up the valley below – a small band of figures in red anoraks: the Ross and Sutherland Police team, led by Donnie Smith. As darkness was now close at hand Tom decided that he had better start lowering the bodies, since the police party had only limited experience on snow and ice and he didn't want any further accidents.

Combining the length of his rope with the 170 feet which Iain had left by the bodies, he succeeded in lowering the first corpse. The length of this lower was exactly 500 feet – the distance that Iain had fallen.

Tom quickly climbed down the face and joined the police as they were strapping Peter's body to the stretcher. The next day the RAF team recovered the other body.

Iain Ogilvie was awarded the MBE for his part in the attempted rescue of his friends, while Tom received the Queen's Commendation for Brave Conduct.

SIX

We were slumming in what must be the most despicable 'hotel' in the length of the Andean chain: The place, the Ecuadorian town of Ambato. In the courtyard idle peons whittled wood with keen knives, whilst others played cards with our gaunt, wily de-poncho'ed landlord. The game was strategically conducted at the bottom of rickety stairs which led to the balcony from which our room sulked in shadow.

This cell, for it resembled a cell more than a room, had at one time, perhaps when Pizarro was a breadsnapper, boasted white walls. The remaining plaster bore witness to this. The only furniture was three wooden platforms serving as beds. On these lay Joe Brown, Yvon Chouinard and I. We swotted flies and absorbed the incessant cacophony of the market crowd; assailed by a proliferation of smells which is South America. The other 'fixture' in the room was a large rat – it hadn't moved for ten minutes. It looked me over with a calculating eye from its sanctuary beneath Yvon's bed.

We had come to look for treasure and to find emptiness in the Upper Amazon. So far we had discovered flies and had been engulfed by numerous, gregarious, but essentially friendly Ecuadorians – but that is another story.

"You know you were asking about that rescue in the Tetons, Hamish." It was Yvon speaking. I looked up expectantly. He continued, "There's a guy, Pete Sinclair, who can possibly help you. I think he was involved. He's a professor of English now, I'll give you his address."

Well, Pete Sinclair did help. He knew about the rescue all right, he was on it. So was another American climber that I knew, Al Read, who now lives in Kathmandu where he runs Mountain Travel, the trekking organisation.

Both Pete and Al had done a lot of climbing in the Tetons, the range on the Wyoming–Idaho border; compact mountains rising up to 6,000 feet from an alluvial carpet of river flats interspersed with aspen and cottonwood, a veritable 'rock candy' upthrust, studded with pearly lakes. From both sides of the massif water drains to the great Snake River, which, true to its name wriggles 900 tortuous miles to the Pacific. Early trappers called the three main peaks the Grand, Middle and South Teton – Les Trois Tetons, the three breasts, which makes one speculate on the suggested angular profile of pioneering maidens!

Unlike those in the bum's song, these are real peaks, they can be hard, cold and unrelenting. There *is* snow and the wind *does* blow in these mountains.

NOT A PLACE FOR PEOPLE

accident on the Grand Teton by Pete Sinclair

O brothers who through a hundred thousand perils have reached the west, to this so brief vigil of the senses that remains to us choose not to deny experience, in the sun's track, of the unpeopled world. You were not born to live as brutes, but to follow virtue and knowledge.

Ulysses from the eighth sphere of Dante's *Inferno*
(translation by John D. Sinclair)

The back room of the Jenny Lake ranger station served as a country store on stormy days or rest days. The cabin had a stove because in the winter it was used as a patrol cabin; there was also running water. It was a good place to make tea and to talk. Leigh Ortenburger spent quite a bit of his research time there when he was in the valley and since he was our historian, the back room became one of the two storytelling places in the valley. The climbers' campground was the other one. Once Yosemite climbers started coming to the Tetons to rest from the intensity of the Yosemite walls, the campground and ranger station became the communications hub of American climbing through most of the 'sixties.

Late in July, 1962, there was one storytelling session going on with Leigh Ortenburger and Dave Dornan in the group. Dave wanted me to work on No Escape Buttress with him. Mount Moran's south buttresses presented Teton climbers with a chance to do something that resembled Yosemite wall climbing. The easternmost of these buttresses, No Escape Buttress, was the last and most difficult of these problems. I was not in any way prepared for a climb of this difficulty but I had to try. Dornan wanted this climb. He was born in the valley, had been a climbing ranger with me and was now an Exum Guide. He had accepted the Yosemite challenge. That is, he did not expect to become as good as Chouinard or Robbins but he wanted to be good enough to carry on a conversation with them.

There were encouraging signs in the heavens as we rowed across Leigh Lake in a rotting plywood skiff, one rowing, one bailing. I had never seen clouds so massive or as black as those which were piling up on the Idaho side of the range. Such clouds in the morning indicated that this was not to be an ordinary storm; we were sure to be stormed off the climb. The prospect pleased me, we'd do a couple of pitches and then go home. That would give me time to psyche myself up for a serious attempt later. As it turned out, I was to be busy for a while.

In a different part of the range, another climber was discovering that he had backed himself into a commitment which was to prove very serious. Ellis Blade had led a group of nine Appalachian Mountain Club climbers up Teepe's Snowfield on the Grand Teton. The snowfield is steep though not extreme. But the snowfield had become Blade's personal Rubicon.

Dornan was near the top of the first lead when the storm hit us. He rappelled off and we ran for the lake. Crossing the lake in that storm is one of the sillier things I've done. Fortunately, the energy of the storm was released in impulses rather than as a sustained force. The wind and rain combined to beat the surface of the lake down instead of lifting it into breaking whitecaps or we would have been in trouble. Dave, chortling because he was no longer a rescuer, remarked that if there was anybody in the mountains, my day was not over. I wasn't much worried. This storm was severe enough that the most desperate vacationing climber with one day left on his vacation and fifty weeks of being chained to a desk facing him, could not pretend that it was a passing summer shower. It was not only violent, it was cold. There was a smell of the Gulf of Alaska about it. You could tell that an Arctic air mass had penetrated south.

I looked forward to a few quiet days in the ranger station as Dave and I walked and hitch-hiked back to Jenny Lake. The climbers would be out of the mountains and the campers would be heading for motels or the desert. The back of the ranger station would be warm, full of climbers drinking tea. The guides would be in, looking at our photographs of the peaks, planning one more climb, swapping stories.

When we got to the ranger station I was told that the other ranger on duty, George Kelly, had been sent out to check on an overdue party of ten from the Appalachian Mountain Club. This was an annoyance but couldn't be serious. Ten people can't just vanish in a range as small as the Tetons.

The failure of the Appies to return as they had planned was irritating to us. People often get benighted in the Tetons in circumstances like those attending this climb: a large party, composed of people of varying experience, climbing a route that is reputed to be easy but is seldom climbed. In fact, those circumstances are guaranteed to produce a bivouac. At the ranger station we would normally give the party plenty of time to extricate itself from the route and get back before we did anything dramatic. Often there was another party in the same general area who would spot the late party. From where they were last seen, we could make a reasonable guess of how long it would take them to get back. If the missing party exceeded our estimated time of return, as well as their own, then we'd set things in motion. Even then we wouldn't scramble a full scale search. Our first action would be to send out one ranger, or two if there was to be technical climbing, and combine the search with some other activity such as a patrol, if possible. We might also pass the word around to one or two key rescue types that such and such a party was overdue. What that meant to them was that they'd be where they could be easily reached and maybe pass up the second beer until the word went about that everybody was out of the mountains.

Sometimes the worried family or concerned friends who were waiting in the valley would take exception to this stalling for time. But there really is no other way to do it. If we'd scrambled a full-scale search and rescue operation every time a party was overdue, the expense would have been enormous but, most important, tremendous pressure would be put on the party in the mountains to get back in the time estimated and the result would be many more injuries and deaths.

In the case at hand, we actually did not stall as long as we normally would have. There were a lot of people in the Appalachian Mountain Club encampment who were concerned enough to bring down word to us of the overdue party. They certainly expected a response from us. Second, the storm increased the possibility that the party could be stuck for some time. One detail was worrisome, the party was not well equipped for cold weather. So, very soon after we were notified, Ranger George Kelly was on his way into the mountains on a patrol. He would stall by organising a search party from the Appalachian Mountain Club encampment. It's not that we didn't worry. We always worried. Worrying was a major component of our work. It is not difficult to imagine the worst, even after a hundred repetitions of one's imagining's turning out to be worse than the reality. We worried, but we had learned an orderly, logical procedure to follow in these cases and kept our imagining at a distance.

The leader of the party was Ellis Blade, not himself an Appie but a recognised leader. Blade was not really what Europeans would regard as a guide. Americans do not hire guides in America, they hire authorities. Glenn Exum, the founder of the Exum Guides, has a kind of genius for spotting young men who carry an aura of personal authority. And that is part of the reason for the success of his guide service, a success which is unparalleled in America. The Exum Guides at that time ranged in age around late twenties to early thirties. Blade was in his fifties. The rest of the party varied greatly in experience. Steven Smith, quite young but a good rock climber, was the assistant leader. The other able rock climber was Lester Germer, who was sixty-five. Charles Joyce was a good recreational rock climber, very respectful of the Western mountains because his experience had been mainly on the cliffbands of the East. Janet Buckingham was an experienced hiker, with Lydia and Griffith June, Charles Kellogg and John Fenniman in various stages of learning rock climbing. Mary Blade, Ellis's wife, was also along and was an experienced mountaineer. The route they were to climb was known as the Otter Body Route, after the shape of a snowfield in the middle of the east face of the Grand Teton.

The party got off as planned at four am Thursday morning, a good sign.* There had only been a couple of minor problems in the days prior to setting out. Blade hadn't been able to generate much enthusiasm for conditioning climbs. The time to get the party into condition

*For many details of events, I did not personally witness, I am indebted to James Lipscomb's account in two issues of *Sports Illustrated*, 1965, '72 Hours of Terror', June 14 and 'Night of the One-Eyed Devils', June 21.

had been scheduled, but things hadn't quite worked out. This is not surprising in view of the fact that the encampment was the size of a tribe, but one with random membership. Going into the wilderness to set up a new society is an American passion, but it takes a lot of energy just to eat, sleep and talk in a situation like that. There are new people to meet and hierarchies, liaisons and enmities to be established before the group can truly focus on its stated purpose. It requires the genius of a leader like Shackleton to select team members who accomplish the settling-in work quickly and in such a manner that the resulting organisation is the one that's needed to do the job.

The problem, other than conditioning, that Blade might have had on his mind at four am that Thursday morning was that Steven Smith, the young assistant leader, was suffering from an attack of no confidence. He didn't like the looks of the weather. He had vomited the evening before, and had confided his doubts to Charles Joyce. Blade was fifty-four and Steven Smith twenty-one. They never became co-leaders in any meaningful sense. It was Joyce who broached Smith's worries to Blade. If there was to be any rapport established between these two, it would have been up to Blade to establish it. Presumably part of his responsibility was to train the next generation of leaders. It is also true that mountaineering in America was undergoing a tremendous growth in rock-climbing skills; hundreds of good young climbers were, within three years, learning to do moves on rock routes that older climbers had thought only feasible on boulders in campgrounds. Blade would be an unusual man indeed if he did not feel his authority somewhat undermined by this new generation.

As for Smith, it's possible that he had a touch of the 'flu or had picked up a bug from the water. It happened to me at least once a season in the Tetons and to all the guides and climbing rangers I know. Whatever the cause of Smith's loss of confidence, the events of the first day conspired to keep it that way. They did however make an early start.

Four and a half hours later, at 8.30, they started up Teepe's Snowfield. A pace twice that fast would be regarded as slow by most climbers. Blade had plotted the climb with a five-hour margin of daylight. Half of his margin was gone before the party roped up.

Janet Buckingham broke out of her steps in the snow, and although Smith held the fall easily, Janet's feet flailed away at the snow use-

lessly. Anybody who has taught climbing beginners is familiar with
the scene. The student or client literally loses contact with his/her feet
and thrashes away hoping that a miracle will occur and one of them
will stick. Perhaps Smith didn't know how to deal with the situation,
perhaps he hadn't the chance. It was Blade, leaving his own rope, who
talked her back into confidence in her steps again. The incident with
Janet would have been soon forgotten by all involved except that
disturbing incidents began to accumulate.

The lead rope of five made it to the top of the snowfield half an hour
before noon. The second rope, Smith's, didn't join the lead rope at the
top before lunch. They stopped on an outcropping about three rope
lengths below. This area is scarred by debris fallen from the cliffband
and two snowfields above. This detail did not go unnoticed by Joyce
at least, and he was the one who spotted the falling ice first and gave
the warning yell. One block carried away Fenniman's ice axe.
Another glanced off Kellogg's foot. Joyce had two blocks to dodge
and only managed to dodge one. He was hit hard and knocked into
the air. Though briefly stunned, he was uninjured.

To this point, Joyce, though he was Smith's confidant, had been
maintaining a neutral stance on the question of whether the climb was
advisable or not. After being hit, he still wasn't as shaken as Smith,
whose hands were trembling, but he was now of Smith's opinion that
this was an ill-fated climb and they ought to go down.

Blade had gone down to check that everybody was all right and
then quickly climbed back up to his rope, before a discussion could
ensue. The lower party, wanting to get out of the track of falling
debris even more than they wanted to go down, followed quickly.

While they were getting underway, Joyce said to Smith, "Let's get
out of here." Smith replied, "He'll kill us all."

As the entire party reached the top of the snowfield, a storm hit. It
was noon. This was not the familiar late afternoon thunderstorm but
the arrival of one that had been threatening since the previous evening.
The party took refuge in the moat between the top of the snowfield
and the rock which at least sheltered them from the wind. Smith
finally confronted Blade with his desire to retreat. Blade responded
that the snowfield was hardening and had become dangerous. As the
heavy rainfall and hail from the first huge cumulus cloud passed and
the rain moderated, Blade gave the word for everyone to put on their
packs and start moving up. Joyce sought out Smith.

"What's he doing? Is he nuts? We've got to go down. You're a leader. Tell him we've got to go down."

Eventually it would be Joyce who would take command and make the decision to go down, but that was to be two days hence.

The party traversed the top of the snowfield to the base of a rock couloir. Blade sent Germer ahead to scout the route, asking him to report "how it would go". The wording is significant. Phrased that way, it is not the same as asking "Ought we attempt it?"

This couloir, carved in the interstice of the east face and the east side of the Grand joins the Otter Body Snowfield to Teepe's Snowfield. It is rather alarmingly free of the debris which packs the bottom of most Teton couloirs. It is too steep, too water, ice- and rock-washed to hold anything much in it for long. Obviously the rock is not particularly sound which is why a couloir developed. Griffith June saw the couloir first as a bowling alley and then found in his mind the inscription from the *Inferno*, "Abandon hope, all ye who enter here." Wet, cold, late, tired, with weather threatening and tension in the group growing, it can not have been a cheerful party that geared themselves up for rock climbing.

Germer returned with his report which he recalls thus: "I told him it looked easy. I know now he was asking for advice, and I gave him a rock-climbing opinion. It was easy rock climbing. I was not considering the safety of the party. The camp had chosen Blade as a leader, but I should have said something." Possibly there was something else at work here. The opening sentence in the description of the route in Ortenburger's, *A Climber's Guide to the Teton Range* (1956 edition) is: "Petzoldt (who did the first ascent) ranks this as one of the easiest routes on the Grand Teton." Twenty-seven years after the first ascent, an Eastern cliff climber of Germer's stature could not in good conscience rate this climb as more difficult than the first ascent party found it to be. Unless Blade had reason to think that he was seriously off route, which was unlikely, he knew what Germer's reply was to be.

Ellis Blade retorted when Smith once again said that they ought to go down, "I've been on that glacier before in weather like this. It's as hard as ice. If we go down, someone will get killed."

Smith pressed the point, "We can't climb the mountain now."

Blade's response was, "You keep your mouth shut."

"Well, I'm assistant leader of this group," said Smith, "and I think my opinion should be considered."

"Well, don't you forget that I am the leader and I know it is safer to go up."

In the hours that follow, they all got soaked, Lydia June had a shock from a lightning bolt, Smith avoided a rock avalanche only by leaping across the couloir into the arms of Griffith June, and Kellogg was hit by a rock which drove his crampons through his pack and into his back. Griffith June considered leading a splinter group back, a serious responsibility. He had the authority within the AMC organisation, but not as a mountaineer, and they were very much in the mountains now. He urged Blade to lead them back but Blade replied that they were committed.

Blade now climbed quickly and well, getting the party three-fourths of the way up the couloir. Griffith June arrived at a huge boulder two pitches from the top, big enough for them all to sit on. Joyce secured them with pitons and they all bivouacked there except Blade who had reached the wide ledges and easy slabs at the top of the couloir. There was no reconsideration of Blade's decision. There were complaints, perhaps fewer than there might have been had Mary Blade not been part of the group. A decision to go down would have been a decision to abandon Blade on the mountain.

Three inches of wet snow fell during the night. They had no down garments, no dry clothes, and virtually no food. In the morning, Germer asked Smith what he thought, Germer didn't like the rotten rock and had been weakened by the bivouac. Smith replied that he didn't know the route.

It took all of the next day, Friday, to get the party up the remaining two pitches to the top of the couloir. Joyce and Fenniman climbed up to Blade. June slipped on the ice just below the point where the angle of the couloir eased. He tried repeatedly and fell repeatedly. He cut steps, almost made it, and fell again, this time further and over an overhang. There was danger of his being strangled by the rope. Smith muscled him over to the bivouac pillar where June collapsed exhausted.

Germer then went up and set up an intermediate belay position where he stayed until all six remaining climbers were up the couloir. (This was during the time when Dornan and I were being driven from Mount Moran a few miles to the north.) Though fit enough, Germer was in his sixties and this was too much; he had lost all reserves. His hands were claws; he clutched a piton in each and made it up the ice.

Blade moved on but was called back. Germer announced he was dying.

Blade assessed the situation and had a new plan, but not a new direction. There can be an infinite number of situations, tactics and explanations but there can only be one conclusion. He, Joyce and Smith would go up. They might find climbers at the top. If not, they'd go down the Owen-Spaulding Route and get help.

There was twice as much snow above them as they climbed on Teepe's Snowfield and beyond was another cliffband.

When duty ranger, George Kelly, got to the AMC camp at the Petzoldt's Caves, there was no word of the missing party. By the time he radioed this news down, we were back in the ranger station and instructed him to organise a search. We were getting a little nervous. The search was to a certain extent window-dressing. These people couldn't be sent up on any difficult terrain. In other words, any place they could be allowed to search would be a place where the missing party could get out of by themselves. What they could do was to look and listen. They did and what they saw was three members of the party up on the Otter Body Snowfield.

The need for a plausible explanation for what was happening with that party was increasing by the moment, while the prospects for getting such an explanation were decreasing. At their present rate, it would be two days before they got to the top. We were at first inclined to believe that these three could not be from the party we were seeking, but a review of the facts available to us convinced us that they had to be three of the ten. There was no way to make sense of it. It was hard to believe that if there had been an injury, accident or a fatality someone couldn't have gotten out to tell us. If there had been some kind of horrible disaster and these were the only survivors, that would explain why we hadn't heard from them, but not why they were going up. Only one thing was clear, we had to get serious about finding out what was going on.

There had been a short rescue the evening before involving a client of the guide service. The guide service had provided most of the manpower for the rescue. Barry Corbet was one of those who had helped. He was to take a group up the Grand on Saturday but another guide had taken his party to the high camp at the Lower Saddle earlier in the day while he got some rest. He was on his way up to join them when he met George Kelly and was pressed into service. As they followed the track of the party up the snowfield and into the couloir, the storm renewed itself. Barry was equipped and George wasn't. They were, as we later determined, within 400 feet of Blade's group when they turned back, Barry to join his party.

Doug McLaren, a district ranger and member of the rescue team when it was originally organised a decade earlier, was our supervisor, though no longer an active climber. It was he who organised and co-ordinated rescue activities. Doug ordered a pack team to move as much equipment as we could reasonably muster up to Garnet Canyon. Garnet Canyon is the cirque rimmed anticlockwise from north to south by Disappointment Peak, the Grand Teton, the Middle Teton, the South Teton and Nez Perce. Doug, Sterling Neale, Jim Greig and I left in the advance party at seven pm. Rick Horn and Mike Ermarth, the remaining strong climbers on the park team were to follow with more equipment. All the available Exum Guides volunteered, Jake Breitenbach, Pete Lev, Fred Wright, and Al Read; and they were joined by four other volunteers, Dr Roland Fleck, Bill Briggs and Dave Dornan, who were soon to become guides, and Peter Koedt, who later helped me in organising the Jackson Hole Mountain Guides until the Vietnam disaster forced him into Canadian exile. These guides and volunteers were to come up in the morning. Another guide, Herb Swedlund, was holding at the Petzoldt's Caves, awaiting developments. The majority of the professional mountaineers in America at the time were to carry out this operation.

The four of us got a little sleep at the end of the horse trail about an hour's climb below the encampment at the Caves and started up around four am. We arrived at the top of the snowfield at about 10.30. Here I made a serious mistake in route-finding. The party had to be either on the cliffband between Teepe's Snowfield and the Otter Body Snowfield, or possibly at the top of the Otter Body just above the point where the three climbers had been spotted. There were two obvious routes up the cliffband. One was the couloir to the right of the cliffband, dark, wet, rotten, and the other was a nice sunlit rock line straight up from where we were.

I'd never been here before, but I'd been nearby six weeks earlier, looking at it from a col about 400 yards to our left at the southern edge of the snowfield. I had come to take a look because the climbing pressure on the standard routes was becoming such that I was interested in finding another easy way to the summit to recommend to those climbers who mainly wanted to get to the top of the mountain. What I had seen in June was far from being the easiest route on the mountain. The sun reflected off the snow into the couloir to reveal a mass of contorted ice, as if a section of rapids in the Grand Canyon of the Snake had been instantly frozen and set up vertically in this evil-looking crevice in the mountain. Debris, both ice and rock, cascaded out of it. It seemed the picture of unpredictability. There was no pattern other than a headlong, downward plunge. The mountain seemed to be saying, "Here I keep no pacts." At the same time, I did note the comparative warmth and orderliness of a sunlit route up an open chimney just to the south of the icy corner. I had decided this was the route Petzoldt had gone up and though it may have been easy for him, it wasn't easy enough for the type of climber I had in mind. I descended from the col without bothering to traverse the snowfield to take a closer look.

Now the ice was gone and water poured down the couloir. My comrades were of the opinion that the route went up the couloir. I said that was impossible, anybody could see that that was no place to be. It was not a place for people. My memory of my first look at the couloir in June coloured my present perception of it considerably. Thus I persuaded them to follow me up the route I had seen, which is in fact not the Otter Body Route but the Smith Route.

The discussion had planted enough doubt in my mind that I wanted to make sure the climbing went as easily as I had claimed it would. I've never worked harder to find the easiest possible line. I scanned the rock almost frantically and climbed with as nonchalant a motion as I could. However, the climbing, while easy, was not trivial and at the point which in the guidebook account of the Smith Route is described as "the difficult overhanging portion", the climbing became seriously non-trivial. As we paused to deal with this shocking appearance of fifth-class climbing on what was supposed to be a third- and fourth-class route, we heard voices unmistakenly coming from the top of the couloir.

We rappelled down and decided that only two us would go up to investigate, partly because of the rockfall danger and partly because the voices we heard seemed to be singing! Sterling Neale and I had travelled together, worked together and climbed a lot together. I wanted him to stay at the bottom with Doug because it looked like that was going to have to be the organisation point. I didn't know what the tremendous barrier was between where we were and where they were, but there must be something keeping them from descending. Sterling could practically read my mind and I wanted him where he would be in a position to do something if things got complicated. Also, Jim Greig was bigger and stronger than either of us and there were at least seven of them up there someplace.

Angry because of my mistake, I climbed carelessly and managed to break my hammer soon after we got underway. I remember the climbing as being more difficult than does Jim. The last two pitches, bypassing the overhang and crossing the ice, could be psychologically intimidating to a climber, or a party, not in good form.

The route lay up the right-hand or east side of the ice at the top of the couloir. The party was on the slabs at the 'tail' of the Otter Body, about thirty feet above and half a rope length in distance. There was about seven inches of snow on the ice almost heavy and wet enough to adhere to the ice while bearing our weight. We weren't able to protect the pitch in a manner which could stop a fall short of the overhang. We had neither ice pitons nor crampons. A rope from above would be just the thing.

For the first time, we turned our attention fully to the party we'd come to rescue. They seemed surprisingly calm. Did they have a climbing rope? They did. Would they toss us an end? They would. The young man Fenniman stiffly approached the lip of the ledge with a rope. He seemed a bit perplexed. We instructed him to give the coil a healthy swing and toss it down to us. He swung the coil back and then forward but failed to release it. He did the same thing again. And then again. And again. There was something odd about the motion. He wasn't swinging the coil to get up momentum, but swinging indecisively almost as if he wasn't sure he wanted to cross over to them and disturb the calm which reigned there. The swinging motion became mechanical. He'd forgotten that he was not only to swing the coil but also release it. We hadn't told him that he had to do both. We told him. The coil, released in the middle of the swing instead of at the end of it, dropped in front of his feet. Jim and I exchanged glances. Perhaps if he climbed down the slab to the next ledge toward us?

"I won't! I won't!" He spoke not directly to us but first to the air at our left and then to the rock at his feet.

"Stay where you are!" we said in one voice we just managed to keep from rising. We were in for it, no doubt about that, we'd really gotten into something which promised to be very strange.

Jim "went for it" and we made it across and joined them on their ledge. They undoubtedly had been badly frightened and were probably making an effort to recover their wits. Possibly they were somewhat embarrassed. The resulting impression on me was of an unnatural calm. It seemed to be an effort for most of them to acknowledge our presence. There was a polite smile, a curious, almost disinterested gaze, the sort of thing I'd experienced in New York subways. Mary Blade seemed positively cheerful. They'd been singing, she told us. She also told us that Lester had been having a difficult time. Lester wanted to know if we'd brought any strawberry jam. We hadn't. We should have. According to Lester that's what we were supposed to do, bring strawberry jam and tea. He was a little put out with us and seemed doubtful that we knew our business.

I was offended. My first thought was, "Jesus Christ, Lester, if I knew what we were going to find up here I would have brought the Tenth Mountain Division!" I had just enough presence of mind to realise that I was feeling defensive and said nothing. The Grand Teton National Park Rescue Team was and still is the best rescue team in the country. Where did Lester imagine he had gotten the authority to lecture us? From a book, a book on European practice? I had a picture of the members of these large climbing organisations sitting around in their meetings *imagining* rescues with the old New England obsequiousness toward things British and Continental. The European teams were unquestionably better than ours. Gary Hemming used to urge me to go to Europe and learn from them and I wished I could. But what we'd been able to glean from books we found unadaptable to our circumstances. There was a more immediate reason for my defensive response to Lester's suggestion that we didn't know what we were doing. What were we going to do?

I signalled to Jim. Under the pretext of moving to a better radio transmission site, we climbed up to the next ledge and walked behind a boulder to talk.

"What in hell are we going to do?" he asked.

Jim later told me that I calmly lit a cigarette and replied, "We're all going to die, that's what we're going to do."

I guess I had to say it to get it out of the way. I'm glad I did. Life doesn't provide many opportunities to deliver a line like that. Anyway, the notion was not that far-fetched. The radio wouldn't work and we'd managed to get off without taking an extra battery. I restrained myself from throwing the radio down the mountain and satisfied myself with shouting into it, cursing and shaking it.

Eventually, by moving about from rock to ledge to chimney and bouncing our voices off the walls on the East Ridge, we found a place where we could shout out of the couloir and have some words heard and, we hoped, understood by Sterling and Doug. All we could tell them was to stay out of the couloir. What we wished to have been able to tell them was that we would be setting things up, up here, while they organised the equipment and men coming up from below. At some convenient moment, we would freeze all motion in the upper couloir while they set up belaying and lowering positions below us. Then we'd have a bucket brigade of various techniques, fixed ropes, maybe a litter or two, rappels, belays and so forth, depending on the terrain and condition of the members of the party. It could have been very elegant but it was not to be. Jim and I would just have to start moving the group down the mountain any way we could until we were back in communication with our team-mates, or until they could see what was needed and we could see that they could see what was needed.

We started. There was a ledge big enough for the whole party below us but it was further than the two short pitches Jim and I could manage with the equipment available. Could Fenniman, the only one of the party who was reasonably ambulatory, help us? He'd have to. The fact that we had to use Fenniman in the shape he was in gave me a feeling like what I imagined the French Existentialists meant by the absurd. A little ironic repartee crept into the conversation between Jim and me, something of Hemingway, a bit of Camus' Stranger. Jim would lower one to me, I'd lower that one to Fenniman, he'd belay them to the ledge.

I had anchored Fenniman to a slab about thirty feet above the big ledge and gave him very precise instructions about what to do which I repeated several times. While doing so, my sense that things were absurd became a feeling that things were desperate. The entire operation had to funnel to and through this eighteen-year-old youngster just out of high school who was headed for Dartmouth. I'd once been a kid just out of high school headed for Dartmouth and couldn't imagine what I'd have been able to do if I were then in the position he was now in.

He had been there, within a stone's throw of this place, for two nights and now nearly three days. He was in what must have appeared to him as the most precarious position he'd been in during the entire nightmare. He was, in fact, quite securely anchored, but he had only my word for that. It would not be surprising if he had come to doubt the word of people who claimed to know better than he the position he was in. He might have been bound to a rock over an abyss by a strange god or demon for all the events of the past three days might have taught him.

It was no wonder that I wasn't quite sure if I was talking to the whole Fenniman or to a messenger the whole Fenniman had sent to hear me out. The messenger seemed reliable, even heroic. I felt that Fenniman would get the job done, but had the odd thought that I'd like to meet him some day. It occurred to me that he might untie himself from the anchor and step off the mountain. That had happened a few years before to a guide with a head injury on this same peak, three ridges to the south. I moved the knot tying him to the mountain around behind him, where it couldn't be reached accidentally as he tied and untied the people we sent down. I made my instructions simple, precise and routine and tried at the same time to speak to him as a peer who could of course do what we were asking of him.

It worked. He did it exactly as I instructed; exactly the same way every time. When I had seen him swinging that coil mechanically back and forth when we'd asked for the upper belay some part of my mind had registered the potential in those precise movements and the potential in his, "I won't! I won't!" There must be a way that he could be made to say "I will! I will!" There was, but as the sequel was to show, something very different might have happened.

We first assumed that they could provide their own motive power and set the pace of the descent if we belayed them down a fixed rope. The least experienced of them would not have found the first pitch at all troublesome under normal circumstances. Now people were falling down on flat ledges, falling into a stream two feet wide and three inches deep and spending thirty seconds trying to figure out how to step over an eight-inch rock. Sometimes you see this in a beginners' rock-climbing class when the client is really frightened. There are ways to deal with it. But these people did not look frightened. What we were seeing on their faces and hearing in their voices wasn't fear but confusion, as if the problems of balance and motion were intellectual problems entirely. We had to give up trying to talk them through the moves. We were becoming exasperated at the ineffectiveness of our explanations and instructions and knew that our exasperation would only make things worse.

Tactfully at first, and then less so, we relieved them of their autonomy. Staggering, slithering, stumbling, as long as they kept descending, they could pick their one way down. If they stopped too long, a tug, a nudge and finally steady, unrelenting pressure kept things moving as the sun got lower.

After the first of them had gone down the snow-covered ice, it was snow covered no longer and all pretence of down-climbing was abandoned. They got soaked; sliding down the ice and water and I shivered for them. Speed was becoming imperative. Fenniman caught on. I overheard someone explaining to him that they had lost a foothold. To which Fenniman replied insistently, "They say you have to keep moving."

Speed under these circumstances is a relative term. We who were trying to imagine that we were in control of things were tying, untying, handling the rope with one hand, gesticulating with the other and talking and thinking as fast as possible. Those who were being controlled were rudely precipitated off a pitch, tied to an anchor and then left to a shivering halt of a half hour or more before it was their turn again.

Once down on the big ledge, things seemed better. Perhaps the ledge they'd spent so many uncomfortable but relatively safe hours on had been difficult to abandon. There was less of a feeling of us and them. There was some conversation. We found out all we could about what had happened as the opportunity arose. I began to learn their names and to take account of them as separate people. I noted that the Junes seemed to be holding together. That doesn't always happen to couples under stress in the mountains. I wondered if Germer was recalling warm summer days rock climbing in the Shawangunks. Janet was the wettest, coldest, seemed most out of place, but I was impressed by her endurance. I wondered if Mary Blade was worrying about Ellis, and if so would she be more concerned about his safety or the repercussions that seemed obviously destined to come to him. Kellogg appeared to be not too badly off, something like a nice young man just recently embarked on a course of dissipation.

There was little time for these thoughts. Above all was the fact that we could make a mistake and kill one of them, or not make a mistake and still have one of them die. Lester Germer was the obvious candidate, the one everybody was worried about, but there were others. And what of the missing three? We had to take Mary's word that they were in pretty good climbing shape, but what did 'pretty good' mean? The best we could hope for was that they would be spotted by Barry who was on the summit today. The trouble was, Barry would be down by now. Perhaps Doug and Ster already had news?

I chafed at our slow pace. My earlier route-finding mistake had cost us about two hours and that was going to make the difference between day and night in this gully, between warm sun and 32° granite, between wet pitches and icy pitches, between snow you could heel down and snow as hard as ice. My mistake had the appearance of meaning the difference between life or death for one or more of these people. Once you parade yourself in the world as a rescuer and once you take charge of the party, everything that happens after that is on your head.

We made another effort to communicate with Doug and Ster. We tried to impress on them the mass of equipment that would be needed and reiterated the point about them staying out of the gully. It was frustrating for them, and we could see that some of the guides had arrived too, to watch the shadow of the Grand move out over the valley at an increasing rate, while we appeared not to be moving at all. But the rock falls we were setting off were fairly convincing. The main thing we wanted to happen was to have the snowfield all set up for lowering so that as each of the party arrived at the top of the snowfield they could be lowered quickly from anchor to anchor.

Just before dark, Jim called down to me the news that two of the missing three were coming down from above. The significance of the fact that there were two, not three took hold slowly. I couldn't imagine how the third could be rescued. If we stopped everything to bring a litter and eight climbers up through us, I was sure somebody would die of exposure, there would be rock fall both above and below and there'd be nobody left to help us get these seven down. I also found myself fervently hoping that I wouldn't have to go back up the mountain.

When Blade got to me I interrogated him fairly fiercely about the condition of the third. It was Smith and he was dead. I was in danger of feeling relieved and that made me ruder. Also, it was difficult to believe. "Are you sure he's dead, because if you're not, somebody has to go up. How did you check? How long did you wait before leaving him?" Blade told me that the body had started to get stiff. I didn't believe that but whether he was dead when they left him or not, he was certainly dead by now. I sized up Joyce. He was clearly in better shape than anyone else. It was a little startling to see a normal person apparently unaffected by this place.

I had pulled Blade aside to question him. I could imagine what the impact of the news that the strongest member of the party had died of exposure might do to their will to survive. Furthermore, if someone else was going to die it was unlikely that they'd do it quickly and allow us to go on. I had a horrible image of being immobilised there in that gully helplessly watching a slow chain reaction of dying. I ordered Blade not to talk about it.

He moved across the ledge and gathered everybody there around and made a little speech about how we were trying to help them and they'd have to co-operate with us. I found that astonishing and a little amusing. Astonishing that he still was functioning as a leader and amusing as I tried to imagine how they could not co-operate with us. Then I had an awful insight.

What from their point of view would we be doing if we were not trying to save them but kill them? I was a little ashamed of my rough treatment of Blade. I had my own mistakes to worry about.

Janet got soaked again. She lost her footing while being lowered, swung into a waterfall and was too stiff and cold to roll out of it without help. I began to feel that she might not make it and I had to do something personally to give her heart. The distance the rescuer maintains between himself and the victims makes stepping out of it a more effective gesture.

I made her squeeze in behind a flake which would not only protect her modesty if that was necessary but mainly protected her a little from the cold evening westerly pouring down on us from the snow-fields above. I made her take off her Levis, lectured her about the fact

that denim was the worst possible material to wear in the mountains
and wrung the water out of them as much as I could. They were new
and stiff. I imagined that she'd bought them down in Jackson, in
honour of her visit to the West. I gave her some food I'd been saving
for someone it might make the difference to, including possibly myself. Then I took my favourite sweater out of my pack and made her
put it on. I tried a little levity. I told her that it was a twenty-five dollar
sweater and she'd better not get it dirty! She took me seriously – so
much for levity. Whatever was going to happen was going to happen
without interference from me.

There were shouts from below. They were coming up and we were
to be careful about rocks. It was worth being a climber to feel the
cameraderie that I felt then, an emotion that embraces much more
than mere bullshitting around a table in a tavern.

First to arrive were Pete Lev and Al Read. Lev is the picture of
earnest strength. Read is a man in command of himself. Witty, quick
to perceive the ludicrous as the ironic, he is a natural leader and an
unobtrusive one. Lev is very compassionate and was taken aback by
what he saw, including me and Jim. Jim and I were emotionally numb
by this point and I saw concern in their faces. But suddenly it seemed
possible that most of us might escape from this place. Suddenly the
mountain seemed covered with people who knew what they were
doing. Herb Swedlund was down there, Swedlund who would joke
with the Devil. I couldn't wait to get down to hear him say something
like, "Sinclair, you're quaking like a dog passing peach pits." Rick
Horn was down there, probably performing great feats of strength
and daring while screaming, "The world is contrived to drive us
insane."

The next pitch below ended in the middle of a slab which bulged
out from the base of the couloir. Every rock that came down the
couloir had to hit that slab. Jake Breitenbach was at that anchor. When
I got to him, I was afraid for him, a fear that seemed familiar. Then I
recalled the boulder in the great ice gully on McKinley that seemed to
pursue us. He, however, was ebullient, as he was most of the time in
the mountains. For him, this was what it was all about. How often do
you get to have fun like this, up here in an interesting part of the
mountain with practically all your climbing and guiding buddies? He
was good for the people we were rescuing too. He told them, as he
prepared to send them down the vertical slab below, "We always

arrange to have these rescues at night so you won't know what you're stepping off of." He picked them up and kept them going. For one or more of them it is likely that Jake made the difference.

The man I was most eagerly waiting to get to was Sterling, because once I got to him and passed below, he would take charge.

I asked Pete and Al if they'd set up the snowfield. They hadn't. It turned out that the guides, Jake Breitenbach, Al Read, Pete Lev, Fred Wright, Dave Dornan and Herb Swedlund, Mike Ermarth and Rick Horn of the rescue team and Dr Walker from Jackson had arrived at the base of the couloir just minutes after Jim and I reached the top of the couloir. Even if the radio had worked, the word that we needed masses of gear would have gone out too late. Again, the critical two hours I had lost. There went my hopes that things would soon speed up. It had taken Jim and me five hours to get the party down five pitches. It was another seven hours to two am when the last victim was to reach the top of the snowfield. Just two more ropes would have cut that seven hours nearly in half.

Al and Pete tactfully suggested that Jim and I go on down to the snowfield, they could handle matters up here. They received no heroic protests from us.

My last image of the gully is of Horn working on the pitch exiting the couloir. I was rappelling down a steep slab and Horn came racing up by me, foot over hand it seemed, to help someone who'd gotten hung up on a ledge. He was muttering to himself and lunged to the ledge just as I realised that he was climbing unroped. I asked him if he thought that was wise. He didn't, but there weren't any more ropes.

At the top of the snowfield, a huge platform was being cut, large enough to hold all the rescued and some of the rescuers. I described the situation above as best I could to Sterling after telling him he looked good enough to me to kiss. I told him that it wasn't at all clear they all were going to make it. Lester Germer had expressed a sentiment to be left alone to die. I'd be tempted to let him and was glad it was out of my hands. Actually the fact that Germer had the whole party dedicated to keeping him alive certainly gave them a badly needed focus for survival. Germer was, I believe, in some degree conscious of this because, as we later found out, he had spotted the rescue team coming up Teepe's Snowfield and had said nothing to his companions.

Jim and I stood around on the ledge until the first victim arrived on it. There was some debate about whether to set up a series of anchors down the snowfield a rope-length apart or fewer super anchors to which we would just add ropes. I tried to join in the discussion and realised that I couldn't think very well and that it was no longer our show. Jim and I decided to go down.

I got as scared as I've ever been descending that snowfield. We were without ice axes and crampons. The surface was so hard that we couldn't kick steps deeper than half an inch. The rock hammer and pitons we had to stop a fall weren't convincing. I couldn't judge the surface either by sight or touch. I had difficulty keeping my body balanced over the pitiful footholds we were kicking because there was no elasticity left in my legs. At any time I could have moved on a marginal hold to a place where I quickly needed a good hold to find that I was on water ice and that would be it. All the way down my thought was, "And I said we wouldn't need crampons. You stupid son of a bitch, if you fall you'll deserve it."

In those circumstances we paid little attention to the commotion going on above us except cynically to remark that we hoped our mates didn't bomb us with one of the victims.

At this point we shall leave Pete Sinclair for a while and let Al Read take up the story:

Pete Lev and I had climbed up several leads in the late afternoon and were the first to meet Pete Sinclair and Jim Greig who were coming down from the Otter Body Snowfield lowering the helpless people, all suffering from hypothermia. We did not reach them until late afternoon or dusk as I recall. Pete and I were quickly joined by other rescuers and we all participated in the lowering process down the rock wall to the top of Teepe's Glacier. We were all wearing headlamps and the shadows of the victims and the rescuers against the walls were quite dramatic. I remember Jake Breitenbach (killed on Everest the next year) strapping one man to his back and rapelling down. Some were in very bad shape and two, it seemed at the time, rather near death. Anyway, there was no time to wait for litters because it was still snowing and all the victims were absolutely soaked through.

A crew lower down at the top of Teepe's Glacier had hacked out a large platform just below the rock walls and were receiving the Appies as we lowered them or brought them down on our backs. All finally were sitting on the snow tied to a number of ice axes driven in to the hilt just above the platform. The snow was extremely steep and quite hard. A slip would have meant a 2,000-foot slide down the glacier (really more of a steep snowfield but technically a glacier) into the rocks of the moraine below and certain death.

We all were very concerned we would have more hypothermia deaths unless we got the people down to the rescue group waiting at the bottom of the glacier with medical attention, soup, sleeping bags, etc., and the helicopters which would be there at dawn (no chance of pickup at the top of the glacier). We decided to lower everyone – really just slide them – down the glacier from our top stance to a lower stance several hundred feet below. Here we decided to make another platform from which a final lower could be made to where the angle of the snow eased and the Appies could be carried or dragged to the edge of the glacier and assistance. Herb Swedland and Jake went down to make the lower stance – perhaps 500 feet down. Meanwhile, Peter Lev, Sterling Neale, Rick Horn and I tied five loops in a climbing rope and placed five Appies in them. Each victim was tied about ten feet apart. We belayed this expeditious arrangement from two ice axes driven into the floor of our platform. I stood on one and let out the rope while Sterling watched the system and prepared to add additional ropes. Pete Lev (wearing crampons) descended to assist the Appies as they were being lowered. We slid the victims one by one off the platform and began lowering. They were heavy and I wished we had had a better belay.

Suddenly Pete yelled up to stop. He said there was an empty loop. There were only four people on the rope. Obviously one had fallen out of his waistloop. Dead, we thought! But after yelling down to Herb and Jake, nobody had seen or heard a body whirling by. Because everyone was working in the fall line, obviously a falling person *would* have been noticed. Pete then saw someone in his light about fifty feet to the right. He yelled at him. No response. He ran over to him and told him to return to the rope and safety. Pete immediately began to cut a platform as the person was wearing no crampons – only his mountain boots. Of course he had no ice axe. Pete told him to follow him back to the rope. The victim, John Fenniman, said nothing but looked as if he understood. Pete began cutting steps back to the rope, which we had by now stopped lowering. Rick Horn was preparing another climbing rope to throw down to Pete, so he could tie in the victim. We all knew he could come off at any minute.

As Pete began cutting steps back to the rope, Fenniman ignored him and went the other way instead. Pete stopped and climbed back to him, Pete insisted he follow him. Then Fenniman suddenly grabbed Pete's ice axe and they began grappling and struggling. Pete yelled up to us for help.

Rick Horn, also wearing crampons, who had by then readied a climbing rope, quickly lowered himself down and diverted Fenniman's attention. Pete scampered away, still retaining his ice axe. From behind, Rick managed to tie a quick bowline around Fenniman's waist and get away. He quickly returned to our ledge and put a belay on Fenniman. We all looked down at him with our headlamps. He began slowly to climb up towards our stance. I was still holding the remaining four Appies on belay through the two ice axes.

As Fenniman approached our platform his eyes were bulged out. He was ashen and looked as if he had gone mad. He had! He said very slowly, "You are the Devil. You are taking me to Hell" – or words to that effect. I could hardly believe what I was seeing and hearing. All at once he jumped up on our ledge and began hitting us. We believed he was trying to reach the several ice axes still stuck in the snow behind us. I remember thinking, as his fists were banging into my face, that I might have to let go of the belay to keep myself from being thrown off the platform or hit by an ice axe if he ever got hold of one. I remember yelling to Rick, "Kill him if you have to!" One of the Appie victims still on the platform yelled back, "No, no, don't kill him!" It was all quite incredible.

Rick finally managed to give Fenniman a shove and he went over the edge, but was caught at the lip by the belay, secured by Rick, who yelled we were only trying to help him. But when he continued to resist, Rick had to knock him out with a kick to the side of the head. The frontpoints of his crampons missed by a fraction. Fenniman went limp, Rick dragged him over to the rope, tied him in, and sat on him. The lowering was renewed.

Coming up from below, Jack Turner describes the scene as first seeing four people being lowered out of the darkness – limp and facing every direction, some upside down. Suddenly he saw a victim being ridden by Rick. Rick was hitting him with his fists and gagging! What was happening was every time Fenniman showed signs of

The Tatra avalanche cone seen from the plateau of the demolished hut. The bare slope, right, was devastated by the pressure wave, John's tree is middle distance left, at the furthest group of people.

Below left, the ice wall which blocked the mouth of the second valley. Below right, Miloš Vrba demonstrating avalanche probe techniques in Glencoe.

Markus Burkard at the controls of
his Alouette.

The helicopter at the scene of the
Dossenhütte accident.

HB-XFF

The severely frostbitten Robert Burnett being dug out of the avalanche on Beinn a'Bhuird. Skin exposed to the snow came off as the snow and ice were cut from him with a penknife. His two dead companions were dug out a short way below.

Burnett after being entombed for twenty-two hours, the longest anyone has survived an avalanche burial in the British Isles.

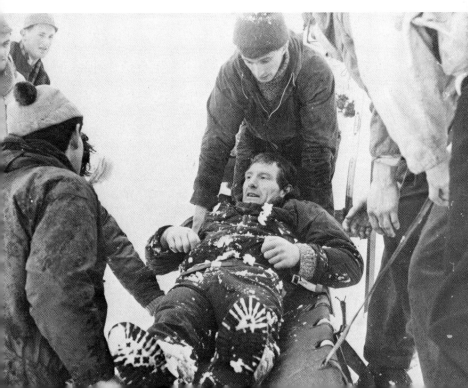

The Grand Teton showing the North Face and Mount Owen.

The West Ridge of La Perouse from the Cook River, with Mount Cook behind, left centre. Below, taking Ruth Adams up ice cliffs near the summit of La Perouse, top left, Bill Beaven and Ed Hillary; below, Norman Hardie and Harry Ayres.

The western aspect of Mount Cook (from the summit of La Perouse), showing the main, middle and low summits and the Hooker Face. The Gazley-McCahon avalanche area is above the climber right. The accident to the two Australians who called from the Empress hut took place just below the main summit.

The final slope of the Krylenko Pass, Pamirs, the day before the avalanche off Peak Lenin.

Pinned in their tents for three days by a blizzard on the Saukdhara Glacier at 17,000 feet.

Searching for Tony Tighe in the Everest Icefall, 1972.

The Ogre: A, Doug Scott's first abseil point to regain peg crack 150 feet below left at B; C, point of swing impact 100 feet across the gully; D, tie off point where Scott waited for Chris Bonington; E, their bivouac ledge. Below left, crawling down in a storm with two broken legs, right, Scott at Base Camp.

coming round, Rick had to put him out again without actually killing him, and the tension and desperation of the experience had nauseated him. According to Turner this remains as one of the most amazing scenes he has ever witnessed.

The rest of the victims were lowered without incident and all fully recovered. I saw Fenniman later that morning being carried in a litter down to the helicopter landing site. He remembered nothing and could not have been nicer or more thankful. He simply had momentarily lost his mind and was trying to protect himself. I rather imagine he had thought he was dead or dying and that we indeed were trying to take him to Hell.

Pete Sinclair and Jim Greig had spent twenty-two nonstop gruelling hours on their vital first part of the rescue. But the next day something had to be done about Steve Smith's body. Pete Sinclair takes up the story again:

We didn't want to bring the body down. The Chief Ranger, Russ Dickenson, and the Superintendent contacted Smith's parents and asked for permission to bury Smith on the mountain. I don't know how they found the words to ask them and I don't know how the Smiths found words to grant it, but they did. I felt awful about it, as if we were violating the code that Achilles violated in refusing to allow Priam to give Hector a proper burial. Achilles relented, we didn't. I knew the Smiths would probably recall that Steve had loved the mountains and might wish to be buried there. That might have been his wish had he died in the heat of action. But life had not ended in glorious action for Steve Smith, it had oozed out of him, sapped from him by an insidious worm of self-doubt that had gotten lodged in his soul, giving him no opportunity even to struggle.

On Monday, Rick, Jim and I were transported to the Lower Saddle by helicopter. The weather looked lousy. Soon it started to snow. We stayed in the guide's hut, lounging on several layers of sleeping pads and drinking tea, chocolate and soup. Rick told us about his adventures with Fenniman. He still hadn't quite recovered from that experience and obviously didn't relish the task at hand. Our plan was to go up the Owen-Spaulding Route, cross over the top of the mountain just south of the summit and descend the snowfield to the shoulder of the Otter Body where Smith's body lay, bury him, and descend the route taken by Joyce, Blade and Smith and then on down the evacuation route, cleaning up as much of the debris as we could. The snowstorm was not an auspicious beginning. This was turning out to be one of the worst climbing seasons in memory. Jake used to say that the Owen-Spaulding is both the easiest and the most difficult route he had climbed on the Grand, easy under normal conditions, difficult under the conditions currently prevailing. That worried me some but that wasn't what was worrying Rick, much the strongest climber. Every hour or so Rick would inquire as discreetly as possible as to what we thought *he* would look like when we got to him. It dawned on Jim and me that this was to be Rick's first corpse, and I have to confess that we laid it on a little. We weren't unsympathetic but we knew that nobody can help you through that experience. The best you can do is to gain what distance you can by finding what humour you can, not laughing at the death but laughing at what your imagination is doing to you.

It snowed throughout Monday night and for much of Tuesday and then began to clear. We would leave for the summit before dawn on Wednesday. It was not an unpleasant prospect. We were well-rested, in good physical condition and we'd spent most of the past four days high in the mountains.

The Owen-Spaulding Route is on the shaded side of the mountain. It was bitterly cold for midsummer that Wednesday morning and the whole upper part of the mountain was completely iced over. It might have been November. Jim and I climbed slowly and cautiously, protecting every high-angle pitch but Rick found that maddening. He seemed almost frantic to get to the summit ridge, out of the cold and into the sun.

Over the crest of the ridge we found a beautiful summer day in the mountains. Not hot of course because we were in fresh snow above 13,000 feet, but the sun opened our down jackets and eased into our tensed muscles. We called a halt for an early lunch. The partially mown hay fields made squares of light green between the darker green willows along the Snake and the Gros Ventre rivers and the greenish-grey and light brown sagebrush flats of the valley. The snow was clean and too bright for unprotected eyes. We had passed from winter to summer in the space of a few moments and a few yards.

We moved at normal pace now, picking out a route with caution in the couloirs we had to cross to reach the snowfield and then descended with an occasional belay down the East Snowfield to the rock above the body. Some scrambling and a short rappel brought us to Steve Smith. Near him was an empty matchbook, the matches lay scattered about. Each one was tried, none had lit. Much later, we heard the story of how at Smith's death Charlie Joyce rebelled, took Blade by the shoulders and told him that they were going down, all the way down.

We took what personal effects we thought his family might like to have, tied a rope to the body and manoeuvred it over the moat between the base of the cliff and the Otter Body Snowfield. Getting it adequately protected was something of a problem. We looked for a place near at hand where the snow pack was thickest and least likely to bare the rock in even the driest year. Rick was above anchoring the body. From a stance a few feet above the corpse I guided the rope to a position where it would drop directly down a small chimney to the debris at the base of the cliff. Jim straddled the rope at the body with his knife out.

"Well," said Jim, made the sign of the cross over Steve Smith and cut the rope. I had forgotten to bring a Bible. We covered the body first with small rocks, in case there were any carnivorous rodents up there, and then with larger boulders.

SEVEN

At the beginning of time, according to Maori legend, the children of Rangi, the Sky, came down to earth and Aorangi, one of the sons, set off to explore in his canoe with three of his brothers. The canoe ran aground forming the South Island of New Zealand and the four children became four great peaks of the Central Alps. Aorangi, which means 'sky-cloud', is now better known as Mount Cook (12,349 feet/ 3,764 metres) though the old name is still used by the Maoris. The South Island does indeed look like an upturned canoe, with the spine of the Central Alps running up the centre. Though these mountains are not so lofty as other ranges on earth, they are heavily glaciated, with the ice creeping down to 2,000 feet above sea level. They also get more than their fair share of precipitation. The moist air sweeps across the Tasman Sea, sucking up moisture like a sponge, only to wring out its soggy clouds over the western flanks of the Alps. Higher, like a good wife's washing, it is a uniform white at the colder elevations. To the south-west in Fiordland the peaks are rain washed, vertical and smooth; in places even the all pervading jungle cannot cling. While to the east of the Alps the rainfall is slight, the ground parched and the country baked brown. Indeed, it is a memorable experience to travel over Arthur's Pass, on the road or rail link between the two coasts and witness these changes. As one drops down to the western seaboard, the encroachment of the bush is felt. It is everywhere, elbowing in, the offspring of the two hundred odd inches of rain per year. It is varied and picturesque country, with tree ferns, cabbage trees and lancewood, to name but a few of the junior members of a lofty family with such big brothers as rata and rimu trees.

The main chain of the Central Alps forms a baffle wall between two great seas, the Pacific to the east and the Tasman to the west. It is from the latter that the violent storms sweep in, usually preceded by their advance packs of hogsback clouds, sure get-back-to-the-valley signs, recognised and feared by all Kiwi climbers.

A range of mountains which provides possibly the best Himalayan training ground in the world must inevitably be a rough, tough place. It is. The mountains are both dangerous and difficult. There are inevitably accidents.

During my stay in New Zealand I got to know several of the mountain guides who were employed by the New Zealand Government Tourist Board. Harry Ayres was then chief guide at the Glacier Hotel at Franz Josef and together with Mick Bowie and that earlier generation of founder guides, Peter and Alex Graham, they had a fine tradition and safety record. It was Harry who gave me a job after an abortive gold prospecting trip on the West Coast in the early 'fifties.

The New Zealand guides have never been exponents of Grade Six climbing. The emphasis in their training was on knowledge of the peaks, basic mountain craft and the well-being of their clients. They could cut steps for twelve hours a day and Mick Bowie would still have enough spare energy to puff away at his pipe whilst doing so! One wonders how many modern 'tigers' would stand up to such physical exertion?

It was with this backbone of guides, Mick Bowie and Harry Ayres, that a rescue was successfully completed from close to the summit of La Perouse which will probably never be equalled in sheer protracted effort. Over the years I've witnessed the transition from sweat and toil rescue to the quick whisk by helicopter. I can't say that I regret this change – it's a lot easier – yet something has been lost. Before, it was team effort, where men worked as a closely knit unit, often exposed to danger themselves, always subjected to the grinding, arm-stretching work obligatory in taking a casualty off a mountain. But with this hardship an understanding and compassion was generated which isn't a part of the clinical and remote evacuation by a helicopter.

The accident on La Perouse was before the days of helicopters in New Zealand and from the men on that rescue a powerful nucleus of Himalayan climbers was born. The name of Norman Hardie will be forever linked with that hard core of Kiwi climbers that explored the remote area to the south and east of Everest. In that fascinating wild country our paths crossed on several occasions, in the depths of the Hongu valley and in the steamy Choyang, but I met him first in Christchurch. Norman, like his colleague, Ed Hillary, is an unassuming man. Here he gives his account of the La Perouse rescue of Ruth

Adams, still vivid to him over the intervening years, and an enduring monument to the determination of a small group of men:

I

LONG HAUL ON LA PEROUSE

by Norman Hardie

The peaks near Mount Cook are named after Pacific navigators. Some, such as Tasman, Drake, Torres and Magellan preceded Captain Cook in time, and others came after him. Among the latter are Vancouver, Hicks, Dampier and La Perouse. On the ridge to La Perouse are three peaks named after British Admirals, Sturdee, Beattie and Jellicoe who were not Pacific navigators.

At the beginning of 1948 Mount Cook had been climbed seventy-four times and La Perouse merely twelve. On 6th February the South Ridge of Cook was ascended for the first time by Ruth Adams, Ed Hillary and the two guides, Mick Sullivan and Harry Ayres. (Through Ed's inability to get leave at Christmas, when most amateur New Zealanders do their mountaineering, he had made several climbs with Harry). Three days later the same party set off at four am to climb La Perouse. The normal route in those days involved three hours' travelling from Gardiner hut, up the Hooker Glacier, then over Sturdee, Beattie, Jellicoe and Low before the ice ridge to the main summit. It is generally a long hard snow and ice climb, with several big pitches of fragile rock on the buttresses of the British admirals, and on the slopes to Low. Mount Low was named after R. S. Low of the Scottish Mountaineering Club, who was in the party that made the first ascent of La Perouse in 1908.

These four made good progress on a fine morning until they encountered an ice wall on the descent from Low to the last col before La Perouse. Hillary and Ayres got down the wall but, on finding it far from easy, called to the rear pair to divert round the end of it. Ruth and Mick cramponed to a steep slope and were working their way down this when Ruth slipped. She slid down the ice slope out of control, passed the position where Mick was firmly placed and, to his horror and that of the two spectators, their rope snapped in what was really not a major fall. Ruth slid onwards about sixty feet, dropped over a short cliff and was stopped by a projecting rock – the only obstacle which could have prevented her going a further 4,000 feet.

Mick had been given that rope by a client from Europe in 1938, and he regarded it so highly that he locked it away for safekeeping on the outbreak of war, bringing it out again in 1948 for the special climbs which he and Ruth undertook that year. Although the rope looked in good condition, it had apparently rotted in the damp atmosphere of the West Coast.

The three climbers rushed to Ruth, secured her to the slope, and made their assessment of the situation. She appeared to have a broken wrist, possibly a damaged back, and definitely bruising and concussion. Clearly without further assistance the party could not carry her over the long tortuous route they had ascended. In 1948 there were no helicopters in New Zealand and no climbers carried radios. Getting the news out, and assembling the rescue team in this remote site was to be a major effort. The injured woman was a long day's march for a climber from the first telephone; and Christchurch, the nearest centre for mountaineers, was a further 170 miles away.

Ed Hillary stayed with Ruth, and spent most of the day cutting an ice cave and lining its floor with rock slabs, to give some security for the night. His patient regained consciousness and although cheerful, was quite unable to walk. The two guides had rushed back down their ascent route to Gardiner hut, where Mick picked up food, a cooker, two sleeping bag covers, a bag for Ruth, and climbed solo back up to the accident scene, doing the last hour in the dark. They all sat in the cave, ate a bare meal, and huddled together for the night, two without sleeping bags. In fact, Mick Sullivan spent the subsequent five nights without a bag. Meanwhile Harry had run on down to the Hermitage Hotel at the foot of Mount Cook and reported to the chief guide, Mick Bowie. Immediately a call was put through to Christchurch, so that late on the night of the accident a strong group of climbers received the bad news.

Mick Bowie was nearing the end of his distinguished guiding career. He had been chief guide for many years. He had once led a mountaineering expedition to southern China and had spent several war years with the New Zealand Army in Egypt and Italy. Mick led the whole rescue operation. Also at the Hermitage were three trainee guides whom he brought in from other climbs, as they returned to the

Hotel in the dark. Equipment was packed for an air drop. Before dawn they all set off for the climb to Gardiner hut and then right on to the accident site, which they reached as darkness was falling, on the second night.

During that day a single engined plane had dropped three loads in accurately placed positions and with minimal damage. Thus the patient, Ed Hillary and Mick Sullivan received a stretcher, a tent, food, fuel, a long rope and another sleeping bag. Apart from receiving this equipment there was very little they could do for the day.

On this same complex day the Christchurch party drove to the Hermitage in the dark hours of the morning. I was then a junior engineer at a hydro-electric construction project on the way to the Hermitage. At five am Bill Beaven, from one of the Christchurch cars, woke me vigorously and said, "The Mount Cook South Ridge party has had an accident on La Perouse. Can you come?"

"I've got a busy day. But Bill, you appear quite cheerful for a search party member!"

"Well, yes. It should be an interesting trip. If we act quickly everyone should get off safely – and it's a good team."

"I'll try my best. Start without me, and I'll catch you if I can."

I rushed to the Chief Engineer's house, explained the situation as I saw it. He said he would drive me to the Hermitage, but first he had to eat. I then ran to the rooms of two of my work mates and handed to them the duties that were to have been mine for the next few days. My climbing gear took just a minute to gather.

In this early morning activity the local policeman, who was not a mountaineer, was woken from his slumbers. As the police had just been given the responsibility for rescue operations, he announced he was also coming. Ted Trappitt, a good friend of mine, is now in one of the senior police posts in New Zealand, but on that occasion I felt his presence on such a technical climb could be a great embarrassment. The policeman, my boss, and I, drove with some speed to the end of the road. For the last few miles La Perouse became visible – a great ice peak towering above multiple shining cliffs. Between the cliffs are steep gullies, and even from fifteen miles away I was able to point out the great cones of avalanche debris at its base. Ted Trappitt became silent.

At the hotel we obtained more information. Harry Wigley, the pilot, had read a message stamped in the snow when he made his air

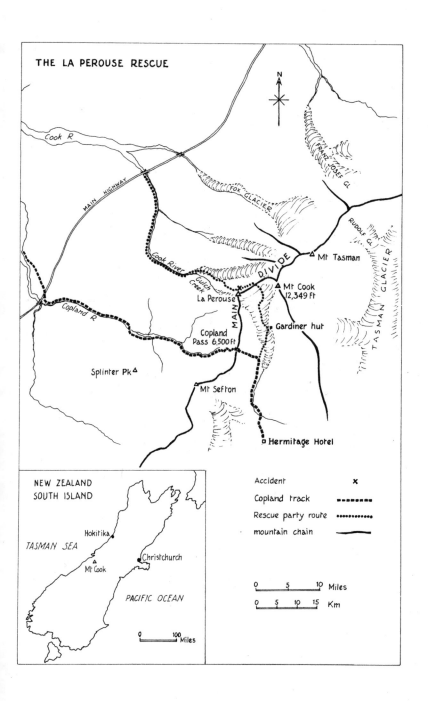

THE LA PEROUSE RESCUE

Cook R

MAIN HIGHWAY

FRANZ JOSEF GL.

FOX GLACIER

RUDOLF GL.

Mt Tasman

MAIN DIVIDE

Cook River

Gulch Creek

La Perouse

Mt Cook
12,349 Ft

TASMAN GLACIER

Copland R

Gardiner hut

Copland
Pass 6,500 ft

Splinter Pk

Mt Sefton

Hermitage Hotel

NEW ZEALAND
SOUTH ISLAND

Accident   x

Copland track   ------

Rescue party route   ·········

mountain chain   ▬▬▬

Hokitika

TASMAN SEA

Mt Cook

Christchurch

PACIFIC OCEAN

0   5   10 Miles

0   5   10   15   Km

0   100
          Miles

drops, and it stated, "O.K. all well." He also reported, the three on the site were about a hundred yards on the west side of the main divide.

Ted looked at me, with a brief smile, "That hundred yards is a relief. The accident is outside my boundary of operations."

Carrying as little as possible, I set off alone, some two hours behind the Christchurch party. Fortunately for me, the long car journey in the dark had taken its toll on the others and I was able to overtake them before I became committed to any really technical climbing. Some were passed, returning, having decided they were not fit enough, straight from office desks, for this type of major rescue. Our Christchurch party had now Harry Ayres, the guide, at its head. He had replaced broken crampons from his run down the glacier the previous day, stolen a few hours sleep, and was on the way up again. The whole tourist and climbing operation from the Hermitage was to be left without any climbing guides for a week.

We were astonished to find a long line of steps cut up the face of Jellicoe, not to Harper's Saddle, the normal route. Mick Bowie had made a new direct route to save time and all of us followed these widely spaced footholds in the fading light of the second night after the accident. Darkness overtook us as we were working our way up the icy face. Our group scattered in pairs on this unknown territory, and I was relieved to be roped to Bill Beaven who had been one of my main climbing companions for several years. We pressed slowly upwards assisted by the light of one feeble torch. It was bad enough, looking after our own safety, recognising the correct positions for our boots and ice axes, but every few minutes we were alarmed by the whistle of rocks passing over us, like cannon fire.

"Bill, that mountain is mighty loose up there."

"We should stop at a crevasse lip every time they start. Each climber ahead is 'gardening' when they reach that hundred feet of black rubble at the crest of the ridge."

"Yes, a good idea."

But when the next group reached the rocks we were not near a protective crevasse. There was no option but to keep climbing. Needless to say, strong words were hurled up the slope as each rock barrage descended. I heard later that Mick, leading his three new guides up that first ascent took time off to give just one command to those further down the rope.

"No bloody mistakes here."

At midnight, at the crest of the ridge, our group of eight unrolled sleeping bags on the ice and slept until daylight. Two were still on the face and they spent the night there. With the weather remaining fine so far, the absence of tents and snow caves did not matter. Breakfast was a slender snack in swirling mist. We struggled along the crumbly ridge and then there were stretches of guide-cut bucket steps, until at ten am we were at the accident site.

Thus, forty-eight hours after the fall the team was fully assembled. In total we were sixteen climbers and one patient. Among the climbers was Dr Gerry Wall, now a Member of Parliament, who had been a student at medical school with his patient, Dr Ruth Adams. His examination revealed no alterations to the original diagnosis by Ruth's climbing companions. She was put securely in a stretcher, given sedatives and prepared for the long journey. We rummaged among the air-dropped supplies and it appeared that Ruth would have all that she was likely to need, but it was more than evident the sixteen climbers were destined for a very hungry journey.

Mick Bowie had given much thought to the two known routes off the mountain. The one we all knew by then, over Low, Jellicoe and Sturdee, was long and steep, involving many risks from further accidents with such large numbers moving about on great areas of rotten rock, and much New Zealand rock is very treacherous. The weather seemed to be deteriorating, and on that route there appeared to be the likelihood of two more nights on the ice at above 9,000 feet.

The alternative was to descend to the West Coast side where the route off the mountain was technically easier, and by the second night the party should be at the Gulch Creek Rock, an enormous glacial erratic which could shelter the party under its overhangs. There would be alpine scrub for fuel there and we would be secure, but still some three days of trackless forested gorge from civilisation. In the interests of getting everyone off the mountain safely, as fast as possible, Mick chose the West Coast route, down to the shelter rock and then out via the Cook River. La Perouse at that time had been climbed only three times from the West, but in our party was a man who had been on one of these climbs. Doug Dick had been in a trio, including David Lewis, later known for his solo yachting, that had climbed La Perouse in 1938. For this expedition-type climb no real tracks had been cut through the bush, and for ten years no one had returned to the Cook River. Carrying the stretcher in this country would be a formidable task, but there would be fewer risks of a fatality by this choice of route.

To reach the North-West Ridge of La Perouse it was necessary to climb a further 500 feet, to a point not a 100 yards along from the summit before beginning the descent. That climb was hot and frustrating, with ropes being trampled, big packs having to proceed forward and three vertical ice walls to be scaled. In the morning the guides had gone ahead, cut steps and put ropes and belays at the worst places.

It soon became apparent that the six, or sometimes four, handling the stretcher could not also carry their full packs. Nor could they be roped together and hold coils of slack rope. Progress came to a halt just 200 yards from the accident site. Men on each side of the stretcher, working on very steep snow, bumped their heads into the packs of those ahead. Crampon spikes tore into climbing ropes. Previously silent complaints were now sometimes murmured. We halted. The guides approved the removal of the climbing ropes, and delegated jobs to most of us. Some without packs were to do the stretcher work. Others were somehow to manage the additional packs and be available for a turn on the stretcher carrying, sliding and pulling. Consequently there was much travelling back and forwards for packs and equipment; some climbed with two rucksacks. In weather which had earlier been threatening, seventeen people emerged at four pm just beside the summit of La Perouse. No one seriously considered diverting to bag that rarely climbed peak.

As the clouds dispersed it was comforting to hear Doug Dick telling Mick, "When we came up in 1938 we used this snow ridge ahead. One can't go to the end of it. We have to go down a steep face to the west to avoid the enormous bluffs which drop away from the ridge end. It's all rather steep but reliable for quite a distance. But lower down there is loose rock where we had troubles ten years ago."

For the descent along the ridge, new techniques had to be tried and adopted. Our giant leader, Mick, tied 400 feet of air-dropped rope to the stretcher. He established a firm anchor and the carriers moved on to the extent of the rope and then rested, as Mick walked forward to anchor for a further move of 400 feet. In the late afternoon the slope steepened and by winding in and out of a crevassed area we eventually reached temporarily easier ground. As the light was fading we emerged on to an exposed but rocky terrace at about 8,000 feet. Here we stopped for the night.

Throughout the day I had been hungry and I had frequent misgivings about our food supply. As each of us scratched a groove for laying out a sleeping bag, Mick came round and issued us with a slice of cold corned beef, two slices of bread and a portion of tinned fruit. This was washed down with water from the ice-cold pools, only feet from our stopping place. Very little was said that night and few had a sound sleep. Several light showers fell on the mountain, but there was no severe wind. I dozed off several times, and eventually I came to full life with Mick's gruff voice beside me, "Wake up, Hardie. The day's half gone. The sun will burn a hole in your arse."

I opened my eyes, and it wasn't daylight yet. But the clouds had gone and the full extent of our exposed eyrie soon became apparent. The almost totally unclimbed Balfour Range was across the La Perouse glacier from us. The sun later touched Tasman, Malaspina and Vancouver far to the east. But to the west, far below us, the still scarcely lit bush on the Cook River cliffs promised much gloomy struggling before the journey ended.

We had been cramped on a tiny hard and damp terrace, with a tent for Ruth, and saturated clouds for us. At one stage Neil Hamilton rolled over and committed a terrible crime. He crushed Mick Bowie's pipe! Mick, always a heavy pipe smoker, surveyed the damage as he was putting on his boots and said drily, "I had hoped this rescue would have got through without a disaster." Neil, the only other pipe smoker in the party, unveiled his own, and handed it to Mick, who puffed on it at every stop.

Breakfast consisted of another slice of cold tinned meat and two of plain bread, again without a hot drink. The hard work continued and it took a full day to get down to the Gulch Creek Rock. First there was a long descent of a loose rock couloir, and the only way to handle this was for climbers to go down in pairs, using the long rope as a handrail, then scrambling clear at the bottom. Eventually the stretcher was lowered, being guided by two men to avoid injuring the rescuers. Another hazard was the likelihood of sharp rocks tearing the fabric of the stretcher.

Gerry, the doctor, did much of the attending to Ruth. She was tightly strapped in with just part of her face visible. For most of the travelling she was heavily sedated, so there was very little conversation with her, and discussions about the look of the next downward hazards were held away from the likely range of her ears.

It was not until nearly lunch time some three whole days after the accident, that there was a general acceptance that the operation would be successful. We stopped on a terrace by a small tarn, munched the normal slender ration, and more openly discussed the prospects. Before leaving the Hermitage, Mick had sent a message to people on the West Coast, requesting a team to cut a track through the bush for us, if we were not seen descending the ice slopes on the east side. Mick now seemed confident the track work would have started and he said, "For a strong party not carrying much, it is possible to struggle through without a track. In fact we might even see someone tonight."

There is a lot of difference between a man pushing through hard country alone, and six men carrying a stretcher with a patient whose injuries required delicate transportation.

In the afternoon we carried and slid the stretcher down a further 2,000 feet of loose rock and snow grass, aiming all the time at the vast sheltering rock which had been visible most of the day. At four pm sixteen tired and very hungry people struggled through the first small patches of alpine scrub, and lowered their loads at the rock. Here at last under the overhangs there was shelter, and, what seemed more important, fuel was available for the first time. Great billies of tea were produced, damp gear was put out to dry, and Ruth was temporarily released from the cramp and heat of the stretcher.

Mick Bowie's forecast was right. We were still settling in when four men appeared from the moraine which gives access to the Cook River.

"Are you carrying a body or a patient?" was the first question.

"She's alive and not too bad, but she'll have to be carried all the way."

"Anxious relatives, and hordes of reporters are down at the highway, desperate for news."

The four new arrivals emptied the food they were carrying into the joint pool. They hadn't brought very much, as they had come up in a hurry, and they had to bring their own sleeping bags, climbing gear, a tent, and clothing.

"We had no idea you were short of supplies. From all reports, the outside world thinks tons of it were dropped from the plane when you got the stretcher."

Within an hour two of them set off for the road, carrying the news of Ruth's relatively satisfactory state, confirming our outward course, and requesting food to come up the fast forming track.

One of the four who came up the Cook River was Earle Riddiford. This was the first time he met Ed Hillary. These two were subsequently on three Himalayan expeditions together and it was Earle and Eric Shipton who in 1951 first broke through to the crest of the Western Cwm and confirmed the easiest way to the Nepalese upper slopes of Mount Everest.

After numerous introductions Earle joined Bill Beaven and me. His first remark to us was, "This new track will open up some great climbing for our four next season."

Bill said, "We've had exactly the same thought."

For several years we three, Earle Riddiford, Bill Beaven and I, had been part of a highly successful group which climbed in the more remote valleys of New Zealand, accomplishing many first ascents, from places where we would have to carry loads for a week, before putting in a base for an expedition-type climb. In fact our group was to use this new Cook River track ten months later, when we completed the climb of La Perouse, and several other mountains.

At the Gulch Creek Rock, Earle, always one for looking ahead and planning ambitious schemes, said, "What's Ed Hillary like on the mountain?"

I replied, "This is the first time we've met him. But he seems very good to me."

Then Bill added, "He's fit and he worked really hard on the mountain. You know he's also got expedition ideas for the Himalayas."

Earle had been pressing us for years to set our eyes on the Himalayas, but the giant problems of costs, sponsorship, permission, oxygen and publicity appeared forbidding. We never did all join forces in the Himalayas, but within seven years, three of us, and of course Ed Hillary, each made first ascents of peaks above 23,000 feet.

The warmth of dried bags and the lower altitude gave everyone a better night at Gulch Creek. But Mick, who for the whole journey had been pressing us with the gruff command for an early start, now added to the previous strong words, "There'll be some streams to cross and some likely wading in the Cook River. It'll be low in the mornings, and high each afternoon with the melting snow." From the rock we all scrambled to the moraine which covers the lower few miles of the La Perouse Glacier, before the Cook River begins. Like all moraines, it is a jumbled mess of sharp rocks, steep slopes, mostly bedded on ice. Fortunately, the further down the glacier one goes the less ice there is visible. Gradually, the going improves.

In mid-morning, when the worst of the moraine was past, a single-engined aircraft was heard, and then seen, coming up the valley. A tiny homemade parachute dropped out and landed safely near us. I looked up. "That doesn't look like much of a food drop." Tied to the parachute was a brief hand-written message. "Wave a parka if Ruth is safe." Evidently last night's messengers had not travelled in the dark. We waved. The plane departed. Again we picked up our burdens and struggled onwards.

Soon the plane returned, did several circuits round the group, and another parachute dropped out and opened. It also looked small. Someone collected it and returned with a big carton. It was eagerly opened and inside was a giant fruit cake. What a joyful sight! Ruth's father, Ernest Adams, runs New Zealand's main cake bakery.

After a big cake morning tea, the team performed better. Soon the valley closed to a steep-sided gorge and we were forced into an area of enormous river-washed boulders, originally dropped there by the glacier. With the roaring river lapping their sides, it was usually necessary to climb over them. Where this was done the route was through the bush. As soon as we entered it we could see that the first upward helpers had at least cleared a slender track for our outward passage.

But the difficulties were enormous. There would seldom be fifty consecutive yards of normal stretcher carrying. The total width of men on each side of the stretcher was too wide for the initial narrow track cut through the trees. Great tree roots, thousands of boulders, steep bluffs where ropes had to be used, wet moss-covered rocks and a raging river had to be negotiated. Frequently the stretcher had to be moved from hand to hand, in circumstances where men were unable to move with the main vital load. Those coming behind, having their turn at relaying the pack loads, or carrying two packs at a time, had fewer problems, as the bushmen's route was better suited to persons travelling singly. But it was still extremely hard work.

As time went by, more helpers came up the valley. They included Ruth's three brothers. More bushmen were working on the track and there were obvious improvements the further west we travelled. Also food began to arrive in great quantity. But still it took us three days to get out from Gulch Creek to the West Coast road.

At one camp, in the depths of the humid rain forest, we were sitting round a fire, shortly to crawl into our sleeping bags, when one mountaineer spied an axe, picked it up, and began to chop firewood. Immediately an enormous bushman with immense arms bulging out of a black singlet leapt up and grabbed the axe. He looked at the keen edge as a professional golfer may inspect his putter. Then he took a heap of logs, laid into them with immense skill, and sprayed us all with showers of great chips as he rapidly produced a stack of firewood. I sat in wonder, and one of my new associates whispered in awe, "He's the toughest man on the Coast – won last year's Australia and New Zealand downhand chop. No one can ever touch his axe."

It was on the seventh day since the accident when Ruth was transferred to the greater comfort of a car. Soon she was flown to Christchurch – and eventually she made a full recovery. In fact she completed a medical degree, married a doctor, had three children and is at present in medical practice in Sydney, Australia.

The rescuers and ever willing bushmen were given a great welcome at the small town where they emerged. After an enormous feed, a thorough clean and a good sleep, I stated I intended walking back to my work at the hydro dam. This meant a two days' walk on tourist tracks and a crossing in snow of a 6,500-feet pass, emerging at the Hermitage, where I could easily arrange a ride to work. The guides were horrified at this. Yet another crossing of Copland Pass meant no great joy to them. One came to me and requested, "Keep away from the bosses at the Hermitage and don't say where we are. We've been offered a ride through by car and train to Christchurch. We'll get back to the Hermitage a day after you."

They enjoyed their comfortable journey the long way round, and they certainly deserved the rest.

2

ACCIDENT – EMPRESS HUT

In 1955, when I was climbing down near the base of South Island's spine in the Darran Range, I met a colleague whom I hadn't seen for

years. This was John Hammond who, together with Chris Bonington
and I, had started his winter climbing career in Glencoe in Scotland. I
arranged to meet John a week or so later at the Hermitage Hotel. But
when I arrived, I discovered that John and his companion had fallen on
the western side of Mount Cook and their bodies had not been recovered.

Some time later, when making a solo attempt of Mount Cook from
the other side, I reached the Haast hut late one evening. There was
no-one there and though it was possible to get a weather report from
the Hermitage using the hut's two-way radio, which had a hand
cranking generator for transmitting, I realised that I was too late for
this. After a spartan meal of dry biscuits and a can of beans, I snuggled
into my sleeping bag, resolved for an early night as I intended being
off by three am.

I can't say why I later got out of my warm bag and switched on the
radio receiver. It was operated by a spring switch, so that it couldn't
be left on, thereby running the battery down. During those few
seconds that I depressed the switch there was a crackle of static, then
the weak hum of a carrier wave. A faint voice, but it was definitely a
voice, crackled from the small speaker.

'Accident – Empress hut, urgent . . .'' Then there was silence.

I was dumbfounded. With those few words the sender had imparted
to me his desperation. But had I been hearing things? No, I told
myself, I was quite awake. I wasn't conscious of any telepathic
message, but still, for no apparent reason I had put the radio on
although I knew there could be no possible traffic on that frequency.
But as I pondered, I wondered why the message was so brief, why
wasn't it completed? I sat astride the generator seat of the transmitter
and started to hand crank the generator. It had a double handle which
required quite an effort to turn to give sufficient power to operate the
set. Usually two people use the transmitter, one to give the message
and the other to provide power via the treadmill, or rather the hand-
mill. I didn't get any response from the mystery operator. However, I
continued and somewhat out of breath, managed at last to contact the
Hermitage and told them of the weird message. I also said that I was
quite convinced that something terrible had happened on the other
side of the mountain at the Empress hut. Fortunately, they believed
me.

Mick Bowie who had put the Ruth Adams rescue into motion was still chief guide at the Hermitage. He was a big man, quietly spoken, who, you felt, could bare your soul with his glance. As soon as he got the message he guessed who had sent the distress call. Two Australians, Cooper and Murphy, of the Sydney Bush Walking Club had asked him a few days previously if Mount Cook was in condition. Mick had told them that it wasn't and warned them against attempting it. I had also met the two Australians at the Unwin hut close to the Hermitage a few days before and had spoken briefly with them, but of course I had no idea of their objective. Despite Mick's warning they went up to the Empress hut on the west side of the mountain with the intention of attempting Mount Cook by Earl's Route.

On the 25th February, 1955 at three am they left this refuge in overcast calm weather and reached the low peak of Cook at seven am. It's about a mile between the low and the high peak. They reached the main summit and returned to the low peak by midday. A wind had now sprung up from the west and it was this wind and the poor snow conditions which had deterred me from making an ascent of the mountain. Thick cloud and rain came in on the back of the wind and visibility was poor. They were descending the steep couloir leading towards the Hooker Glacier when they slipped on snow-covered ice. The snow avalanched with them, for it had virtually no anchorage due to the thaw, and they were both partially buried. Cooper was killed in the fall and Murphy suffered back and head injuries as well as breaking his wrist, but he managed to dig himself out. Due to his injuries, he couldn't dig down to his friend, but after a great effort managed to reach the Empress hut by descending a rock ridge. It must have been a gruelling experience.

When he reached the hut he collapsed on the floor and it was two days before he was able to move. It was on the third day that I providentially received that weird weak signal from him. Due to his injured arm he hadn't been able to operate the generator properly, indeed it was difficult enough for a fit person with full capabilities, as I had discovered, and it was that short message, about four seconds long, which I had intercepted that saved his life. Murphy was taken down in a distressed state by Mick Bowie's rescue party. The body of Cooper wasn't recovered.

I also had a frightening experience in that same couloir down which the Australians fell. The next year I made the first ascent of one of Mount Cook's ridges with two Americans, Dick Irwin and Peter

Robinson. When we had finished the climb, we took the rope off and soloed the last section to the summit of Mount Cook. On the top we met a party of two guides from the Hermitage and a client. It was the first time that two parties had met on the summit. As they had ascended from the Empress hut by Earl's Route, we decided to return that way. It was, they said, in good condition. They, on the other hand, were going back down the normal way, by the Linda Glacier, also making a grand traverse. Still travelling unroped, we started to descend the couloir that had proved to be the downfall of the Australians when Peter Robinson caught his crampons on his trousers and hurtled head-first down the ice. By a stroke of luck he stopped after a fall of about 300 feet and, being only bruised, he managed to continue, though much more slowly than before, and with the rope on! We had to bivouac above the Empress hut that night, as we were caught by darkness.

Mick Bowie would have been able to observe our early progress through a telescope and was no doubt going to be annoyed that we had thrown precaution to the wind and gone unroped up that final section of the mountain. When we arrived at the Hermitage the next day I saw Mick standing outside smoking his inevitable pipe and in all probability waiting to give me, as ringleader, a piece of his mind, so before he could take his pipe out of his mouth I hailed him.

"Hello, Mick, we did the climb, the new ridge, and we've decided to call it Bowie Ridge. I hope you don't mind?"

Later, Mick, when he was guest of honour at a dinner, related this story and concluded, "How could I give the blighters a telling off when they named a ridge of Mount Cook after me?"

There have been countless other dramas enacted on the great stage of the Central Alps of New Zealand. Even today, though helicopters and modern rescue methods assist the evacuation of climbers, they don't prevent accidents. As long as there are mountains there will be accidents. Paul Gazley, a talented young man, a pilot with the Royal New Zealand Air Force, was a national springboard diving and squash champion. He and Karen were married only seven and a half months when he was tragically killed in the second of two freak accidents. In the first he was buried for twelve hours under one of the biggest avalanches ever to come off Mount Cook. The second he didn't survive. Karen and Paul tell their story:

3

BURIED ON MOUNT COOK

by Karen Gazley

At home in Auckland I was bursting forth with all the news of my first South Island trip. I was so thrilled to see the family again and still highly exhilarated by the wonderful adventures I'd experienced during my discovery of the South. Three girlfriends and I had toured by car and thoroughly enjoyed some tramping in Fiordland, but Mount Cook particularly held a strong fascination for me.

By chance I had met Paul for a few minutes in Hokitika on the West Coast just as his party was departing by bus for Christchurch after their three strenuous weeks of tramping and climbing in the Southern Alps.

Now, a week later, the magnetism of those mountains still overwhelmed me. The prospect of returning to work the following day was far less inspiring and brought me abruptly back to earth, but I also realised that there was a lot more to life than just working.

It was while listening to the eleven pm radio news that I first learnt that something was very wrong in those mountains. Paul Gazley and Olly McCahon had been caught in a massive avalanche off the South Face of Mount Cook at five am that morning. Olly had managed to free himself and had raised the alarm and by the time I heard the news broadcast Paul had been found. Certainly, I had been spared earlier anxieties, as I had been driving for most of that day from Wellington to Auckland.

Suddenly, my world seemed shattered! Feelings of utter loss, despair and anguish seized me. I seemed so helpless and detached, being hundreds of miles away, not really knowing what was happening except that Paul was alive; these thoughts tortured me for the rest of the night. I prayed fervently for him.

It was five am on January 14th when Olly heard a cheerful call, "Look at that," from Paul who was in their bivouac above the south side of the Noeline Glacier where they had spent the night. It was an ideal site, a horizontal rock-rimmed platform with fresh water a short distance away trickling down the rocks. They were now making preparations to climb Nazomi (9,716 feet/2,961 metres), over-shadowed by Cook's glistening South Face.

Paul had been stuffing his gear into his tiny climbing sack when he looked up and saw the top cliffs breaking off the South Face of Cook 1,500 metres above. He yelled to Olly who was some distance away.

Paul later wrote.

> When I looked back, the plummeting ice hit a shelf part way down the face and exploded like a bomb. Powder snow was thrown high into the air and in front of me thousands of tons of it began crashing on to the glacier. Huge hunks of ice, as big as houses, began smashing themselves to pieces. I dismissed the thought of it sweeping half a mile across the glacier and burying us because we were too high, but I crouched down behind the rocks securing myself against the expected wind blast.

Olly was fifty metres from the bivvy site attending to nature's wants. Crouching comfortably he raised his head as Paul called out. Olly recalls:

> I looked up. The South Face of Cook was shedding its top ice cliffs directly opposite and above us. The avalanche grew huge as it thundered down, hit the bottom shelf on the face and exploded across the glacier. I crouched, staring fascinated, as it filled the whole sky and the world became a roaring wilderness of white, crashing, crushing snow bearing down on my head and shoulders. Hard things smashed on to my right hand and hit the back of my bare head, squashing me helplessly into a huddle on the rocks.

Paul's last impressions before he was buried were . . .

> The blast came and scattered our gear over a wide area. Then it happened – what I hadn't counted on, being bombed from above. I tried to stand up, but try as I might, the onslaught was too much. I was crushed into the snow, completely immobilised.
>
> I tried to move, but it was impossible. I was jammed down into a kneeling position with my chest on my knees, my right hand caught up by my head, and my left hand down by my side. Air was essential; I had to be able to breathe. I began to call for Olly,

thinking that his position would be far worse than my own. Then I began swearing at myself, calling myself every name under the sun and struggling in vain to free myself from my icy tomb. Somehow, although I don't remember how, I managed to free my left hand and, by clawing away at the ice, cleared a small hole in front of my face. By reaching out as far as I could, I was able to reach within about fifteen centimetres of the surface. At least I was now able to breathe.

My left hand looked dreadful. The fingertips were missing and bleeding, steadily staining the snow red. I was determined not to scrape with them any more but soon found myself doing so. I then began punching at the snow but it was frozen solid and the effort was useless.

Meanwhile, Olly had been partially buried:

The world was hushed, no sound broke the awful stillness. Where there had been warm, red rock there was now a desert of hard-packed snow and nowhere could I see gear, bivvy or Paul. Shocked and dazed by a blow on my head, I was buried up to the waist, my smashed right hand was spreading blood over the snow.

Panicky, desperate digging and heaving got me clear and the resulting freedom helped me fight off my new and overwhelming fear of the South Face towering over me. Inspection of my right hand revealed smashed knuckles and a badly cut palm. It looked as though I could write off my first finger. Closing my mind, I wrapped the hand in bog paper and a handkerchief.

Above, the South Face was now showing grey ice and bare rock where there had been ice cliffs. The whole width of the Noeline was a jumble of blocks with great slide tracks sweeping off down the glacier. Around me the scene was almost unrecognisable, especially as I had partial amnesia and had to concentrate hard just to remember where I was and who I was with. Dread of the South Face stimulated my efforts to climb up to the bivvy site. I was soon well above it, although it was some time before I realised this and came down again. Finding the bivvy brought little joy for everything was buried.

I could see no sign of Paul, although I guessed he must still be there. But it was now at least an hour after the avalanche and with one hand and no gear I couldn't dig. After some desolate soul-searching I left him for dead and headed for the Gardiner hut. Obviously the best way back was to follow Saturday's tracks, but they were across the glacier under the South Face. With my heart in my mouth I scrambled across the debris, in terror of a repeat performance. As I reached the other side and turned down the tracks I heard a crump and looked round to see a little avalanche coming down further along. Fear lent me wings and I headed down the glacier at a very rapid trot.

Signs of the avalanche were everywhere. To my left the glacier was heaped with avalanche debris and where I was travelling the snow had been swept bare by the blast. Things went well until I reached the steep slopes above Gardiner and there, in sight of the hut, I found my way blocked by slopes of very hard snow. How I longed for ice axe or crampons and I wasted some thought on which I would rather have before deciding that crampons would be best.

Fortunately it was now quite late, and the slopes further over were in the sun and presumably softened, but between lay the steep hard snow, criss-crossed with slots. These turned out to be the solution to my problem for I found that I could balance along the lower lip of one, then scramble down to the next using a pocket knife as an ice dagger and then repeat the performance. After that it was o.k. and with the sun warming my back I hurried down to Gardiner and the radio.

At 10.35 am on January 14th Barrie Thomas, chief ranger at park headquarters, received an urgent message from Olly McCahon at Gardiner hut. A practised rescue procedure swung into action. Senior rangers Irwin and Thorne aided their chief, now field controller. Fortunately there was an Iroquois helicopter at Tekapo, fifteen minutes' flying time away. The helicopter left park headquarters at 12.22 pm and carried a team of R. Whitely (leader), M. Dorfliger and Eric Saxby. Olly was collected from Gardiner and they flew over the search area. The wind was increasing and the weather was fine and hot. The high temperature caused such lack of power at 2,600 metres that the helicopter could not chance a landing at the bivouac site. There was no sign of life below. So the search party was unloaded at

Gardiner hut at 1,700 metres, some one and a half climbing hours to the bivvy.

At 2.15 pm the helicopter flew a second rescue party to Gardiner. This consisted of Paul von Kanel, Colin Monteath, Etienne Kummer and Hans Muller who followed the first team up the Noeline Glacier. The helicopter now flew Olly to park headquarters. Suffering from shock and in need of medical attention for his hand, Olly had remained with the rescue teams for as long as he could be of use. At headquarters, he was attended by Dr Anne Hall and Dr Jock Staveley who were both holidaying in the park and, as soon as the accident was reported, had told headquarters of their willingness to help.

Paul, still trapped under the avalanche, continues his story:

I decided the only way to free myself was to try and turn over so that I could push the ice off with both hands. To do this I had to free my right hand and I began desperately yanking it back and forth trying to free it. Every time I pulled it, I scraped a little more skin off it leaving an ugly raw area. Finally, when I freed it, the fingers were too cold and useless even to pull back my parka sleeve to look at my watch. In vain I began using my left elbow as a hammer, smashing it against the ice, trying to free my knees so that I might have been able to turn over. I could not give up hope. I had to keep trying. I didn't even know that Olly was alive, let alone that anyone was searching for me.

I had no idea of time, but resigned myself to the fact that if I ever did get myself free then I would most likely have to spend the night there as it would be too dark to walk down the glacier. My feet were getting cold and I began wriggling my toes to try and warm them. My right foot was the worst. I couldn't even feel it. The prospect was frostbitten feet.

At 2.30 pm the leading team reached the area where Paul was believed to be buried. What had been so clear from the air was entirely different from the ground. Snow had melted and there was no sign of blood from Olly's gashed hand which might have helped in pinpointing the location. Olly's and Paul's climbing gear was spread over a wide area, such had been the force of the windblast created by the avalanche. All likely places in the vicinity were searched, but to no avail. Then the searchers climbed up to some rocks where they had seen a sling and karabiner. They decided these had been swept down from above as the sling was not tied.

On the arrival of the second team, the searchers combined their efforts. Two climbers searched towards the head of the Noeline Glacier, while the others concentrated on the area above the previous search site. It was in vain. All seven searchers converged on a convenient spot to eat a hurried lunch while they discussed further search plans. They decided to ask the Air Force to fly Olly back to locate the burial spot more precisely. Two searchers were sent to Gardiner to call them. Meanwhile, the others resolved to concentrate their efforts at a higher level and in closer groups. Here they noticed some tracks made by Olly on his way down to summon help.

Eric Saxby left the searchers to pick up some surplus gear he had unloaded at a lower level. On his return he stopped at the lunch spot to drink from a rock pool. As he bent to scoop water into his hands, he heard a faint shout for help. He was immediately alert to the possibility that one of the two returning to Gardiner had fallen into a crevasse. He straightened up and called,

"What is it? What do you want?"

"Over here! Over here," returned a muffled shout. Eric scrambled over the rough terrain towards the call. He stopped, puzzled. There was no sign of anyone.

To Eric's anxious cry, "Where are you?" there came from beneath his very feet the quiet answer, "Don't tread too hard, you are directly above me."

Eric dropped to his knees and frantically dug away ice and snow with his ice axe and hands, calling to his companions while he did so, but they were too far away to hear. He uncovered fingers issuing through the ice some thirty centimetres below the surface. Eric dug deeper. He could now see part of a head. He uncovered it, a metre below the surface of hard-packed snow and ice. It was now five pm.

Paul recalled:

During one of my bouts of scraping, hammering, punching, yanking and twisting I heard voices. I recognised one of them. I yelled as loudly as I could. There was an instant reply. I yelled again but this time there was no reply. My heart sank. I began yelling again as loud as I could. Then came a reply from right on top of me. At last a hand came through the snow.

Eric had been unable to make himself heard to the other searchers. He left Paul for a brief period to rush to them and yell exultantly, "I've found him! I've found him! He's alive! He's OK!"

Disbelief gave place to relief, then to ecstasy. The five whooped deliriously as they raced to the bright, relieved voice and grin from the hole in the ice. Eric continued digging. As the other rescuers arrived they began to dig, prepare the stretcher, arrange a safety line and unpack food. A radio message was sent to the hut-bound pair to request the return of the helicopter.

Half an hour's digging was still required to release Paul from the rock and ice that had imprisoned him for twelve hours. He could never have freed himself alone. He was lifted out and a jersey laid out for him on the snow.

Paul said: "I remembered very little of the whole operation. When freed, I tried to stand up but my legs just collapsed under me and I fell in a crumpled heap on the snow."

Attention was given to his left hand and he was fed some peppermint chocolate. The rescuers dressed him in warm clothing and placed him securely on a stretcher for the long haul down the glacier.

Paul recounts: "They had to sledge me down the glacier. This was done with celerity but it seemed an endless journey for me. My whole body was cold and my hands were freezing. I stuffed them down my trousers to try and warm them but there was no warmth in me at all."

The condition of the glacier and its ever-present risk of avalanche, the gathering darkness and the need for speed in man-handling the heavy stretcher demanded consummate skill from the rescuers – particularly as much of the route was taken at a run.

On the way down the glacier the helicopter flew above the returning party and made radio contact, but conditions prevented it hovering and winching up the stretcher. So the downward haul continued. At Gardiner hut, Paul was given hot tea but his hands could not hold the mug, nor could he sit up to accept it. Here, his hands were bandaged and he was wrapped in blankets.

At 8.30 pm the helicopter came back up the Hooker Glacier to determine whether or not a pickup was possible. Darkness was rapidly falling, but the crew knew the urgency of the occasion. Firmly supported under each arm, Paul stumbled up the rocks as the helicopter was landing. He was hurried aboard and made secure by the loadmaster.

When Paul arrived at park headquarters, he was in a state of severe shock. He was conscious but hypothermic and pulseless, with frostbite to both hands, left elbow and left knee. Dr Hall and Dr Stavely decided he should be treated on the spot. They set up a drip bottle on the end of a broom to supply intravenous Dextran to help counteract the shock. Park rangers hugged him to raise his temperature by direct body heat. His feet, which were very white, were immersed in a bedpan of warm water. Dressings were applied to the frostbitten areas.

After two hours, his pulse could be felt and his body temperature had risen to near normal. At one am he was given Bactrim capsules and went to sleep on a mattress between two electric blankets, which Barrie Thomas had borrowed from private houses. Dr Hall stayed with him through the night. Her main concern was the acute kidney damage that could be expected from the crush injuries and the low body temperature he had suffered.

The next morning Paul was transferred by helicopter to Christchurch Hospital. He was minus the tips of his index, second and third fingers of his left hand and was frostbitten on his right hand, left elbow and left knee. Initially, he was treated for acute renal failure which had resulted from both muscle crush and disintegration of striated muscle fibre. Other factors considered important were hypothermia, dehydration and a degree of hypoxia (abnormally decreased oxygen supply). A week later he was transferred to the plastic surgery unit at Burwood Hospital and for the next seven weeks was treated for the frostbite damage, particularly involving two serious operations to his left hand.

One had to admire him for his cheerfulness amid physical discomfort, immobility and the knowledge that his future held so many uncertainties – was this the end of his flying career? However Paul recovered completely and, despite a pinned ring finger on his left hand, was able to return to diving, squash, tramping, climbing, skiing and flying.

Paul's remarkable survival appeared to be something of a miracle. The medical world attributed much of the complete recovery to his extreme fitness. But was he now living on borrowed time?

We eventually married in December, 1974, a few weeks after I had qualified as a medical laboratory technologist at Middlemore

Hospital, Auckland, and we then very happily settled in Blenheim. Paul was stationed here as base adjutant and pilot for RNZAF, Woodbourne.

July 19th dawned as a Saturday morning with prospects of a reasonable weekend; certainly a full one so typical of the life we had been living. My morning was taken up with working in the lab at Wairau Hospital and general lassitude was sweeping over me by the time I returned home; probably increased by the knowledge that the inevitable end of week housework had still to be done. The previous day Paul had run in a cross-country marathon at Trentham with the Air Force and was exhausted – not only did he appear weary, but actually admitted it. Regardless, he was playing in another squash tournament on both Saturday and Sunday in which Blenheim was host to Nelson and, as I was unable to watch the Saturday match, I promised to watch him play on the Sunday.

It was while baking that afternoon that an excruciating stomach cramp suddenly pierced my system with such violence that I almost collapsed on the kitchen floor. The pain remained as a constant throb and on awaking on Sunday morning I felt dreadful. However, I had a strong urge to attend mass. I mended some dachstein mittens for Paul which kept me occupied for a while before stirring myself for the eleven am mass at the Catholic church at the end of our street. I hadn't been for ages, as many other things had temporarily assumed equal importance. I may as well not have bothered. The priest's words I did not hear. I felt detached and alone. Voices thundered in on me and washed over me. Eventually the mass ended and once again I was caught up in the surging tide, everyone moving towards the door. Then it happened. As I walked out of the church I experienced what I can best describe as a premonition. I looked down at myself as a message flashed through my brain, "My God, you're wearing widow's clothes." I immediately erased this from my mind and didn't think anything further about it until three days later, but that morning I had worn my favourite slacks suit – black slacks, black and white woollen jacket over a red skivvy and complete with red accessories.

The same day I watched Paul play one of his most dynamic squash games. He was a very strong player with particularly powerful shots and his superb fitness allowed him to spring across the court with such agility that it appeared effortless.

Paul's mountain experience was invaluable to the Air Force and he was asked each year to assist in the training on a particular Air Force survival course. He was to instruct a party this week, an aircrew from No. 40 Squadron Whenuapai, which flies Hercules aircraft to Antarctica. He took a considerable time packing his old faithful canvas pack.

"I'm going prepared for anything," he assured me, putting in plenty of warm clothing and several pairs of mittens, as his hands readily suffered from the cold since being frostbitten two and a half years previously. My baking was not only to be a special treat, but more important, was a survival 'stand-by'.

Monday morning at work was a struggle. Finally, I had to acknowledge that I could no longer persevere and so biked home at lunchtime. Sadly, I had just missed Paul who had been home earlier in his lunch hour after being refused a warrant of fitness (or test certificate) for our Fiat. However, the necessary arrangements were made for me to take the car to a garage the following day. We had a brief chat over the phone and by mid-afternoon Paul was on his way to Wigram, Christchurch. How I wished I was going with him – just to be there. Paul seemed uneasy about going alone, even pleaded with me to join him – but we knew this would be impossible on an Air Force exercise. I was so grateful when he rang me that night from Christchurch.

The nine pm news on TV featured heavy snows in Christchurch. I immediately and somewhat anxiously thought of Paul, but realised of course that he was fine. I had only just been speaking to him and had confidence he would take every care. Before leaving he had emphasised that he would be prepared if they were caught in a storm. After all, he had experience, fitness and the equipment.

Little things started to go wrong the following day. Trivial really, but still big enough for me to wish Paul was home again. Then, the next day, July 23rd, 1975, seemed to be a continuation of trouble. It started with further complications in getting the car through its test – now it was a headlight – later the day merged with night in one shattering nightmare.

I noticed someone dressed in black as I walked out of work at five pm that evening. I was anxious to check the Fiat which the mechanic had delivered. I saw the car parked under nearby pines. Relieved to see that I now had a new warrant of fitness sticker displayed, I leapt in, then remembered the headlight and just to be sure it too had been replaced, decided to take a quick look. The black figure materialised beside me as I bent over. It was the Rev. Dick Simpson, an Air Force padre, and he told me that Paul was involved in an avalanche at Mount Cook.

"I couldn't take a second one,' I murmured to him almost disbelieving what he'd just told me.

Paul had spent Tuesday night at Ball hut at the foot of Mount Cook with the rest of the instructors and students. On the Wednesday morning they had all climbed the ridge behind the hut to do basic snowcraft, self-arrest with the ice axe and generally skylarking in perfect snow conditions. Their final task for the day was to dig snow caves at the head of the Ball Glacier and sleep in them overnight.

The avalanche struck all twenty-five of them just before four pm. Some rode it and swam furiously to keep on top, some were buried with shovels in their hands and even succeeded in digging themselves out, but those who were actually excavating the snow caves at that time were engulfed.

John Moore, Dick Strong, Howard Conway and Olly McCahon had been instructing the climbing on the Mueller Glacier, together with ranger Martin Heine. They returned to HQ to be met by Barrie Thomas, the chief ranger, who told them that several people had been buried in an avalanche on Ball Pass. An Iroquois helicopter which was in the area as part of the course would fly them in as soon as possible. They all piled out of the Land-Rover and raced off to pack their gear. When they returned the Iroquois was waiting and avalanche probes, radios, spare headlamp batteries, food and shovels were being loaded. The rescue team were airborne by 4.45 pm. First they flew down to Unwin hut (the Alpine Club hut at Mount Cook) where the air crew were based and landed on the road outside to pick up a doctor. Then they flew up the Tasman Glacier to Ball Pass where they landed by five pm. As soon as they were on the snow, equipment was ferried to the avalanche tip. Once there radio contact was established with HQ and avalanche probes assembled.

Just below the avalanche debris were a few men in sleeping bags. They had been dug out, shaken but uninjured.

In Olly McCahon's words: "I went uphill with a load of probes and handed them around, then returned for more and met Martin Heine who said that Paul Gazley had been dug out and looked pretty bad, but was still alive. It was a grim moment and my first reaction was a desire to cry, but there was no time, so Mart and I just looked at each other, muttered a few inadequate words and got on with it."

Over the next few hours the Air Force men were organised into probe teams and dug anxiously for those who had been located by the probes. Now the search party relieved them of the digging for these members of the avalanche party were near exhaustion. Theirs had been an emotionally and physically demanding experience and without much direction they had worked as a close-knit rescue team.

A food box was uncovered some six feet down. Then another buried man was located, whereupon Olly and Howard Conway were called over to assist in digging him out. Meanwhile, the rest of the Park's Board team had arrived and now had a probe line operating in an endeavour to locate the remainder. By then the survivors had gone down to the base of the slope and were provided with a well-earned hot meal and then directed to bed in a snow shelter. For them it was to be a night of terror – an overwhelming fear of yet another avalanche taking them in their restless sleep tormented them until daylight. As it was almost dusk it was decided that the helicopter would come in after moonrise to take out the most shocked of the survivors and the body of the man they'd just found. The rest of the night passed slowly in increasing cold, probing the snow and taking breaks for cups of tea and soup until they found another and finally the last body just after midnight on the last attempt before they had decided to give up. There were three dead and Paul who was critically ill – or so they all thought until they learned the next morning that he had died at the Hermitage, despite every effort to save his life.

Olly wrote later: "I can't even pretend to understand why Paul's and my paths should have come together on these two occasions or why I should live and he die. All I can do is to remember him as he was; fit, brown and happy on his way up the Hooker and then so cheerful and courageous in hospital afterwards . . . I remember him as he was and I'm grateful for what we shared in the mountains and what I gained from those experiences."

The weather was good so the helicopter was able to operate, first lifting the survivors. Finally, the search team flew out to Park HQ with two bodies.

When the Rev. Dick Simpson told me that Paul had been involved in another avalanche, I was absolutely numbed of any emotion and I drove home, parked the car in the garage and then went with Dick to his place and didn't for one moment think the worst. It just couldn't happen twice! Minutes seemed endless as we waited for news. At six pm I was relieved to hear that three of the four missing had been found and Paul was one of them and was being flown to Timaru Hospital. At this point I phoned both our families. More waiting. The phone rang. Dick answered it in the hallway as I sat anxiously in the lounge already planning my journey down to Timaru.

Then there was an ominous silence! A firm hand rested on my shoulder; I turned to hear the agonising words, "I'm sorry, Karen."

Every bodily emotion erupted as I sat screaming No! No! in utter horror and total disbelief. My hopes had soared so high. Now crushed so cruelly to a pulverised nothingness. That dreadful phone call was to report that Paul was dead. Shock froze every fibre within me as the world helplessly looked on.

EIGHT

Paul Nunn and I have known each other for more years than we care to remember. In 1970 we were fellow members of an expedition to the Caucasus, that stark upthrust between the Caspian and the Black Seas, a cradle of civilisation and now a playground for Soviet mountaineers. Paul, Chris Woodall and I completed a climb up the forbidding face of Pik Shchurovskiy and at our second bivouac, Paul, usually a human power house, with an exuberant enthusiasm for life, came dangerously close to being an exposure victim. It was probably a blend of two dangerous ingredients which fortify this death cocktail: altitude sickness and exposure.

In the following account Paul's role is reversed and it was he together with others who set off from their base camp in the high Pamirs to attempt to reach Soviet women climbers, encamped and trapped on the summit of one of Russia's highest mountains. All big mountains are potentially dangerous; like fast cars they must be treated with respect. Yet if one uses common sense they can be traversed and enjoyed with impunity. The two popular ranges in the Soviet Union, the Caucasus and the Pamir, are high and subject to violent storms. Also being marooned in a vast land mass they can be grippingly cold.

The Russian climbing bureaucracy appears somewhat ambiguous in its policy. On the one hand they are acutely safety conscious and enforce a control time. Before setting out a party is allotted a number of days or hours to complete their climb. The route itself must be approved by a panel of Masters of Sport, experienced senior mountaineers. This panel and the climbers agree on a reasonable time for the expedition. Should the party fail to return at the specified time, a rescue party sets off immediately, unless of course the overdue mountaineers have managed to advise base by radio or some other means that they have been delayed. It's also necessary to have a simple medical examination before setting off on a major route. To western climbers all this is anathema, although I can see the point of it in such dangerous mountains. But what I can't reconcile it with is the Russians' 'press-on regardless' policy, which advocates that the objective, ie. the summit, should always be reached. I can remember on a previous trip to the Caucasus in 1965 being told off for turning back when we had retreated in the interests of safety, on a relatively low peak, due to adverse conditions. After all, I climb for enjoyment not for death-dicing thrills.

In recent years the Russians have been running organised climbing camps in both the Caucasus and the Pamirs and in this way mountaineers from all over the world have had the opportunity to climb in the Soviet Union. I received an invitation to climb in the Pamirs in 1974 from the Federation of Sport, but couldn't make it. However, many of my friends, including Paul, did and for them it was an experience they won't readily forget.

STORM ON PEAK LENIN

by Paul Nunn

There was little hesitation for me in joining the British Pamirs expedition of 1974. Every member knew me and I them, while some were among my oldest friends. Fourteen years before Clive Rowland and I had a first weekend climbing together in the Lakes, dreaming up Overhanging Bastion and the steeps of North Crag Eliminate, and Kipling Groove on Gimmer Crag in Langdale next day. Our ventures together were always successful. The same could be said of previous experience with Doug Scott and Paul ('Tut') Braithwaite, particularly in our ascent of the North-East Pillar of Asgard on Baffin Island in 1972. Guy Lee impressed by his wide experience, Speedy Smith by his enthusiasm and ability on rock. It was the most able group of climbers ever to leave Britain for the Soviet Union, and also the most piratical in appearance.

There had been only one British expedition to the Pamirs since 1963, when Robin Smith and Wilfred Noyce died and relations became strained for some years. In 1970 Hamish MacInnes, Chris Woodall and I climbed a new route on Pik Shchurovskiy in the Caucasus in one push. In 1974 the objectives were ambitious –

nothing less than an alpine-style climb up the East Face of Peak Lenin
(23,400 feet/7,134 metres) seemed satisfactory, with all the seriousness
and difficulty of commitment at high altitude.

The Soviet Mountaineering Federation had made a huge effort of
organisation in drawing together climbers from many nations in a
huge meet in the Achik Tash valley of Kirghizia. Under the great
domes of Peak Lenin and her neighbours they built a tented village for
more than 150 foreign climbers and many more from the Soviet
Mountaineering Federation. The climbers came in relays from
Moscow after meeting there in early July. While they flew in from all
over the globe, our contingent chugged across Europe on the London
to Moscow express, drinking endless glasses of *chai* (tea). After only a
day or so in the hurly burly of the capital, a whirl of circuses, meals,
intense conversations and meeting both our hosts and other national
groups, we flew south-east from the great plains to the dry lands of
Central Asia, to Osh on the old trade route to Peking and at last to the
Alai Valley. As the climbers spilled from the plane into Asian heat and
the red dust there shimmered a dazzling wall of mountains which
spanned the whole horizon to the south. A few hours jolting by lorry
led us to Base Camp at over 10,000 feet, tired and yet elated by the
journey from Moscow in less than twenty-four hours. Dinner came in
a great military tent only twenty miles or so as the crow flies from
Sinkiang, China.

The Base Camp was run by the Moscow psychiatrist, Michael
Monastyrski, a small weather-beaten individual who could put on a
stern look of disapproval if things went badly. In practice he proved a
sympathetic and likeable man, for whom the International Meet held
many trials in store. Michael organised the logistics of the camp and
was responsible for the smooth running of the establishment and of
supplies which had to be ferried either from the Alai airfield or from
Osh, a twelve-hour dusty road journey.

Mountaineering was arranged in liaison with a small group of
prominent officials of the Soviet Mountaineering Federation, including the veteran of numerous first ascents, Vitali Abalakov, and the
urbane one-time secretary of the Federation, Eugene Gippenreiter.
Both Eugene and Michael spoke excellent English, making our visit
far easier. Also, each group was asked to develop a special relationship
with an adviser, a prominent Master of Sport who would comment
upon plans made and volunteer as much help as possible. There were a

few days settling in, medicals of a simple nature, waiting for gear to arrive and checking on plans. This was all to the good for acclimatisation aided by short walks towards Peak Lenin across grassy meadows or to the yurts of the Kirghizian shepherds tending their flocks of sheep and goats.

Eventually all the formalities were complete, the various climbing groups moved off towards a variety of objectives and we drew our food from the stores, packed our sacks and set off for the Krylenko Pass, 19,095 feet, which had to be crossed to reach the base of the East Face of Peak Lenin. There was quite a crowd on the 5,000-foot north slope of the pass. Apart from the British, who broke the trail up deep snow in three days, eleven American, three or four Soviet climbers and a team of Japanese were moving in the same direction. Though there had been negotiations about precisely which objectives the various groups were to try once the pass was crossed, the eventual outcome appears to have been left to fate and the relative speeds at which the parties moved. Doug and Tut were first up the slope, unsurprisingly as Doug had only recently returned from over 27,000 feet on Everest South-West Face, while Tut generally goes well at altitude. In contrast Speedy and I found 19,000 feet for the first time a terrible graft, but eventually we all made it over and down to a camp on the Saukdhara Glacier at about 17,000 feet.

It was a marvellous but remote spot, ringed in by a line of major peaks and opening up vast views of glacial wastes and more distant and little explored snow mountains. Like a huge Brenva Face of Mont Blanc, the East Face of Peak Lenin looms across the head of the glacier, a mass of hanging seracs and soaring ice ridges. Ever energetic and impatient, Doug and Clive set off late in the afternoon of our arrival on the Saukdhara, to plod out a path through the deep snow towards the face. Doug was some hundred yards from the tent and unroped when he suddenly disappeared from sight. Clive cautiously peered into the crevasse to find him ensconced on a bridge of snow less than twenty feet below. He fed down a rope and Doug emerged snow covered but fortunately unharmed. The plan was that we should push straight onto the face the next morning, moving lock, stock and barrel up the mountain. It was very ambitious and in retrospect likely to succeed for only a couple of members of the party who were better acclimatised. In any case it was not to be.

That evening two Estonian climbers who had come up via the

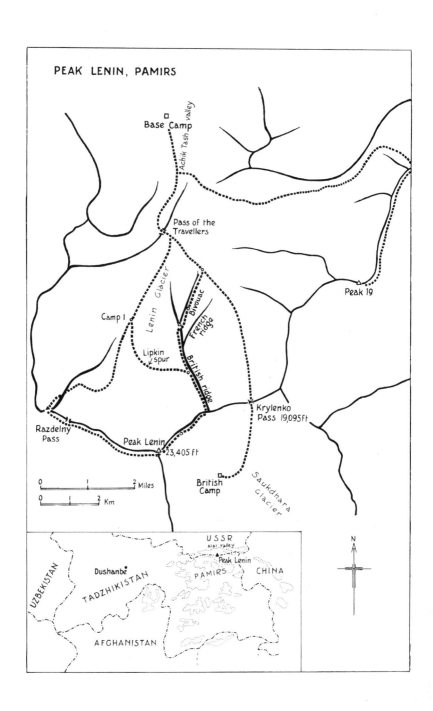

PEAK LENIN, PAMIRS

Base Camp

Achik Tash valley

Pass of the
Travellers

Peak 19

Camp 1

Lenin Glacier

Bivouac

French ridge

Lipkin
spur

British ridge

Krylenko
Pass 19,095 ft

Razdelny
Pass

Peak Lenin
△ 23,405 ft

British
Camp

Saukdhara
Glacier

0   1   2 Miles
0   1   2 Km

USSR
Alai Valley

Dushanbe

Peak Lenin

UZBEKISTAN

TADZHIKISTAN

PAMIRS

CHINA

AFGHANISTAN

N

Saukdhara in support of an attempt on the Heibeler Route on the East Face distracted me from some serious thoughts as we fed them tea and tried to converse. Soon after dark, snow pattered on the tunnel tents, each crowded with three inmates and already white rimed in frozen condensation.

As the third day of the blizzard dawned in the tiny gauze window of the tent, my head ached and my guts seemed wrenched with exhaustion. A pervasive and nauseous chill crept into every cell of my body. Despite excellent equipment, prolonged inactivity and increased dampness was clogging my system and destroying bit by bit the indispensable insulation upon which all depended. The aches from continued overcrowding in the tent were abominable, while deep and constantly falling snow pressed in the walls and roof. An incessant wind depressed the spirits and was isolating in the extreme. Even Guy's endless fund of wit froze, while Speedy had long stopped speaking. Only Doug and Tut remained in adequate physical condition, while everyone else had some form of altitude headache. Our nights were disturbed by the jolting of the glaciers, as huge earth tremors twisted the geological substructures through which they carved. Through the black nights and driving snow great echoing roars thundered all too near. Though we saw nothing, the shaking earth hurled off slabs of snow, sweeping the Estonians from the Heibeler Spur to their deaths and burying an American party on a new route on Peak 19.

I peered out of the tent, moving slowly in the logistics of high altitude brew-making, into a third morning of complete white out. There was no sign of the high peaks, or of anything more than a few yards away. Ambitious plans had dropped us into a trap, as Abalokov had feared. The way up was barred, food was becoming slender and we had to get out. To go downhill would lead via the Saukdhara, close to China, though how close or how far it was we did not know. After some shouted deliberation it had to be the Krylenko again, two miles away and 2,000 feet above. Some of the equipment would stay behind for the next attempt, so the crossing had to be as fast as possible to avoid a tentless night out.

Unhappily, we had assembled in the driving snow outside the tents. Doug and Tut shared the lead, plodding in calf-deep snow at the front of the long rope of six. As we set off into the opaque haze, painfully tramping towards the Krylenko, the Estonians were dead or dying a mile or two away and Jon Gary Ullin was deep under the snow of Peak 19.

After a couple of hours of glacial tramping the caravan stopped for the fortieth time. Through the murk ice cliffs barred the way. "We've missed the upper glacier, have to go back, youth," came from Doug. So down it was, and then up at last into the ice corridor leading between Lenin's East Ridge and its eastern neighbour. Mercifully, the snow abated and about midday the sun shone for a little while, but the snow softened and dehydrated bodies protested. Doug and Tut still went well, but everyone else suffered headaches. Guy plodded on self-contained but tired, Speedy lost psychological clarity so that urgings made no impact, while I remained mentally lucid but found my knees folding frequently. Clive took up an effective rearguard position and chaperoned us to the Krylenko and a view of the Achik Tash as massive black clouds swept up the valley and boiled into the basin of the descent route. It was six or seven hours after leaving camp with only five more hours of daylight.

From the col the rope split, and while the others sped ahead I remained roped to Speedy, and Clive kept us company on the descent. Only a few hundred feet below the col a great wind-slab avalanche had broken away to a thickness of four feet and several hundred yards wide. Vast areas of slab remained hanging on all sides of the upper basin and, tired as we were, we moved down as fast as possible, so that our enthusiasm led us to go too low at one point, and there followed a painful pull back uphill to reach the crevasse in which we had left eleven Americans, four Russian climbers and a tent a few days earlier. The site of the camp at 17,400 feet had seemed protected, or at least more nearly so than anywhere else on the 5,000 feet of climbing to the col. The overhanging lip had proved only just sufficient defence. From mounds of snow only a few broken tent poles and tattered rags emerged. Speculation about the fate of the residents seemed pointless. Doug scraped around for morsels of food and found Molly Higgins' diary. There was little knowing whether this tough little blonde was alive or dead with her companions under the compacted avalanche debris. After more despondent pokings around there was no alternative but to continue down, as our cooking equipment, tent and food had shared the fate of the Americans.

With very few hours to darkness the urgency became the greater as we lacked tents and even down jackets or sleeping bags in some cases. The bank of battleship-grey clouds enveloped everything and in premature dusk we fled very fast as altitude diminished, hopping crevasses and sliding through avalanche debris with manic energy, with no time for ropes or delay. In only minutes I slid down a huge avalanche runnel a thousand feet to the edge of a steepening in the slope, every moment conscious of the recent high temperatures above, ears cocked for a roaring in the mist as the Krylenko discharged its next bombardment. As I peered down, Clive shot out of sight down another avalanche runnel into the gloom. Speedy was close behind, so I did the same, sacrificing caution to speed. Once I turned upside down in the massive careering swoop down the ice-backed runnel, but so much deep snow abounded below that the eventual landing was deep and soft. In the mist I could hear voices and, staggering with fatigue, I joined the others as the snow blew in and the temperature began to plummet. Speedy was still to come and there was a small icefall to negotiate before the glacier which led to a place where we hoped some French tents remained.

The minutes ticked by and our bodies froze. We cursed and muttered at the delay and eventually Tut, earliest down and thinly clad, preferred to go back onto the slope to find our companion. In not too long he returned with Speedy. We had gravely miscalculated in leaving him alone as he, unlike everyone else, had not regained mental clarity as descent proceeded. Only a little way up the slope, after making the slide, he had stopped, at a loss as to what to do next. We roped and in the last light negotiated the icefall and in a black night groped down the lower glacier. To my relief as the site of the old camp on Krylenko moraine came in view there was a light, and soon we found ourselves in an American pyramid tent eagerly swilling brews.

Al Steck and Mike Yokell were resting there after escaping the avalanche in the Crevasse Camp above, at the cost of cracked ribs and a battered knee. From them we learned that all seven Americans there had survived, though it had been a close call. Bruce Carson, Fred Stanley, John Evans and Al Steck had been hit by the same avalanche as they fled the Crevasse Camp, and Steck had almost been buried, while all were lucky not to die. Sleep came with the deadness of relief. Masses of snow fell overnight and even the interminable moraine heaps leading to the Pass of the Travellers and Base were heavy going next day.

An earth tremor had started the great avalanche. The Americans had been prevented from crossing the pass on their second carry by the bad weather and were left to the mercy of the Krylenko slope. It almost caught them. The Japanese party had not yet committed themselves to the slope and merely lost gear dumps low down. In the same earthquake a four-man party on Peak 19's North Face was hit by a similar avalanche and despite frantic efforts to dig him out Jon Gary Ullin died.

After that storm no one dared enter the jaws of the Krylenko, as avalanches streamed down in procession. A mountain of valuable equipment was lost on the slope while we could not get back to the East Face. All subsequent planning was conditioned by tent shortage and by dreadful snow conditions. The Soviet advisers were now acutely worried and understandably anxious there should be no more accidents. At Base Camp there was an atmosphere of pessimism and exhaustion as we rather frantically tried to get permission to get back by a low level route to our equipment, and the camp directorate concealed their grief and preoccupation at the loss of the Estonians. The weather was very bad and a little multi-national group could only ease into black nights with the aid of the national beverages of Scotland and Russia. It seemed justifiable, despite the health rules.

After days of bad weather the shortness of our month long visit pressed, the routines and food of Base palled, and we persuaded our adviser to let us look at the Krylenko again. There was just a possibility of reaching it by the traverse of a 20,000-foot peak to the east and by that circuitous route reaching the camp on the Saukdhara Glacier. It boded ill as we plodded the Pass of the Travellers in driving rain and crossed the miserable and characterless moraines to Moraine Camp.

Early next morning Doug and I tramped up the glacier, but the avalanches on the Krylenko proved no more attractive at close quarters, while the crossing via the spur of Peak Lenin's outlier was a major venture in itself. Time was short and we needed action, which fortunately suggested itself in an elegant snow ridge of no great difficulty which eventually merged with the East Ridge of Peak Lenin itself. Three Scots, Bruce Barclay, Alan North and Greg Strange, had intended to join us in crossing the Krylenko and now, as a nine-man British party, we changed our plan. The ridge provided a route from below 16,000 feet to the summit of Peak Lenin. It had not been climbed, but ran parallel to a narrower ridge which a French party had ascended while we were on the Krylenko, eventually joining it and the classic Lipkin Route up the main summit. A baking day was spent in making the few preparations, for we had little equipment and only two tents for nine climbers, though we were lacking in neither food nor fuel.

The crocodile of climbers set out early next morning, climbing solo across initial ice slopes onto the ridge and then beginning the most formidable soft ridge plod that I have ever encountered. Almost everyone took turns to make steps, knee- or thigh-deep in the crusted snow. One thought only of the next ridge top, which might be reached in a three- or four-man lead, or of the next few steps upwards, firmly placing the ice axe, no rope, no insurance. At least there was not too much to carry. Gradually the ice jumble of the upper Achik Tash fell below, the sun rose higher in the sky and by late morning a small tower loomed ahead. Doug and Tut ploughed an insecure route direct, while Clive and I also used a rope to outflank its steep section. In such a large group there seemed scope for variation. Above, Clive took the lead on the deepest snow yet, waist deep, softened by late morning sun. No one could sustain more than a couple of hundred feet leading in such stuff.

At last, as the subsidiary peak of Lenin began to look nearer, everybody stopped for a brew, a few sweets, and a slice of smoked sturgeon from the yellow fillet which hung from my rucksack lid. After plodding in front lower down, Clive, Bruce Barclay and I spent about an hour in the afternoon in semi-slumber, while Alan North, Greg Strange and the others pressed on up the upper ridge. As the sun slipped behind the peaks to the west the snow solidified a little and we followed the tracks up small steep steps and round crevasses serrating the upper peak to a shoulder which offered a safe camping place.

The caravan had kept going from dawn to dusk, through morning frost and midday sun, gaining over 3,000 feet and considerable distance in bad snow conditions. It was reason for satisfaction as Doug, Guy, Clive and I all hacked away at the snow cave in which two of us would reside to relieve the tent shortage. There was a bitter wind which urged on the outdoor activities and Clive and I were glad to slide gingerly inside, trying to avoid the tendency to knock crusts of snow onto down gear. Clive snuggled into his duvet, with only a blue hat and hooked nose emerging from the down cocoon, as I resuscitated fingers frozen in the efforts with a snow shovel. With all hands on deck the five-foot cave had taken two hours of breathless effort and it was almost dark when a hot brew attached to a long arm emerged from the tent.

Overnight it was fine, bitter cold and deep frosty, and the dawn a brilliant blue, with magnificent views east into Sinkiang and north across the arid yellow foothills of Central Asia. A cup of tea again emerged and eventually we struggled from the powdery hole. As always it was difficult to get going. It took an hour to get rigid boots onto cold feet, frozen gaiters onto stiff boots. Speedy poked a nose from the tent he shared with big Bruce Barclay, Greg Strange and Alan North. People just wandered off up the ridge, knee-deep and breathless still, as they were ready. After a few hours a minor summit found the whole party sitting thawing in the sun, brewing and gnawing without conviction at the salted sturgeon.

A few steep little gendarmes of rotten rock decorated the crest of the continuation ridge which would lead to the Lipkin Route up Peak Lenin. The tottering pinnacles looked difficult and time-consuming, and Clive, with a quick eye for a feasible route, led onto a long evasive traverse across unstable slopes of snow. We crossed them before the sun destroyed their cohesion by the same techniques as before, with those out in front who had the energy to gasp and plough through deep snow. At last the ridge broadended and the whaleback leading onto the Lipkin stretched ahead. Leaders changed more frequently as fatigue took its toll and midday haze and heat wore down our tired bodies, but still the weather held. There was more tea and a long stop after an especially tiresome rise, while the site of the camping place on the Lipkin was visible a mile or so away. Most people were feeling the altitude and each progressed at his own pace through the deep snow and patches of afternoon mist.

I stopped hurrying on this relatively safe ground, as there was no tent to arrive at on the spur. Tired and in a reverie I looked across the seracs of the North Face of Lenin, above which the Lipkin Route threads a traverse of almost two miles. It was all very big, but curiously rounded and superficially inocuous, deep plastered in new snow everywhere except where avalanches had already swept down after the recent bad weather. Apart from ourselves almost all the climbers in the Achik Tash had been channelled onto the Razdelny and

Lipkin Routes up Peak Lenin. It had not appealed to our group at all, and I was pleased with our variant which twinned admirably with the Eastern Rib ascended the previous week by Vincent and Benoir Renard and their friends.

The last pull to the camp seemed hard work. I still felt the weight of the Krylenko exhaustion as I slackened my boots and the others climbed into the tunnel. It was a stony, bare, windy place, with little tent platforms. Clive and I slid into a bivouac sheet as the easterly wind battered at the tents. Tea and food filtered from the over-crowded tent as the wind hammered away at the slopes. Fine powder snow got into the top of the envelope and swirled wildly inside, sticking to Clive's beard and getting even into the top of our sleeping bags, making us cough and suffocate. I failed to get my toes back to life as the wind howled through the darkness. Clive and I had shared many a dangerous and icy night travelling by motorbike. But this was a miserable night. Neither of us said much about it.

In the morning my feet would not revive, and I remembered the months it took before they came back after the Caucasus Shchur-ovskiy climb in 1970. The two bivouacs on that were the worst that I have ever encountered, desperately uncomfortable, wet to begin and frozen solid by morning. I was not prepared to go so far again, even with better equipment, although the summit was only 2,500 feet above. Clive was in better condition and seemed to be standing the altitude better. I did not want more nights over 21,000 feet without a tent. It was windy and cold but the sun was coming. I announced my decision to Clive, put on outer boots and spoke briefly to those in the tent. Of our group I thought I was now weakest, though judged most of the other tent less able to continue. Without many words, wishing everybody luck, I set out slightly uphill on the first leg of the Lipkin Traverse, across the North Face to the safe descent spur.

The shelf of the Lipkin Route is about a mile wide, cutting across the North Face of Peak Lenin and traversing over a long band of ice cliffs. There was little loss of height before it merged into a steeper ice and snow slope. As I trod out a deep rut, resting frequently to catch breath, a mysterious row of masked figures slowly came into sight. There was not an inch of human face to be seen, but they all appeared very short in stature as they slowly pushed their upward furrow to meet my descent. "Good morning," in English evoked the same response, and a pleasant female voice went on to tick me off for wandering the big mountains alone. They explained the whereabouts of their ice cave camp of the previous night. Tired and still chilled as I was, I felt better, though I was still near level with our miserable bivouac. Later I was to become familiar with this morning lowpoint at altitude and with the subsequent recovery. The eight masked Soviet women turned away and began to climb on very slowly and steadily, and I headed out onto the vast avalanche-rutted slope leading down from the mountain. It took time to get crampons fixed but then the loss of altitude was rapid and the deep snow of the lower slopes of the Lipkin occupied me for the rest of a morning.

There were two more meetings. Above the ice cave Eugene Gippenreiter and two other climbers appeared. He produced an apple and told tales of his fall on Chimney Route on Clogwyn du'r Arddu in North Wales, while I swallowed half of it – the apple, that is. After a few jokes we parted. Eugene was going up to try and keep count of the climbers on this route. I aimed for lamb stew at Base Camp. The sun made the 5,000 foot descent to the glacier very tough, but on a lower plateau Al Steck's tanned face and twinkling eyes peered from the underside of a gnomic hat which he never seemed to take off. With Jock Glidden and Chris Wren he was intent upon reaching the summit, despite an earlier avalanche injury. Loaded with great pack frames which I thought must be full of down, they laboured up through softening snow.

Ironically, after crossing numerous crevasses, I came near to being pipped at the post. A curious man-sized hole gulped me in within yards of the Lenin Glacier. Fortunately, as it appeared bottomless, my arms shot out and I stopped, nor was it particularly difficult to escape. The glacier and the Pass of the Travellers I took at full speed. Flowers carpeted the meadows below and I was in Base Camp for supper 10,000 feet below the spartan purgatories of the ridge.

The remaining eight British climbers moved up with their two tents onto the harsh plateau of Peak Lenin on the day of my departure. Clive, Doug, Guy and Tut reached the summit the following day after an early start, but Alan North was the only member of the other foursome to do so. Leaving later than the others, he almost lost his life on the return as cloud and high wind obscured his retreat. As the eight came down the Lipkin two more Britons, Graham Tiso and Ronnie Richards, were among a number of groups reaching the summit via the Razdelny

Route to the west. The Soviet women met them from the east and camped on the summit, intending to descend the Razdelny next day and make the first female traverse of the mountain. Now a major storm was forecast and the wind rose, clouds scudded across the high peaks and the temperature dived even at 11,000 feet. Over fifty climbers remained scattered over the two standard routes. Japanese, Soviet Ladies, and Steck's group of Americans were all very near the summit of the mountain. Very large groups were also high on the Lipkin Route and at the Razdelny Pass.

On August 5th the Base Camp radio had advised all groups remaining on the mountain to retreat as an exceptional storm had been forecast. Next day in atrocious weather came a radio report that the International Women's group were in difficulties high on the Razdelny route. One of them, Arlene Blum, had already gone back in deteriorating conditions the previous day with Jed Williamson to Camp 3 on the Razdelny Col. The weather was now extremely bad with very high winds and blizzard conditions, as a small party led by Pete Lev moved up to help the remaining three down. They met the Bavarian, Anya, retreating after the night of violent storm and she was escorted down by Michel Vincent of the Grenoble group. François Valla and Jed Williamson went on to find the other two women, Eva Eissenschmidt and Heidi Ludi, unable to move down as Eva had collapsed with symptoms of advanced hypothermia. They were at about 21,500 feet in a very exposed position. Lev and Valla decided that there was no alternative but to attempt to move Eva down, and after trying to get her to drink, wrapped her in a tent and lowered her down the ridge with great difficulty. In practice they had to make a sequence of diagonal lowers along the north side of the ridge in a wind of about eighty miles an hour. After a series of such lowers a Bavarian, Sepp Schwankerer, came up from Camp 3 alone after retreating earlier because of the bad conditions. With his help it was possible to lower her a little further through deep snow, but only at the cost of getting further and further out onto the North Face rather than keeping to the ridge. Tired and worried about both the women, they stopped and Valla went to Camp 3 with Heidi Ludi to get more help. Eva had stopped breathing and Sepp Schwankener and Lev gave her artificial respiration but despite considerable efforts breathing could not be restored. As the place was dangerous they secured her body and escaped from the slope onto the descent route, meeting Jed Williamson and others coming up to try and help. All then retreated to Camp 3 where some of the lighter tents were destroyed by the wind.

Meanwhile, Jeff Lowe and John Roskelley had at last completed the American Route on Peak 19 where Jon Gary Ullin had died in the earlier attempt, but there was little respite in the Achik Tash. So many parties of such varied experience were on the mountain and in conditions so bad that it seemed inconceivable there would not be trouble.

The eight Soviet women I had passed on my way down remained camped overnight from the 5th to the 6th of August on the very summit of the mountain. Initially, while the attempts to rescue Eva were going on, Elvira Shataeyeva contacted Base to say that one member of her group was sick and that their tents were unable to withstand the ferocious winds. Though they had been instructed to retreat like everyone else, they had initially persisted in their long prepared plan to descend by the Razdelny. But after an exhausting night they set out back down the Lipkin Route as directed, taking the sick woman with them. It appears that one woman died of exposure belaying the rest of the group down and the whole group stopped only a little way down the slope. By the evening of the 6th several more of the climbers were suffering the symptoms of exposure. The leader contacted Base in the evening and was instructed to continue down, even if it meant leaving those unable to go on. The weather remained diabolical, and late on the evening of the 6th only five of the eight women remained alive.

Help with a rescue party was volunteered by French, Americans and British. Our hosts were desperately anxious and understandably wanted to handle this cruelly evolving tragedy themselves. Four strong Soviet climbers were already at Camp 1 below the Lipkin intending to render assistance. But so many people were still on the mountain and exposed to risk, at Camp 3 on the Razdelny, or very high on the Lipkin Route where there were embattled groups of Siberians, Japanese and Americans, that it made little sense not to put more experienced helpers back into the field. The senior Soviet climbers agreed and also called for help with helicopters from Dushanbe. But everyone who threw together gear for a rapid departure on 6th August knew that there was little chance of the remaining Soviet women surviving even if the conditions improved. At best we might save one or two survivors or help other climbers in trouble on the mountain.

On a sleet-driven grey afternoon the rescue party plodded off across the Achik Tash towards the Pass of the Travellers. Cloud hung in great banks over the foothills and Lenin was shrouded totally. The path down to the Lenin Glacier was muddy red, soaked with rain and snow in the days of storm. As the group of English, French and Americans reached the Lenin Glacier a harsh November-like wind swept down the moraines. Sleet became snow and Bernard, a tiny animated Chamoniard, donned a huge cape which covered him and his rucksack. This silver grey phantom, hunchbacked and bizarre, produced a few wry laughs even in these grimmest of circumstances. We were all quite fit, everyone had done their bit of mountaineering, so a few days after climbing the ridge, here we were, hiking across expanses of glacier to the foot of the Lipkin, a route down to which the French had skied, by Lenin's North Face, only a short time before. At the camp below the spur three Russian climbers waited amid the bedraggled tentage. The snow swept in great curtains down the glacier and there was a pervasive damp chill. Clive crawled into a soaked tent and we brewed and rehydrated American steaks one after another.

As darkness fell the others heard Elvira, the women's leader, speak from over 8,000 feet above. "Another has died. We cannot go through another night. I do not have the strength to hold down the transmitter button." In fact this was one of several transmissions which our Russian companions had received. Their faces were riven with frustration and grief at being able to do so little. Three of the women appear to have been alive on that storm-blasted plateau, with winds approaching a hundred miles an hour at over 22,000 feet. Later in the evening as we went through the seemingly empty motions of preparing to climb the mountain to their rescue, they came on again. Only two remained alive. By nine pm the storm blew out to be replaced by a frost so bitter that we shivered in our best down so many feet below them.

Early next morning Doug, Tut, Guy, Clive and I, Jeff Lowe, Vincent and Benoir Renard, Bernard and two other Frenchmen moved off early with Boris and the other two Soviet climbers, trekking all day in fine weather up the great slopes leading to the Lipkin Spur. Above, Al Steck, Jock Glidden and Chris Wren emerged from a prolonged bivouac within a short distance of a Japanese party which had adopted similar chrysalis tactics and they all struggled to the summit. They found the women, spread along the ridge leading back from the summit, most of them together in the ruin of their fatal final camp. The Americans, who had known nothing of the tragedy, reported their news on the radio carried by the Japanese. The latter had an inkling of the situation from their companions at Base and had once tried to fight the elements in an effort to find the women, but with no success in the maelstrom.

In late afternoon the final slopes to the ice cave at 17,500 feet were swept by a cold but relatively innocuous Lenin wind. In its depths, still several thousand feet below the plateau, the report of events above was received. Everyone was now in retreat, with Americans coming back by the Lipkin, Siberians far on the descent of that route, and the beleaguered Camp 2 on the Razdelny relieved by John Evans and others from the American party. There was not a lot more to be done by us – in death it became a domestic tragedy. Guy Lee and I remained at the Lipkin ice cave for only an hour or so. The cave was crowded and the necessity which had brought us back dissolved. Several of the French had turned downwards already and while Tut, Doug, Jeff, Vincent, Bernard and Russians opted to stay up for one night to plough a path with the Masters of Sport to meet the retreating parties, we turned back towards the valley, speeding down in a few evening hours to the camp from which we had emerged with so much toil that day. Next morning we fed tea to the groups fleeing from the Razdelny, storm-battered, shocked men and women – Heidi Ludi with blackening finger ends. In the late afternoon Tut and the rest came down and we quitted the Lenin Glacier for the last time, crossing the Travellers' Pass, strolling down the Achik Tash Pamir past goats and flowers into Base.

It was the worst storm within living memory in the area. High wind and a bare terrain threatened even the most modern tents on Peak Lenin. The wooden poles and zipless doors of the Soviet Ladies' tents stood no chance so near the summit, despite the strength of the materials. Tactics, too, were a problem. The Soviet approach to climbing insists not unreasonably on the unity and cohesion of the party. The ladies had moved up Peak Lenin quite slowly, acclimatising gradually. Even in a team of eight this might have assured a successful traverse in less adverse weather. But the plateau is very high and long and to remain there long is risky for any party. In bad weather it is potentially highly dangerous, not least because of the possibility of losing the way, if the party has to move, and with risks of sickness, deterioration and even death if the group is caught in a storm. The ladies had been ordered back by Vitali Abalakov. They stuck too rigidly and bravely to their planned traverse in the teeth of ferocious weather. Nor would they consider leaving the summit with the last groups descending the Razdelny as the storm lashed into the mountain, after the fatigue of their ascent with loads to the summit.

Possibly that was the critical point. Once one or two members became sick in the first day of the storm, only quick descent might have saved all or some of the party, as their equipment would not enable them to survive. Their commendable team spirit prevented them doing this as individual members weakened. Bluntly, descent would have meant leaving someone behind. They could not do it even when ordered to do so from below. Perhaps it was already too late and few would have had the strength to cross the plateau in such a blizzard. The likelihood of them meeting Japanese or Americans embattled in their tents on the lee of the peak was not great. About the entire event there was a fearful logic.

As the tragedy unfolded in Base Camp emotion ran high. In particular there was a belief that helicopters might have speeded rescuers up the mountain with a hope of being effective. In practice this was not likely to have been of much real help. High winds, even low down, combined with poor visibility, could easily have caused a helicopter to crash at these altitudes. At most it might have taken a group of rescuers the day's walk to the Lenin Glacier. Probably the main hope was that the lost Japanese might have found the party when they heard of the plight of the retreating group. But tough and resilient as they were, it was a condition of their survival that they did not stay out searching long or they, too, would have lost their way back and with it their lives. Even had they found the women, they might have had neither the strength nor the numbers to get them back to their camp, nor the equipment to shelter so many.

The official inquest seems to have reached a similar conclusion. It was a bitter finish to a disastrous summer. Yet as always new things grew out of the wreckage. Speedy Smith married one of the Dutch contingent, a good number of the Americans turned towards the Himalaya where John Roskelley made an oxygen-free ascent of K2 in 1978, while

NINE

I

DEATH IN THE EVEREST ICEFALL

I first met Doug Scott in 1972 when we joined forces with Don Whillans as members of Dr Karl Herrligkoffer's European Everest Expedition to the South-West Face of the mountain. To say that the expedition was a fiasco would be an understatement. It started with waves of suspicion amongst the rival factions and ended on the open sea of hostility. Though Herrligkoffer didn't particularly want us as members of his team, he wanted the money which I had been promised by both the BBC and the *Observer*. We were quick to rename the doctor Sterlingscoffer when he was out of earshot.

My opinion of German efficiency declined early on in this expedition when there was an obvious lemming-like rush to get to Base Camp and a disregard for the need to acclimatise. The main group survived this, but Horst Vitt, a German diplomat who was on his way to visit us, died of pulmonary oedema. Professor Huttl also fell victim to the altitude on his way to Base Camp to conduct physiological experiments and had to be evacuated to Kathmandu, then back to Germany.

Despite international differences, we three were eventually established at Camp 4 at approximately 24,000 feet with the purpose of establishing Camp 5 some 1,500 feet above. It was here that we had what is probably the highest high altitude quarrel in history. The Big Four, Werner Hiam, Adolf Huber, Leo Breitenberger and Felix Keun, argued the toss with us. Felix as the climbing leader didn't give us much choice.

"You must down go," he pounded the edge of a box platform with his ice axe to give extra emphasis to his words and only added over and over again, "I vont give one millimetre . . ."

The Big Four had returned to the fray as they felt the summit was looming closer in good weather; they were determined to be at the sharp end from now on. For the past week they had been whooping it up at Base Camp where they had gone to welcome their leader, Karl, who had just returned from a flying visit to Munich to collect down clothing for the Sherpas. The Sherpas had refused point blank to go above Camp 2 without it. When Karl returned with his feathers he helicoptered as far as Pherichi at 15,000 feet. On arrival at Base Camp it was found that he had suffered a mild heart attack. Full use was made of the helicopter flight for Leo Breitenberger was sent back to Kathmandu as he was suffering from pleurisy. Hans Berger had gallstone trouble and Peter Bedner, who had been suffering from a cholera injection gone wrong, both retreated to Base Camp, but later returned to Camp 2. A Persian, Mischa Saleki, who was a member of the expedition (making its working title something of a misnomer), had been constantly bullied throughout the trip by the Big Four and now decided he could stand it no longer. According to a German press report, he stowed away in the helicopter at Pherichi, an extremely difficult thing to do, especially at 15,000 feet when even the passenger seats have sometimes to be removed to lighten the machine.

On such an expedition you get to know your companions well. You live in close proximity for months, get used to each other's smells and habits and share danger and pleasure, be it a super-cold high altitude view with peaks standing out as if fresh from a mould, or a piece of well-travelled cake which somehow escaped the hungry gauntlet of climbers in lower camps.

Well, the Big Four, or rather the Big Three, as Hiam injured a knee near Camp 3 and had to be evacuated down the Western Cwm by improvised stretcher, didn't get up the South-West Face. Felix, poor chap, later committed suicide back home in Austria. We didn't have many laughs on the Herrligkoffer expedition; it wasn't that sort of a trip. But an amusing incident happened on the bleak ice of Camp 1. One of the Big Four who suffered from constipation – an uncomfortable affliction in the cold of high altitude – was squatting in solitary splendour on the glacier close to camp. Imagine his dilemma when a crack appeared in the ice between his boots.

Doug, I discovered, is an idealist, a great companion on a big trip. He trained as a physical education teacher and taught in his home town, Nottingham, for ten years. His long hair didn't endear him to the crew-cut Germans, but it was inevitable that eventually they respected him.

We had acquired an assortment of rather useless items of clothing from the Base Camp coffers. Doug amassed a large pile of this jumble, not in the least suited for use on the mountain. No doubt it had been donated by well-meaning hausfraus back in the Fatherland. Realising that there was a ready market amongst the Sherpas for such draperies, Doug negotiated with a wily Sherpa called Dorge. Dorge, like most of his tribe, is a born trader. For example, on the steep wall between Camps 4 and 5, at over 25,000 feet, we had watched him wander nonchalantly over the face retrieving tatty bits of Japanese fixed rope, remnants of a previously unsuccessful expedition. A Sherpa, I concluded, who went to so much trouble to find tethering for his yaks was obviously a formidable business man. He cornered Doug's clothing market by offering slightly higher prices than his companions on condition that the clothing was left with him at Base Camp and the money was collected from his wife at Ghat, a small village south of Namche Bazar.

On our way to Kathmandu when Doug called at Dorge's house, his charming spouse confessed that she didn't have a rupee in the place. Somewhat disconsolate, but philosophical, Doug shrugged his shoulders and said that he'd call later.

We had only been back in the UK for a week or so when Chris Bonington asked Doug and me to join his expedition to the South-West Face of Everest. He was due to leave in about four weeks. We didn't hesitate. We both felt that we had a score to settle with that prodigious heap of rock and ice after all, we thought, it would be a pleasant change to be on a properly organised trip. Chris doesn't leave things to chance – or leave the Sherpa's down clothing back home. Chris's expedition now gave Doug a heaven-sent opportunity to visit Dorge again on the way back to Everest. But heaven had taken more than Doug under its ample wing. Dorge had gone into retreat, his wife told Doug when he called this time; he had taken up the god business and was going to be a lama. Once again Doug went away philosophically. It wasn't until we went back to Everest again with Chris in 1975 that Doug at last caught up with the elusive lama. Tut Braithwaite and I were with him when we called at Dorge's quaint house above the river. Dorge was at home. He had returned from his cave of meditation. He certainly seemed pleased to see us and we felt the same way, for we had shared hardships high on the South-West Face. He didn't have any money now, he told Doug, but he had good *chung*, would we like a glass? We did, then another and another and eventually parted in good spirits, Doug telling the impecunious lama that he could forget about the long-standing debt.

The highest point reached by our 1972 expedition was no higher than that reached by the Big Four, or that other ill-fated assualt, the International Everest Expedition of 1971, which was even more infamous for its discord, rocks and verbal abuse flying in rarefied air. When the Bonington expedition was defeated in 1972 we remained good friends after a great fight in hellish conditions of high wind and temperatures of −40°C.

When we started to clear the mountain, Dougal Haston and I went down ahead of Chris and Doug. It was 16th November when we left Camp 2. Mick Burke had descended the previous night so that he could get some film of us arriving at Base Camp. The Icefall was particularly dangerous. Earlier in the expedition Dougal and I had spent many cold mornings fixing ropes and placing ladder bridges over crevasses. We would set off at three am to do this work as the Icefall seemed to doze at this time of day and we were usually back down at Base Camp in time for a second breakfast. One section of the Icefall was so treacherous that I had put up a sign urging anyone crossing the area to clip on to the fixed rope which Dougal and I had secured across this passage of horrors. The ice seemed to be constantly moving, albeit slowly, but its groans resembled those of a great snake writhing in its death throes. Seracs leaned like Saturday night Glaswegians and we sneaked under these. When we had enough energy, we passed them at a run, not easy at almost 20,000 feet.

When Dougal and I came down that day at the end of the expedition this passage was worse than ever. I had spoken with Colonel Jimmy Roberts about it. Jimmy was Deputy Leader and in direct charge of the Icefall porters. I had told him that I thought the area would collapse in less than a week. Now over sixteen days had passed and it was complaining, with its belly-aching rumbles, even more persistently than before.

Dougal and I angled down on to the home straight to Base Camp, with only the minor worry of an avalanche from the Lo La to trouble us, peanuts compared to what we had just come through, and I said, "Thank Christ that's behind us."

"Aye, Jimmy," said Dougal, "it's no the place to dither about."

Tony Tighe, a friend of Dougal's, was just setting off for Camp 1 when we arrived. Tony was an Australian, a warm-hearted lad who had been working as a barman at the Vagabond Club in Leysin in Switzerland where Dougal lived. Though he wasn't a climber, he was fit and had unbounded enthusiasm. He had been doing thankless jobs at Base Camp for the past two months and though he wasn't an official member of the expedition and not supposed to go above Base Camp, Chris had agreed to allow him to go up to Camp 1 so that he could see the Western Cwm. We all thought this was the least that could be done to reward Tony for all his chores. There were about twenty Sherpas going up as well to collect loads from the camp. Though the Icefall was highly dangerous in places from falling seracs and subsidence, technically it was easy with all the crevasses bridged and ropes in the trickier sections. It was in fact as safe for one person to go up or down as fifty. We wished Tony a good climb and with a wave he was off, a colourful figure. He had been pestering Chris for weeks to visit Camp 1 and this was his big day. Unfortunately, it was also his last and he never saw the Western Cwm.

Chris and Doug met him as they came down. Despite his fitness he lagged behind the Sherpas, who with the end of the expedition in sight had wings on their crampons. At Base Camp we had our first wash for many weeks and were sitting in the main tent when I said to Chris, "Well, thank goodness it's all over safely, Chris."

He flared up, a look almost of fear on his face. No doubt the memory of Ian Clough's death on Annapurna was still fresh on his mind. Ian, a good friend of both of us, had been killed in literally the last hour of the expedition by a falling serac.

"There's still some to come down that last bit!" Chris said tersely.

He was right of course and I wonder if just then he had a premonition. A short time later there were murmurings from the Sherpas. Though we hadn't heard anything at Base Camp the Sherpas suspected that there had been a big collapse in the Icefall. This was confirmed presently by Phurkipa, our Icefall sirdar who had just returned. He told Chris of the subsidence.

An hour or so later Barny Rosedale, our doctor, came into camp. He and Tony had been the last Europeans on the mountain. He looked distraught and told us he had managed to get round the collapse by a dangerous diversion. He had seen no sign of Tony. Phurkipa, it transpired, had been the last person to see him. We tried to piece together the information we had on Tony's movements and came to the reluctant conclusion that he must have been caught in the fall of ice. Barny told us that he had heard a deep-throated graunching noise at about one o'clock at Camp 1. This had been followed by a great mushroom cloud of ice particles. Some Sherpas had just left Camp 1 to go down to Base Camp and had almost been caught in the fall. An ice ridge on which they had been walking had collapsed beneath them. They came rushing into Camp 1 saying that Ang Tande, one of the Icefall porters, was hanging on the safety rope which Dougal and I had installed. He was swinging seventy feet above the new and equally unstable floor of the Icefall. It was fortunate that the Sherpas had made a point of clipping on to this rope and Phurkipa had duplicated my warning board in Nepalese for their benefit. Barny, acting decisively, managed to dash down to the scene of the accident with two good Sherpas and succeeded in rescuing the suspended porter. He then took all the Sherpas from Camp 1 down to Base Camp by a circuitous and hazardous route. He saw no sign of Tony Tighe on the way, however, and he didn't think that there was another route through the chaos. It was obvious to us all that Tony had been buried.

As Mick Burke and Dave Bathgate were the freshest of our group they volunteered to go up and conduct a quick search. It was already late but they set off with some Sherpas. The Icefall was bathed in moonlight when they arrived at the scene. Crazy shadows reached out from the seracs and the crevasses were black slits. In the moonlight they could see that some of the seracs were still in a critical state, leaning Pisa-tower-like, which to any experienced mountaineer spells death. There was no sign of Tony, only the ominous grinding of the mills of the Icefall. Mick Burke said afterwards that being amidst that scene of destruction was the most frightening experience of his life.

Though Barny had taken all the Sherpas from Camp 1 down with him to Base Camp the previous day, there had still been fourteen Sherpas at Camp 2 doing a final clear up. They had now reached Camp 1 and somehow they had to be taken down. Also a further search for Tony was required in the stark light of day. Doug Scott and I volunteered to do this; Dougal had taken Tony's death badly and had gone down to Pherichi to be on his own.

The scene at the lonely hanging rope was one of devastation. It was as if the immediate area had been subjected to saturation bombing. As Dave and Mick had reported, some of the ice towers were ready to fall at any minute, but when we picked our way under these, we tried to take our minds off the danger and made as systematic a search as possible. We had taken several Sherpas up and they were obviously terrified. So were we, but we tried not to show it.

As we neared Camp 1 Doug complained of headache and pain in his eyes and I thought he must have got snow blindness. Eventually, we reached Camp 1 to be greeted by the remaining Sherpas who had spent the night there, having arrived after Barny and his group had left. They had tried to go down through the fall, but had turned back at the site of the danger.

We quickly made up loads to take back to Base, leaving all but the most essential equipment. The Sherpas, who normally leave nothing of even the slightest value on the mountain, raised no objection. I was concerned for Doug; his sight was deteriorating and I tried to contact Base on the walkie-talkie but without any luck. I thought extra man-power on the lower stretch of the Icefall would help us.

We retraced our route through the great blocks of ice, a valley of death. I remember at the time thinking that it looked like the destruction of a city of glass. Though we also searched on the descent there was no sign of Tony. There was no question of his being alive under such debris; the smallest of the ice blocks must have weighed several tons. We threaded our way down under a broiling sun, for the Everest Icefall can be one of the hottest places on earth in mid-morning.

Two years later we were back again, with Chris's 1975 expedition to the South-West Face. Now we were successful, with Doug and Dougal first to reach the summit, but tragically this time it was Mick Burke who lost his life. Mick was always a prickly customer, but it was Mick who, with Dave Bathgate, had unhesitatingly gone up to look for Tony that night and it was Mick, too, years before, who had played his part on the dramatic rescue on the West Face of the Dru in Chamonix in the French Alps:

Dougal was later killed in a skiing accident close to his home in Switzerland. Doug called at my house in Glencoe shortly afterwards when I was out, but he left a bottle of wine belayed to my front door handle. Attached to it was a note: "Take care, youth, there's not many of us left."

In 1977 Doug was a member of an expedition to the Ogre, a savage mountain in the Pakistan Karakoram. Doug's account of this trip, which is probably one of the most outstanding examples of self-help in the annals of mountaineering, is in striking contrast to the attitude of potential snow-holers and certified climbers who are churned out by institutions. Doug, like me, abhors this approach to mountaineering, which is after all basically a sport of self-reliance.

2

SELF-HELP ON THE OGRE

by Doug Scott

If I think back to the British Ogre Himalayan Expedition 1977, one man stands out in my mind – the Balti porter, Taki, who, after carrying a sixty-pound box throughout a twelve-mile approach march, some of it over moraine waste, produced from the folds of his shorts, smocks and assorted rags thirty-one eggs, none of which was even cracked. How he did it I'll never know. Ostensibly he did it for thirty-one rupees and our favour, but how do you walk over a shifting chaos of moraine rock without breaking such a cargo? Well, I suppose, much more carefully than I could. Eight weeks later, eight more Balti came up the Biafo Glacier to Base Camp and, with as much care as Taki had for his eggs, carried me down some of the roughest terrain imaginable, with hardly a jolt to my broken legs.

Back in June, fit and full of optimism, six of us entered Baltistan, ready to climb the Ogre. The Ogre is the highest point in the Biafo Glacier region of the Karakoram. It was noted by Europeans in 1861, when Godwin Austen first surveyed the area, and again in 1892 when Conway came down the Biafo from the Hispar Glacier and named it. Then, during the 1930s, Eric Shipton and his friends carefully surveyed the whole region. The height of the Ogre stands at 23,900 feet (7,285 metres) and a local name was found for it – Baintha Brakk – but climbers seem to prefer the shorter and more intelligible 'Ogre'.

During the last six years, two British and two Japanese expeditions have attempted the mountain. All four attempts failed in the face of avalanching snow, steep rock and ferocious storms. The highest point reached was 21,500 feet, which was achieved last year when the Japanese explored the South-West Flank. Above their high-point there reared 1,000 feet of steep granite and, beyond that, sheer ice faces, long corniced ridges and a final 800-foot summit rock pinnacle. The technical problems would be quite something in the Alps, but here, at nearly 24,000 feet, the climbing would become a race against physical and mental deterioration in the rarefied air.

During the spring of 1975, Clive Rowland and I reconnoitred the south side of the Ogre. Our high point then had been 16,000 feet on the Uzan Blakk Glacier, where we stood bogged down in wet, sloppy snow, lost in amazement at the sight of the great lumps of rock, 8,000 feet high and liberally covered with snowy ramps and steep ice faces, that characterise the Ogre from the south. It is not a beautiful mountain from down there, being squat and having three small cones, like misplaced nipples, defining the summit, with the centre cone the highest. Yet there is one elegant feature, and that is the South Pillar, a prow of rock 3,000 feet high. While I was excited about the prospect of climbing that, Clive was clearly attracted by the South-West Flank, where there was a possible route up ridges and snowfields that looked the most likely way to the summit area. As a result of this divergence of interest, we put together an expedition with these two routes in mind.

The expedition finally resolved itself into a party of six: Tut Braithwaite and I were to try the South Pillar, while Chris Bonington, Nick Estcourt, Mo Anthoine and Clive attempted the South-West Flank. We were, mercifully, without a leader. The inclusion of such a personage would have been laughable, seeing that all members of the team had had so much expedition experience that they could easily arrive at decisions communally. For some this was their first leaderless expedition and they no doubt found it stimulating to work things out for themselves, while former leaders perhaps found it restful to be without the burden of total responsibility.

Despite an apparent lack of organisation, we had worked hard preparing for our respective routes, but these well-made plans foundered in our case when a big rock smashed into Tut's leg at the start of our South Pillar route. After two weeks of waiting for a large blood clot to move, Tut could still not use his leg for rock climbing. Laboriously, we recovered all our food, equipment and a special hanging tent from the base of the pillar (at 19,000 feet). So ended a two-year obsession – an obsession which had caused me to catch my breath a few times at the thought of taking off to climb with just two climbing ropes and none back down to the ground. But for me, at least, there were still alternatives, while Tut had no choice but to sit the trip out in Base Camp. For someone as active as he is, that wait must have been one of the most frustrating periods of his life.

"Mountain one, climbers none," as Mo put it.

Round Two had already begun, with Chris, Nick, Clive and Mo busy climbing and fixing ropes up the ice rib leading to the West Col. In less than a week they climbed from above Advance Base, at 17,000 feet to 20,000 feet on the col. At the end of this period, Chris and Nick took off for the top, with about five days' food. Finding themselves suddenly alone, the other two descended – Clive because he wanted to reconnoitre a different way via the West Ridge, and Mo because he felt they needed more supplies and more time to acclimatise. Nick and Chris pushed out from the col along a ramp and round on to the South Face. Up to a point above the South Pillar they had followed a line pioneered by the 1976 Japanese expedition. Four days later, they returned, having failed in a very bold attempt to reach the summit. Faced with depleted food stocks and lack of climbing equipment, and suffering from the effects of altitude, they had not felt up to climbing the 800-foot summit cone. They did, however, traverse up on steep snow to the West Summit, before reversing their route of ascent. They set off back down to Base Camp, but on their way came across Mo, Clive, Tut and me at the West Col. We were in the process of making an attempt on the West Ridge which started with a 1000-foot rock pillar. This rekindled Chris's ambition for the top, and he persuaded us to return to Base to give him a rest and also to collect more food.

A few days later, on 6th July, Mo, Clive and I returned to the col and went up to a smaller shoulder, about 1000 feet higher and just under the 1000-foot pillar, where we made a camp. Tut and Nick (unknown to us at the time) had decided not to rejoin the attempt, at Tut's leg seemed to be getting worse and Nick had still not recovered from his attempt with Chris. Chris therefore started out alone, knowing we would be waiting below the pillar. As we put the tents up at Camp 2 on the top shoulder I would have given anything to have been at home. Half an hour later, inside my tent supping hot tea, I looked out of the entrance as the sun set and decided that there was nowhere else I'd rather be but up there at 22,000 feet, watching that sun dipping down, silver lining strands of cloud strung out over Snow Lake and the Hispar Glacier beyond. Range after range of bristling mountain peaks stood out silhouetted against each other, the nearer ranges sharply and darkly defined, while those in the distance faded into the sun's diffused haze of yellow light. Above them all, some 150 miles away, Nanga Parbat caught the last of the sun, whilst everywhere else was plunged into gloom. We zipped up the tent against a strong wind and snuggled content into our feathers.

I thought of the morrow, when we three would at last get on to rock. I looked forward expectantly to covering what ground we could up the pillar, going along hopefully lapping up that granite rock, on the way to who knows where exactly.

During the next two days we got to work on the 1000-foot pillar. This provided some interesting climbing on both faces and in cracks, all carried out at a height of about 22,500 feet. We then descended to the tent to wait for Chris, having equipped the pillar with 450 foot of fixed rope. The four of us eventually took off on 11th July, reclimbing the 1000-foot pillar and continuing to about 23,000 feet, where we dug a snow cave just below the final rocks of the West Summit. During the next day, Mo and Clive took over the lead and went across some very steep ice (65°), made all the more difficult by a thin coating of powder snow. They then continued up to the West Summit Ridge, via a steep couloir. After a stop for a brew, we slowly climbed the ridge and traversed over the summit. We brought the day to a close by digging a big snow cave just below the long ridge connecting the West Summit with the Main Summit. The snow was thick here, but it was lying at about 50° – 55° on ice, giving grounds for concern. Even when we had dug right into it, the thought crossed our minds that the whole South-East Face could easily avalanche and take our snow cave with it. We did dig a bit deeper and a position at the back of the cave was more often sought after than one at the front, but our main hope lay in the face not avalanching, which it didn't until we were off the mountain.

That night, within sight of the summit rocks, we cooked up a big meal of freeze-dried Strogonoff, rounded off with apple flakes and endless cups of tea. The cave was sealed off against spindrift and, despite the 23,000 feet altitude, we slept well. Chris and I set off next morning to break trail to the foot of the rocks. Mo and Clive were to follow later, as Mo wanted to take some ciné film for a BBC documentary he was making of the expedition's ups and downs. When Mo and Clive came up later, they were to be disappointed. Clive recalls, "When we reached the small col 300 feet below the summit it was obvious that we couldn't possibly reach the top that day as Doug and

Chris were taking a long time on the final tower. At three pm we set off back to the snow cave, hoping to try for the top the next day, but fate had other things in store for us . . ."

Chris was feeling the effects of his previous attempt. He was moving well enough, but suggested that I led the rocks ahead, as I should be faster, being fitter. I greedily accepted and soon 'lost' myself climbing two 150-foot pitches up a pinnacle and down its far side to a snow patch on the north side of the summit rocks. From the snow we followed a diagonal break right up to a seemingly blank wall. This turned out to be the crux of the climb, for a crack I eventually found and followed for eighty feet suddenly ended. From a wire chock wedged into the crack, I got Chris to lower me some forty feet so that I could make a pendulum swing across the granite wall. I swung first to one side then to the other, gradually increasing the arc by a sort of gallop against the rock, until I could reach over to another crack which looked climbable. I was just placing a chock when my feet slipped off and away I clattered across the rock. Chris continued to hold his end of the rope firm and, after another session of galloping about, I regained the crack, banged a piton into it, clipped my etrier to that and stood up from the peg, gasping for air after these exertions at nearly 24,000 feet. Chris let out the tension in the rope and by leap-frogging the aid up the crack, I was able to reach a point higher than before. Here the wall relented and I was able to free climb to a point fifteen feet above the pendulum swing, to where a crack went through an overhang to the top of the wall. I climbed this using direct aid from chocks and the odd piton and, just as the 150-foot length of rope adjoining us together had all been run out, I arrived at the top of the wall. Chris then jumared up the rope to join me, and from there we traversed down seventy feet and climbed an overhanging corner into the summit gully.

This final 100 feet took up the last hour of the day, for when Chris had arrived on the top of the Ogre the sun had gone down over the Hunza. As he had my camera, I had been able to sit on the top and take in the new perspective of Snow Lake and the hundreds of snowy peaks stretching off in all directions, without, for once, having to fiddle with camera stops and speeds.

Not having any bivouac equipment, Chris and I were very anxious to get down to the snow cave. However, it had been a good climb, at least above the fixed rope. There had been so much variation – a veritable magical mystery tour of a route, taking in steep rock and ice, a climb over the West Summit and then a traverse across and up to the Main Summit.

We worked our way down a ridge of soft snow to a block of rock. We put a nylon sling round it, threaded our two climbing ropes behind that, and threw both down in the direction of the 150-foot wall. To regain the peg crack, I had to push myself well over to the left as I abseiled, but eventually I got to the crack, just as I was reaching the end of the double rope. I leaned across to fix myself on to a peg, pressing myself over with my feet. I stepped my right foot up against the wall but, in the gathering darkness, unwittingly placed it on a veneer of water ice. Suddenly my foot shot off and I found myself swinging away into the gloom, clutching the end of the rope. Mo saw the fall from below and they then knew that there would be no summit for them the next day.

I couldn't imagine why the swing was going on and on. I had not realised how far left of the abseil sling I was. And all the time I was swinging, a little exclamation of awe, surprise and fear was coming out from inside me, audible to Mo some 2,000 feet away at the snow cave. And then the swing and the cry ended as I slammed into the opposite side of the gully, 100 feet away. Splat! Glasses gone and every bone shaken.

A quick examination revealed head and trunk O.K., femurs and knees O.K., but – Oh! Oh! – ankles cracked whenever I moved them. The right one felt very peculiar: Pott's fracture, I diagnosed, without much real idea – left one, too, but perhaps it's just the tendons. So that was how it was going to be: a whole new game with new restrictions on winning – it was curious to observe my own reactions. I had no fear then, there was too much to do. I banged a peg in, put a couple of wire nuts in, tied off direct from my harness and hung off them while Chris came down the abseil rope.

"What ho!" he said, cheerily.

"I've broken my right leg and smashed the left ankle," I said.

"We'll just work at getting you down," he replied, airily. "Don't worry, you're a long way from death."

Too true! – the thought that I might have major problems of that kind had not then entered my head. I felt extremely rational, remarkably clear about what to do.

We continued our descent as far as we could that night. Chris abseiled down to a large patch of snow on a rock slab. By the time I reached him, he'd hacked a step out in the snow and, for the first time, I put my body weight on my legs and ankles. They both collapsed, the right leg cracking horribly. So I got on my knees, with my lower legs stuck out behind, and kneed across the ledge with no trouble at all.

"So that's how it's done," I thought. And that's how it was done over the next seven days, with a little help from my friends – Chris, Clive and Mo.

Chris and I hacked away at the snow patch, producing a passable ledge on which we could lounge back in a half-lying, half-sitting position. Most of the time we sat facing each other with our bare feet stuck into each other's crutch. Every half hour or so we would reach down and rub a bit of life into each other's feet, a lesson learnt whilst bivouacking on Everest two years before.

Mainly I cursed the night away, moaning and groaning at the cold, wishing I'd brought a sleeping bag and a duvet, afraid that internal bleeding might cut off the blood going to my toes. That thought kept me grabbing at Chris's toes which I would rub furiously, hoping that he would take the hint and rub mine, which he did with gentle pressure. The night passed in these little flurries of action. At 5.30 next morning we abseiled four more rope lengths down to the snow basin of the South-East Face.

Mo and Clive didn't keep office hours either. As Clive noted: "Mo and I went off at first light and passed Chris on the snow slope. Mo went to Doug who was behind and I stopped about two or three hundred feet short of him and hacked out a platform so that I could make him a brew. The rest of that day was spent in returning to the snow cave."

We spent that night in the snow cave and ate the last freeze-dried meal, leaving ourselves with only soup and tea. It was with some concern, therefore, that we found a howling blizzard raging outside the snow cave the next morning. We had to get down to Advance Base to get food and even lower to escape the debilitating effect of the lack of oxygen. But first we had to climb up 300 feet to gain the West Summit. Clive tried first, but after climbing for three quarters of an hour he had only gained eighty feet and packed it in as his goggles, eyelashes and everything else froze up. Mo tried next and returned in ten minutes. As Clive wrily pointed out, "Mo isn't as daft as I am." There was so much snow in the air it had become impossible to see, and the wind made it difficult to stand up, let alone climb steep snow.

The next day, 16th July, there was less wind and we all set off out into the heavy snowfall. Clive took the lead, slowly kicking his way up desperately deep powder snow, angled in places at 60°. Mo went next up Clive's rope, then I, then Chris. It took Clive three hours to climb 400 feet to the West Summit and seven hours for all of us to reach there. Mo then took over the lead, rigging all the abseils, as well as two horizontal sections where I was hauled over on ropes. Clive took up the rear. We eventually reached the snow cave where we had spent the night of the 11th. The weather was terrible – cold and violent. We had to dig out snow that had drifted into the cave, but as it was dark when we arrived no one felt like waiting around in the storm whilst the digging took place. So we ended up with cramped quarters and an inadequate entrance. Mo and Clive already had damp sleeping bags, and these became quite wet during the night with snow drifting in on to them. It was the worst night of all: no food, wet, still above 23,000 feet and me slowing them all down with the 1,000-foot pillar still to come. There was only one way for me to tackle a big, complex problem like that, and that was one day at a time, keeping the broad idea hovering around in my mind that I'd got to get to Base Camp, but each day thinking no further than that day's objective, confident that if each day's climbing was competently executed then the whole problem would eventually be solved.

Next morning, Mo stuck his head out of the cave and announced that the storm was now, if anything, worse. He went off, followed by Clive, then me, then Chris – all of us bent on reaching the tents, for there we had left a pound of sugar, which was something we had not had for two days. That seemed to be a number one priority. But also there was no real resting place between the snow cave and the tents – so we had to make it. It was a nightmare descent. Whenever there was a ridge of level ground, I found crawling painful, seeming always to be catching my legs on protruding rocks. Only on steep, snowed-up rocks did I feel comfortable, for then Mo would have fixed up the abseil ropes and I could slide down with my body making contact with the snow and rock, whilst my feet stuck out, out of the way of obstacles. Clive stayed right by me during the descent, making certain I was belayed, hacking out the occasional steps for my knees and checking my maudlin tendencies. I was apt to moan a lot and lose my temper with myself at which point Clive would come in with "You're always moaning!" and "Who needs legs?" and other punny remarks which brought me out of myself. In this fashion we started to descend the 1,000-foot pillar.

Unfortunately, on the way down, Chris abseiled off the end of one of the double ropes. Luckily, Clive had tied the other off to a rock, so Chris fell only about twenty feet or so, but he still broke two ribs and painfully damaged his right hand. Cold and getting colder, he had no alternative but to continue the descent. Mercifully, he did not at once start to experience the pain in his thorax that was to dog him later. It was a sorry little band that made the tents. Mo was the first and he had to re-erect them, as they were both flattened under three feet of snow.

The rest of us were happy to crawl straight in out of the tearing wind and into our sleeping bags. For me, it was a long and painful process removing gaiters, boots, inner boots and socks. But it had to be done so that I could rub my frozen toes back to life, for circulation was some-what restricted by having my legs permanently bent at the knee. More serious, though, were my frozen finger ends. Crawling about so much I had no opportunity to keep my gloves dry, and not much time to stop and warm my hands when they started to lose sensation. I hoped that things would improve now that we were losing height, and we all kept thinking that the storm could not go on for many more days.

Mo came into the same tent as Clive and me, to warm up, as his sleeping bag was now reduced to a useless clump of wet, soggy feathers. We played cards, hoping the storm would finally blow itself out during the morning, so that we could move the tents down to the West Col later in the day. Chris was now in a bad way – coughing, his throat hoarse, his voice down to a whisper, and every cough increasing the pain under his ribs. He burst into our tent during the morning, announcing that he really must go down as he thought that he had pulmonary oedema. We discussed this with him, but he did not seem to have any of the gurgling noises one hears about. It was probable that he had mild pneumonia which wouldn't have been helped by spending the day out in the swirling spindrift. Neither did the three of us fancy the sub-zero temperature and harsh wind, for Mo announced that he had not felt his toes for nearly a week and Clive's digits were also numb. Despite it being our fourth day without food, we decided to give it one more day. At least now we had enough sugar for the next dozen brews of tea. We had been taking tea without milk or sugar for breakfast and half a curried meat stock cube for dinner, and we were lacking in energy, but now noticed a slight change for the better with the sugar.

It was still blowing hard the next morning as we roped down to the

South-West Col. By now I had become quite expert at knee-climbing. I found that being on my hands and knees was actually an advantage in particularly deep snow, and I did a bit of trail-breaking. Mo unearthed some old Japanese ropes, and we slid down the first 500 feet to the West Col. We went across to our former camp site and dug around until we uncovered a waste bag, in the bottom of which was some boiled rice mixed with cigarette ash, which we ate. We rummaged around some more and found an ounce of milk powder and, in another bag, three packets of fruit sweets and two packets of cough sweets. We shared them out when Clive and Chris arrived.

We moved off to the top of the fixed ropes that would take us to Advance Base the following day. I carried Clive's sack as he had to go and recover a tent that had fallen off his sack higher up. There was now about a mile to go across soft snow, but at last the clouds were rolling back to reveal the mountains all around covered in fresh, sparkling snow down to the glaciers. My arms kept sinking deep into the snow with the weight of Clive's sack pressing down over my neck. Despite following Mo's footsteps, I took many rests, flopping down flat out in the snow. Expeditions are usually good times to sort out a few things in the head – times to drop down a level or two – but it occurred to me then that since my accident I had brought such an iron will to bear on every moment of the day that I had not given such matters a thought. But there had been some compensations, for whenever I shut my eyes I went off into a hallucinatory world of lilac and purple colouring, incredible shapes and forms, caricature people and stylised views of distant times and places. It did not make a lot of sense, but it was one way to while away a few minutes and recover enough to take a further twenty or so crawling paces through the snow.

Mo and I dug out tent platforms, put up one of the tents and then the other when Clive arrived with it. Chris came in very slowly, coughing up a rich yellow fluid from his lungs.

Chris and Mo set off at first light for Advance Base. Clive and I followed four hours later, for by then the sun would be up to warm our frost-bitten hands and feet. Also, Chris and Mo would have had time to cut out big steps at various key places.

Abseiling down fixed ropes was no real problem for me, so I was able to descend 2,500 feet in four hours. Crawling over soft snow down to 17,000 feet was also relatively easy, but after that the snow became thin, and I had to crawl over hard, sharp glacier ice.

We arrived at last to find that Advance Base was no more – either blown away or taken away by Nick and Tut – so there was nothing for it but to follow Mo and Chris down to Base Camp. Clive gave me his down trousers and over trousers, but I went through these after another mile. The next section was the most painful of the whole retreat. The distance was about four and a half miles from the end of the fixed ropes. About one mile was on soft snow, two and a half on ice and one on moraine. Clive was worried.

Just before dark it was evident no one was coming to help us. We didn't want to bivvy on the ice again, so I rushed off to Base Camp to get a torch and some food. I found Chris asleep under a boulder. He told me that Mo had gone off in hot pursuit of Nick who had that same morning given us up for dead.

Nick had left us a note which said: 'If you get as far as reading this, then it presumably means that at least one of you is alive', and added that he was going down to fetch Tut from Askole and form a search party. There was no torch in camp so I got Chris to lie in his pit on top of the moraine ridge above Base with a gas stove burning to light the way for us off the glacier. I then grabbed some food and set off back up the glacier to find Doug. It was pitch dark, but after about an hour we found each other by shouting and whistling. After eating the food it took Doug about three hours to crawl the rest of the way, all the time the little beacon getting closer and closer.

At 10.30 that night (20th June), I crawled over the last of the moraine rocks. My legs were very swollen from knocking them countless times. I stopped to examine them and was horrified to find that I had worn right through four layers of clothing and that my knees were numb, bloody and swollen.

One last bank and I was on the triangle of moraine that surrounded the thick green grass of Base Camp – a little oasis amongst the chaos of shifting rock and ice. I crawled to the old kitchen site. I thought when I saw the meagre supplies that had been left that the others must have really thought we were dead. However, it was good to eat Purdy Cake with a cup of milky tea and then to fall asleep on that little meadow.

Next morning the sun shone on to our wet sleeping bags – you could feel the warmth come right through into the murky interior. Pulling open the draw-cord from inside, putting my head out to see the grass, the flowers and the stream running across, then getting out, brewing a mug of tea, eating a powdered egg omelette and feeling the sun burning my skin: beautiful memories these.

For four days Clive looked after Chris and me, and still there was no sign of the porters that Mo should have sent. On the fifth day, however, when we were down to soup and Tom and Jerry nougat bars, Nick arrived with twelve porters to carry me down, together with the remnants of our gear. Mo, in the meantime, had gone off with Tut and our Liaison Officer, Captain Aleem, to Skardu, in order to dispatch a helicopter for arrival outside Askole on 28th July.

When Mo arrived in Askole, Tut had already been there a week and had made good friends with the headman and many of the villagers. As each day passed it had seemed to Tut and to the Baltis that our chances of being alive were growing increasingly slim, especially when Nick arrived alone. Thus, when Mo walked in, they were all overjoyed to discover that we were safe, if not exactly one hundred per cent. The headman sent off to other villagers to ensure that we had twelve strong and able porters. And that was exactly what we got.

In three days they carried me down to the Biafo Glacier and then along to its snout and on to a flat field near Askole, where a helicopter could land. It was a remarkable journey on a home-made stretcher constructed of juniper wood poles, a climbing rope and sleeping mats. Never once did they look like dropping me, and I seldom felt a jolt. It was good to lie out, listening and waiting as they made decisions as to route finding, choice of camping place, who should fetch wood and water, who should take the heavier part of the stretcher, and so on. They inevitably made the decision after a gentle murmur had gone round the motley band – no one ever shouted or became excited. Their voices blended into a sing-song melody which seemed completely in tune with the rhythm of their village lives. They knew just what to do. And I for one have nothing but admiration for these hardy people, who are all very individualistic and full of character, yet are easily capable of working to a common aim in complete accord. That is how good expeditions can work.

It was sad to be suddenly plucked away from them by the noisy helicopter. Unlike Taki with his eggs and the eight stretcher-bearers with me, the helicopter was not so gentle: coming into Skardu the engine cut out, and we suddenly plummeted twenty feet to the ground some hundred yards short of the helipad. As a result Chris had to wait for a week in Askole while the helicopter was repaired, but eventually he, too, was flown out to Skardu.

Three days later, after fine hospitality at the British Embassy and a first-class flight home, courtesy of Pakistani International Airlines, I was being plastered and pinned in Nottingham General Hospital.

After the expedition, when I heard of Doug's crawl back to civilisation, I sent a note to him at the Nottingham General Hospital: "Take care, youth, there's not many of us left."

INDEX